Germany
and European order
Enlarging NATO and the EU

Adrian Hyde-Price

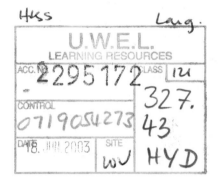

Manchester University Press
Manchester and New York

Distributed exclusively in the USA by St. Martin's Press

Published by Manchester University Press
Oxford Road, Manchester M13 9NR, UK
and Room 400, 175 Fifth Avenue, New York, NY 10010, USA
http/www.manchesteruniversitypress.co.uk

Distributed exclusively in the USA by
St. Martin's Press, Inc., 175 Fifth Avenue, New York,
NY 10010,USA

Distributed exclusively in Canada by
UBC Press, University of British Columbia, 2029 West Mall,
Vancouver, BC, Canada V6T 1Z2

British Library Cataloguing-in-Publication Data
A catalogue record for this book is available from the British Library

Library of Congress Cataloging-in-Publication Data applied for

ISBN 0 7190 5427 3 *hardback*
        0 7190 5428 1 *paperback*

First published 2000

07 06 05 04 03 02 01 00   10 9 8 7 6 5 4 3 2 1

Typeset in Minion
by Northern Phototypesetting Co. Ltd, Bolton
Printed in Great Britain
by Bell & Bain Ltd, Glasgow

This book is dedicated with love to
Lisbeth Aggestam.
Jag älskar dig!

'Har du väntat här länge?

Här står jag nu.
Här står du nu.
Vi står här och bidrar till varandra,
gör varandra möjliga!'

Rolf Aggestam, *Rost* (1979)

Contents

Preface and acknowledgements

This book is the outcome of my long-standing interest in contemporary European affairs, particularly developments in the *Mitteleuropäische* heartlands of Central and Eastern Europe. This interest stirred during the years I was engaged in doctoral research at the University of Kent at Canterbury. It was at this time that I began studying the German language, and, thanks to the German Academic Exchange Service (DAAD), was able to spend two months at the Goethe-Institut in Bremen in 1983. My intellectual journey really began, however, with a post-doctoral research visit sponsored by the British Council to the German Democratic Republic in 1984, followed by a second research trip in 1986. Experiencing the realities of *real existierender Sozialismus* at first hand gave me some sobering insights into the nature of authoritarian state socialism, and fuelled an interest in German culture, history and politics that has remained with me since.

After a year lecturing at the University of Manchester, I moved to the Royal Institute of International Affairs, London (Chatham House) in 1987. For the next three years I was a Research Fellow on the International Security Programme, tasked with studying the East–West conflict in Europe. This gave me valuable experience in working in a policy-orientated environment, at a time of exciting developments in international affairs. It also started me thinking about the nature of European order, and gave me the opportunity to travel extensively in Central Europe. It was at this time that I wrote my first book, *European Security Beyond the Cold War: Four Scenarios for the Year 2010* (Sage 1991).

Moving to the University of Southampton in 1990, I was exposed to international relations theory and developed a passion for this somewhat esoteric topic which has remained with me since. I quickly discovered an affinity for Hedley Bull and the work of the 'English School', the traces of which can be found in this book. At the same time, I began focusing my broad interests in European security more specifically on East Central Europe – the area of greatest transformation and change in post-cold war Europe. The result was my book *The International Politics of East Central Europe* (MUP, 1996).

In 1996, I was appointed Senior Lecturer at the Institute for German Studies at the University of Birmingham. This appointment shifted the focus of my studies towards Germany and *Mitteleuropa*. The result is this book, which has been a real labour of love. Writing it has given me more intellectual pleasure and excitement than anything I have worked on before, and I hope I have been able to communicate some of my enthusiasm and sense of discovery to the reader. At this point I would also like to thank Nicola Viinikka and Pippa Kenyon at Manchester University Press for their encouragement, support and forbearance. I would particularly like to thank Nicola for her friendship and kindness over the years, and to wish her all the best for the future.

The research underpinning this study was made possible by the award of three grants. The first was a personal award from the Nuffield Foundation to study the emergence of a stable peace in *Mitteleuropa*, focusing on Germany's relations with Poland and the Czech Republic (Social Science Small Grants Scheme, ref. SGS/LB/0080). The second was by a much more substantial grant from the ESRC to a research consortium drawn from the Institute for German Studies, Birmingham. Our project is entitled 'Germany and the Reshaping of Europe', and is part of the ESRC 'One Europe or Several?' programme (ESRC Project L213252002). The third grant was the award of an individual NATO Fellowship for the period 1998 to 2000 to study 'NATO's Role in the Baltic Sea Region: Towards Multi-level Security Governance?'

Some of the initial theoretical and conceptual foundations for this book were laid during my research sabbatical at the Swedish Institute of International Affairs (*Utrikespolitiska Institutet*). It was during my time in Stockholm in the spring and early summer of 1997 that I first began to explore ways of applying social constructivist and new institutionalist ideas to Germany's changing role in *Mitteleuropa*. These preliminary ideas were presented at the European Community Studies Association (ECSA) conference in Seattle in July 1997. I would like to thank all at the UI for providing such a warm and stimulating environment for my sabbatical: in particular, Gunilla Herolf, Bo Huldt and Bengt Sundelius. In addition, I would like to thank my friends and colleagues at the University of Lund for their encouragement and interest: Rikard Bengtsson, Ole

Elgström and Magnus Jerneck. Most importantly, I would like to thank Karin Aggestam. Over the years, I have enjoyed our many discussions on social science methodology and the problems of research in international relations. Her doctoral thesis was inspirational, and helped clarify a number of issues with which I had been grappling.

Since moving to Birmingham in 1996, I have benefited enormously from the breadth and depth of expertise in European studies at Birmingham. For those interested in contemporary European affairs, the great strength of Birmingham is the existence of a range of leading research centres and departments in the field of European studies. In addition to the Institute for German Studies (IGS), I have been benefited from the knowledge and expertise of colleagues in the Department of Politics and International Studies (POLSIS), the Centre for Russian and East European Studies (CREES), the Department of Modern History and the School of Modern Languages. Birmingham's expertise in European studies has been formally recognised by the award of a Jean Monnet European Centre of Excellence. With the forthcoming creation of a European Research Institute, the University of Birmingham will be well situated to consolidate its position as a leading international centre for research in contemporary European affairs. I am lucky to be part of such a dynamic research community, and would like to express my thanks to Derek Averre, Judy Batt, John Breuilly, Julian Cooper, Stuart Croft, David Dunn, Colin Hayes, John Redmond, Terry Terriff, Cory Ross and Dan Wincott.

The Institute for German Studies has provided an ideal research environment over the last four years. Being part of a community of scholars sharing a common research focus has been an invaluable experience, and I have greatly enjoyed my discussions with my many friends and colleagues at the Institute. Thanks in particular are due to Willie Paterson and Charlie Jeffery; Lothar Funk, Heather Grabbe, Jonathan Grix, Vladimir Handl, Arthur Hoffmann, Vanda Knowles, Elke Krahmann, Kerry Longhurst, Wolfgang Müller-Funk, Julie Pellegrin, John Roper, Oliver Schuett, Henning Tewes, Wilfred van der Will and Marcin Zaborowski. I also owe a more personal thanks to Gundula Campden and Fraya Grant for their unstinting help and support over the years.

The bulk of this book was written between late 1998 and early 2000, during which time I was able to benefit from a series of research visits to Germany. I am grateful to the Deutsche Gesellschaft für Auswärtige Politik (DGAP); the Friedrich Ebert Stiftung; and the Konrad Adenauer Stiftung. More personally, I would like to thank Karl-Heinz Kamp, Joachim Krause and Ekkehard Lübkemeier. In addition, I would like to thank participants at the Arnoldshain workshop on '*Außenpolitikforschung*' for their valuable comments on this research project. The workshop, held at the Evangelische Akademie Arnoldshain from 11–13 February 1999, was organised by the Sektion Internationale Beziehungen of the DVPW (Deutsche Vereinigung für Politische Wissenschaften). The discussions at Arnoldshain provided an invaluable insight into the latest thinking on foreign policy analysis and international relations theory in Germany, and helped with the shaping of the theoretical framework for this project. My thanks in particular to Gunther Hellmann, Hanns Maull, Hartmut Mayer, Monika Medick-Krakau, Ingo Peters and Thomas Risse.

During the writing of this book, particularly over the last year, I have been kept relatively sane by the diversions offered by the Acock Green Guards and my Southampton friends. My thanks to you all ('we few, we happy few, we band of brothers'!). As always, my parents have been a constant source of encouragement and support, as have my two sisters, Caroline and Julia. I would also like to thank my extended family in Sweden: Gun and Gunnar, Karin, Marianne and Anders (*min vikinga broder!*).

Last – but certainly not least! – I would like to thank Lisbeth Aggestam. She is my muse, and my most constructive critic. Many of the ideas developed in this book owe their origins to Lisbeth. She has encouraged me to think more deeply about the questions I have raised, and given me valuable insights into the many areas of international relations theory and foreign policy analysis with which I am not familiar. In particularly, I am indebted to her for drawing my attention to role theory and its utility as an analytical tool. We have spent many happy months in Germany together, and I have enjoyed discovering Bonn and Berlin with her. Without her constant inspiration and support, this book would not have been written. *Tack så väldigt mycket, älskling!*

Harborne, Birmingham

List of abbreviations

AA	Foreign Office
AWAC	Airborne Warning and Control System
BDA	Federation of German Employers' Associations
BDI	Federation of German Industry
BFM	Federal Ministry of Finance
BML	Federal Ministry for the Food, Agriculture and Forestry
BRD	Federal Republic of Germany
BSEC	Black Sea Economic Cooperation
BMVg	Federal Ministry of Defence
BMWi	Federal Ministry of Economics
CAP	Common Agricultural Policy
CBSS	Council of Baltic Sea States
CDU	Christian Democratic Union
CEE	Central and East European
CEFTA	Central European Free Trade Association
CFSP	Common Foreign and Security Policy (EU)
CIS	Commonwealth of Independent States
CJTF	Combined Joint Task Force (NATO)
CMEA	Council of Mutual Economic Assistance
CREES	Centre for Russian and East European Studies
CSBM	Confidence and Security-Building Measure
CSCE	Conference on Security and Cooperation in Europe
CSU	Christian Social Union
CTBT	Comprehensive Test Ban Treaty
DAAD	German Academic Exchange Service
DASA	DaimlerChrysler Aerospace
DDR	German Democratic Union
DGAP	German Society for Foreign Policy

DGB	Federation of German Trades Unions
EA	European Agreements
EAPC	Euro-Atlantic Partnership Council (NATO)
EBRD	European Bank for Reconstruction and Development
ECJ	European Court of Justice
ECSC	European Coal and Steel Community
ECU	European Currency Unit
EDC	European Defence Community
EEC	European Economic Community
EFTA	European Free Trade Association
EMU	Economic and Monetary Union (EU)
EPC	European Political Cooperation
ESDI	European Security and Defence Identity
EU	European Union
FDI	Foreign direct investment
FDP	Free Democratic Party
G8	Group of seven industrialised countries plus Russia
GASP	CFSP (in German)
GATT	General Agreement of Tariffs and Trade
HCNM	High Commissioner on National Minorities (OSCE)
IFOR	Implementation Force (UN)
IGC	Inter-Governmental Conference (EU)
IGS	Institute for German Studies
IISS	International Institute for Strategic Studies
JHA	Justice and Home Affairs (EU)
KFOR	Kosovo Force (UN)
MdB	Member of the Bundestag
MOOTW	Military Operations Other Than War
MFN	Most favoured nation
NAC	North Atlantic Council (NATO)
NACC	North Atlantic Cooperation Council (NACC)
NATO	North Atlantic Treaty Organisation
ODIHR	Office of Democratic Institutions and Human Rights (OSCE)
OECD	Organisation for Economic Cooperation and Development
OSCE	Organisation for Security and Cooperation in Europe
PCA	Partnership and Cooperation Agreement (EU)
PCC	Partnership Coordination Cell (NATO)
PDS	Party of Democratic Socialism

PfP	Partnership for Peace (NATO)
PHARE	EU economic assistance programme for Central and Eastern Europe
PJC	Permanent Joint Council (Russia-NATO)
RAM	Rational actor model
RIIA	Royal Institute of International Affairs
SED	Socialist Unity Party of Germany
SFOR	Stabilisation Force (UN)
SIPRI	Stockholm International Peace Research Centre
SPD	Social Democratic Party of Germany
TEU	Maastricht Treaty on European Union
UCK	Kosovo Liberation Army
UN	United Nations
UNOSOM	United National Operation in Somalia
UNTAC	United Nations Transitional Authority in Cambodia
USSR	Union of Soviet Socialist Republics
WEU	Western European Union
WTO	World Trade Organisation

Glossary of political terms

Auswärtiges Amt	Foreign Office
Bescheidenheit	Modesty
Bundesbank	Federal Bank
Bundeskanzler	Federal Chancellor
Bundeskanzleramt	Federal Chancellery
Bundespräsident	Federal President
Bundesrat	Upper House of Federal Parliament
Bundesregierung	Federal Government
Bundesrepublik	Federal Republic of Germany
Bundestag	Lower House of Federal Parliament
Bundesverfassungsgericht	Federal Constitutional Court
Bundeswehr	Federal Armed Forces
Bündnisfähig	Alliance-capability
Deutsche Frage	German question
Einbindung	Integration
Epochenwende	Change of epoch
Erklärung	Explanation
Europaministerkonferenz	European Ministers Conference of the German Länder
Europapolitik	European policy
Foedus pacificum	Pacific Union (Kant)
Friedensordnung	Peace order
Gelassen	Relaxed
Gesamtkonzept	Comprehensive concept
Grundgesetz	Basic Law (constitution)
Handelsstaat	Trading state
Historikerstreit	Historians' dispute
Kerneuropa	Core Europe

Land (pl. Länder)	Federal constituent state
Lebensraum	Living space
Luftwaffe	Airforce
Machtbessenheit	Obsession with power
Machtpolitik	Power politics
Machtvergessenheit	Neglect of power
Milchkuh	'Cash cow'
Mitteleuropa	Central Europe
Mittellage	Central geographical location
Nie wieder Auschwitz	No more Auschwitz
Nie wieder Krieg	No more war
Ostpolitik	Eastern policy
Politikverflechtung	Interlocking politics
Rechtsstaat	State based on the rule of law
Ressortprinzip	Ministerial autonomy
Richtlinienkompetenz	The right to determine broad policy guidelines
Schicksalsgemeinschaft	A community of common destiny
Sicherheitspolitik	Security policy
Sonderweg	Special path
Sowohl als auch	As well as
Soziale Marktwirtschaft	Social market economy
Staatsräison	Reason of state
Standort Deutschlands	Germany's external competitiveness
Unbefangen	Un-selfconscious
Verantwortung	Responsibility
Vergangenheitsbewältigung	Overcoming the past
Vernichtungskrieg	War of extermination
Verstehen	Understanding
Vertrauenskapital	'Trust-capital'
Volk	People
Volksgeist	Spirit of the people
Wehrmacht	German army until 1945
Wehrmachtausstellung	Exhibition on the Wehrmacht
Westbindung	Western integration
Westpolitik	Western policy
Zentralmacht	Central power
Zivilmacht	Civilian power
Zurückhaltung	Reserve

'Ich bitte Sie', Ziethen wurde ärgerlich, 'Deutschland ist ein zivilisiertes Land.'

Pause.

Endlich Radek, leise. 'Auch das bedürfte noch eines Beweises.'

Stefan Heym, *Radek. Roman*

---

* 'If you please', Ziethen became angry, 'Germany is a civilised country.'
A Pause.
At last Radek, softly. 'That too needs to be proven.'

Stefan Heym, *Radek. A Novel* (Munich: Goldmann Verlag, 1996), p. 286.

1

Introduction:
Deutschland über Alles?

Not a principle in the management of our foreign affairs, accepted by all statesmen for guidance up to six months ago, any longer exists. There is not a diplomatic tradition which has not been swept away. You have a new world, new influences at work, new and unknown objects and dangers with which to cope.

(Benjamin Disraeli on the implications of German unification)[1]

Heinrich Heine once said, '*Denk ich an Deutschland in der Nacht, dann bin ich um den Schlaf gebracht*' ('When I think of Germany in the night, then I unable to sleep'). German unification in 1990 was one of the most important – and for many, unexpected – developments in late twentieth-century Europe. It has been a primary factor driving the reshaping of the political, economic and strategic contours of the European continent. The Europe of the twenty-first century will be greatly influenced by a Germany which has long been the strongest economic force in the European Union (EU), and which now constitutes the hub of the wider European economy. Once more, Germany has resumed its place at the centre of European affairs – not only geographically and economically, but also politically and culturally.

For some, the re-emergence, in the heart of Europe, of a united Germany with nearly 80 million citizens has rekindled a host of half-repressed fears and concerns – particularly given the transfer of the capital and seat of government from sleepy, provincial Bonn to the Wilhelmine splendours of cosmopolitan Berlin. At the very least, it has generated considerable discussion about the future foreign policy behaviour of a 'Berlin Republic'. Amongst Germany's neighbours, friends and former adversaries, many contradictory worries have been raised about its future role in a Europe no longer divided by an iron curtain – not all of them consistent or rational.

Some fear that Germany will become too strong and self-assertive, and that it will strive to dominate Europe. Others are concerned that Germany will resume its restless wandering between East and West. For some, the worry is not that Germany will abandon its *Zivilmacht* ('civilian power') character and strive for great power status. Rather, it is that Germany will turn in on itself, aspiring to become a large Switzerland and abnegating its European and international responsibilities. Thus Germany's failure to act as a traditional great power pursuing its national interests assertively and unilaterally have led to accusations that it is a 'muscle-bound state with no sense of national purpose' (Judt 1996: 89). Many concerns about Germany focus on whether or not it will be able to manage the competing demands of its *Mittellage* (its 'central geographical location'), and what consequences the dual enlargement of NATO and the EU will have for Germany's *Westbindung* ('Western integration').

This book examines these and other concerns. It explores three interlocking sets of issues. First, the changing nature of European order and the Westphalian states' system in what is best termed the 'age of late modernity'. Second, the implications of the dual enlargement of NATO and the EU for European order. Third, Germany's role in the dual enlargement process and its response to the dilemmas of its *Mittellage*. At the core of these three interlocking concerns is a central question: what is Germany's role in the reshaping of late modern European order? Germany – the 'central capstone of the European system' (Geiss 1997: 16) – is the key to a number of major processes of change in contemporary Europe. By virtue of its size, centrality and influence in the Euro-Atlantic 'security community', the Federal Republic is destined to play a pivotal role in the reshaping of European order. Not surprisingly therefore, the 'German discourse on European order since 1989 has been central to all reflections on the future shape of the continent' (Mayer 1997: 736).

The research puzzle

Germany: still a problem?

The end of the 'short' twentieth century – a 'century of extremes' (Hobsbawm 1994) which has witnessed two world wars and the Holocaust, followed by the emergence of a zone of stable peace in Western Europe – is an appropriate moment to reflect on the changes that have taken place in European international society. Much of the twentieth century has been dominated by the *deutsche Frage*, the 'German question'. In the first part of the twentieth century, Germany was more of a 'problem' than a 'question'. At the start of the twenty-first century, is there still a 'German problem'? Certainly, there are many questions about Germany – about the character of modern German society, the nature and extent of German power, the competence of its political class, the competitiveness of its social market model, its attitude towards the past, its role in Europe, etc.. But is there still a German *problem*?

The assumption underlying this study of Germany and European order is that there is no longer a German *problem*, nor is there a 'German question' in the traditional sense of this term. But there are a myriad of important and interesting questions to be asked about contemporary Germany. In considering the role of a united Germany in Europe, there are two main dangers. On the one hand, exaggerating German power and its ability to determine developments beyond its borders. On the other, believing that unification has had no significant impact on the Federal Republic and that Germany is just one more state among many in Europe. As regards the first danger: Germany is not Europe's superpower, nor is the EU a 'German swindle'. Nor do 'the Germans' suffer from 'angst, aggressiveness, assertiveness, bullying, egotism, inferiority complex, sentimentality'.[2] In many respects they are, as Richard von Weizsäcker has said (1991: 7), 'pretty normal people, just like everyone else'. But, on the other hand, neither is Germany 'just another European country'. It is the 'dominant structural power in Europe' (Hanrieder 1995: 125), with a troubled past, a potent economy, sophisticated diplomatic skills and considerable potential for shaping developments in Central and Eastern Europe – particularly in the historic heartland of *Mitteleuropa* ('central Europe'). Understanding Germany's role in the new Europe thus involves assessing how history and geography will affect the identity of a united German nation-state, in a Europe 'transformed by economic and social integration, and reshaped by the construction of formal institutions' (Wallace 1990: 92).

German questions

Although Europe no longer has a German problem, there are many 'German questions'. The *Bundesrepublik* that emerged from the ashes of the Third Reich was firmly embedded in Euro-Atlantic structures and committed to multilateralism in its foreign, security and defence policy.[3] It was also unambiguously orientated towards Western culture, models and influences. This 'Bonn Republic' quickly matured into a stable liberal democracy with a social market economy and a flourishing civil society. At the same time, it was an 'economic giant but a political pygmy', with a political character marked by a culture of *Bescheidenheit* and *Zurückhaltung* (modesty and reserve). Nevertheless, the Bonn Republic was remarkably successful at shaping its external milieu, and exerting influence inside the multilateral institutions within which it was embedded.

Unification and the end of the cold war, however, have transformed the geostrategic coordinates within which the Bonn Republic operated. From being a divided country in the centre of a divided continent, Germany is now united and at the heart of a Europe growing together. The decisive factor affecting Germany's foreign and security policy is its location on the eastern border of the transatlantic security community and its proximity to the post-communist countries of Central and Eastern Europe. The end of the cold war has thus meant a return to the *Mittellage* for Germany. 'The new Federal Republic', Wolfram Hanrieder has written (1995: 449), 'found itself in a new central location, and its foreign policy had to match up to the new demands this placed on it'. Germany is having to grapple with the new dilemmas arising from its location at the heart of Europe in change. The end of the cold war meant that 'Germany no longer straddled the East–West fault-line. It was once again in the middle geographically and politically, lacking natural barriers, a land of transit to other lands, too small to enforce its will on others, but far too strong to submit gladly to others' will' (Pond 1996: 27).

With unification and the end of cold war bipolarity, Germany has become the *Zentralmacht Europas* – 'Europe's central power' (Schwarz 1994). At the same time, it has begun to think hard about its identity and its national priorities. With the end of the cold war, 'every state in Europe had to ask itself again: What sort of power are we? What do we want to be? What are our national interests? What are our priorities? But nowhere were the questions more difficult than for Germany' (Garton Ash 1994: 380).

These German questions have become entwined with the move of the capital and seat of government from Bonn to Berlin. On 19 April 1999 – in the midst of the Kosovo war – the Bundestag held its first plenary session in the newly renovated Reichstag building in Berlin. This event symbolised the birth of the 'Berlin Republic'. The move from provincial, Rhineland Bonn to the cosmopolitan metropolis on the Spree has prompted talk of the coming of a 'Berlin Republic'. The change from Bonn to Berlin does not constitute a radical break in the political character and underlying foreign policy objectives of the *Bundesrepublik*. Nevertheless, it could have more than a symbolic significance. Unification has shifted Germany's geopolitical centre of gravity north-east, towards

Poland and the Baltic region.[4] Given the loss of its former extensive Prussian *Hinterland*, Berlin will be sensitive to developments in Central and
Eastern Europe (Hacke 1997: 6). This may well lead to some adjustments
to German foreign policy as the German political elite becomes more
conscious of developments in Central and Eastern Europe.

Two further events reinforced the sense of political change in Germany
in the late 1990s. The first was the election of September 1998, which
brought to power a 'Red–Green' coalition under Gerhard Schröder and
Joschka Fischer. The creation of a Social Democratic-Green government
was not only the most decisive change of governing coalition in the history of the Federal Republic, it also constituted a change of generation.
The post-war generation of Helmut Kohl and Helmut Schmidt, whose
experiences were formed by the war and its immediate aftermath, was
superseded by a new generation – the 'sixty-eighters' – whose political
socialisation took place within a democratic Germany securely anchored
in the Western community. The second political watershed was the
Kosovo war. The Berlin Republic, many commentators noted, was 'born
in war'. Bundeswehr participation in 'Operation Deliberate Force'
against rump Yugoslavia constituted another landmark in German foreign and security policy. For the first time since 1945, German forces
were engaged in offensive military operations against a sovereign state.
For a country with a troubled past and a strong sense of itself as a 'civilian power', this was not an easy step to take, and has generated a broad-
ranging discussion on the ethics of using military force to reshape
European order.

These developments have fuelled a lively debate in Germany on its
post-cold war foreign and security policy. This debate has raised
manifold questions. Will the Berlin Republic continue with the 'grand
strategy' of its provincial predecessor, a grand strategy based on multilateralism and the cultivation of a series of strategic partnerships? Will its
choice of multilateral frameworks and strategic partners change? Will the
Berlin Republic pursue its national interests in a more assertive and
increasingly unilateral manner?[5] What is the extent of German power in
Europe? What are the sources and dimensions of this power? To what
extent is Germany able to shape its external milieu, and to what extent is
it the object of globalisation and integration? Will Germany seek unilateral solutions to the dilemmas of the *Mittellage* through power politics
and economic leverage? Will the Berlin Republic exert a hegemonic influence in *Mitteleuropa*, Germany's old stamping ground? Can *Westbindung*
('Western integration') be combined with the new demands of *Ostpolitik*?

'Will Bonn be so tempted by economic and political opportunities in the East, or so absorbed by its own concerns about unification, that it will cease to be the engine of development of the European Community?' (Hoffmann 1995: 251–2).

At the core of this debate is the question of whether the Berlin Republic will be a *Machtstaat* ('power state'), *Handelsstaat* ('trading state'), or *Zivilmacht* ('civilian power'). Will Germany increasingly turn to the traditional tools of power politics (*Machtpolitik*) to pursue a more globally orientated grand strategy? Will it concentrate instead on economic well-being and prosperity rather than great power status? Or will its foreign policy be primarily driven by ethical concerns for human rights and social justice, with the goal of 'civilianising' international politics? (Schrade 1997: 255–6).[6] If there is one central question – one *Gretchen-frage* – that dominates the debate on united Germany's foreign policy, it is the question of its attitude towards multilateralism and integration. As Ingo Peters notes (1997: 362), one of the primary issues in the debate on post-unification German foreign policy is whether Germany will remain multilaterally orientated and institutionally embedded in Western structures – i.e., whether its *Westbindung* will continue.[7]

Germany and Europe: forward to the future or back to the past?

Those reared in the dominant realist paradigm of international relations have predicted that unification (with its consequence increase in relative power capabilities) and the end of the Soviet threat would prompt Germany to pursue a policy of 'autonomy maximisation'. An enlarged Germany, they believe, will inevitably be driven to pursue its national interests more assertively by the structural imperatives of an anarchic 'self-help' system. Germany, they assert, will focus increasingly on relative rather than absolute gains, thereby precipitating shifts in the European balance of power (Waltz 1993: 62–70; Mearsheimer 1990: 7, 32–7). Thus in an oft-quoted article entitled 'Back to the Future', the American neo-realist, John Mearsheimer, argued that Europe would revert to multipolar instability. In this context, he suggested, Germany would seek to balance against its rivals by acquiring nuclear weapons (Mearsheimer 1990).

There are, however, few signs that Germany is responding to its changed situation in the way neo-realists expect. There is a broad consensus that 'Germany has been exemplary in its European cooperation; this has changed little since reunification' (Kapteyn 1996: 141; see also Papcke 1998: 10). Moreover, there is little evidence to suggest that the bleak assumptions they make about 'anarchy' and 'security dilemmas' are of much relevance to understanding the altered structural dynamics of European order in the late twentieth and early twenty-first centuries. There is certainly little indication that Germany and Europe are returning 'back to the future'. Nonetheless, the notion that the demise of cold war bipolarity will be followed by a return to multipolar politics has been the central refrain of a group of influential conservative German historians and political essayists. In a book tellingly entitled *Die Ganz Normale Anarchie* (*The Quite Normal Anarchy*), for example, Jürgen von Alten has argued that in 1990 the world states' system reappeared in the form it was in the year 1910, 'like a Phoenix from the ashes'.[8] Arnulf Baring, an influential conservative historian, has similarly commentated that:

> Between 1945 and 1990 most Germans were convinced that all the dominant features of German history had ended. Something completely new had started ... These zero hour assumptions were revealed as illusions in 1990. In a totally unexpected manner, Germany got back its historical continuity. We are back in the Germany Bismarck created in 1871 ... The new situation facing the country – and the continent – after 1990 resembles much more the constellations of the late nineteenth and earlier twentieth century than the European structure of the last four decades. (Baring 1994: 8–9)

The belief that Europe and Germany are returning to pre-cold war patterns of multipolar politics, characterised by the balance of power and *Realpolitik* calculations, reflects a more fundamental and deep-seated realist pessimism about the prospects for moral progress and human development (Clark 1989: 7–9). Realists tend to see history as cyclical rather than progressive, and are sceptical about the prospects for states overcoming their mutual suspicions and animosities and learning to cooperate together. These assumptions pervade realist thinking, and colour their perceptions of contemporary developments. The argument presented in this book, however, takes issue with the conservative emphasis on historical continuity. It certainly does not accept neo-realist arguments that Europe's future will resemble its unstable, multipolar past. Such arguments overlook the changed structural dynamics of late modern European order. As Ernst-Otto Czempiel notes, while states may continue to pursue what they perceive to be their national interests, 'they do so in an environment marked by levels of interaction and communication, and institutions and cooperation that clearly differentiate it from the environment of earlier centuries that gave birth to the seemingly iron concept of *Realpolitik*' (Czempiel 1998: xi).

As we shall see in chapter 4, late modern Europe has been transformed by a series of deep-seated processes of socio-economic and political change. These have eroded many of the traditional features of Westphalian states's system and pointed to the emergence of a new structure of European order. Although 'Back to the Future' may be a catchy title for an academic article, it provides little or no help in understanding the changed dynamics of post-cold war European order. The problem with arguments that Germany is once again a great power playing the old games of diplomacy and *Realpolitk* 'is that the nature of power has changed since Germany was last a sovereign player. The instruments of the 1990s are not those that Bismarck would have recognised'. Germany has become a 'civilian power', and its 'principal institution for exercising this power is the Bundesbank and and its principal weapon is the Deutsche Mark' (Pulzer 1996: 315). Most importantly, late modern Germany is embedded in multilateral institutions and extensive transnational webs of interdependence and governance. These have transformed both the sources and dimensions of German power (see chapter 5).

The analysis offered in this book is thus based on two convictions. First, that 'Germans today are different from those who supported Hitler. They have accepted democratic values. They have done everything possible to demonstrate their good faith' (Alfred Grosser, quoted in *Newsweek*, 26 February 1990). Second, that Europe itself has changed. Europe, in what is best termed the 'age of late modernity',[9] is different from the Europe of Metternich, Bismarck, Stresemann or Hitler. It is characterised by a dense institutional matrix, extensive webs of cross-border transactions, myriad threads of socio-economic interdependence and novel forms of multilateral integration. Most importantly, the structural dynamics of European order have been transformed by the emergence in Western Europe of a zone of stable peace, with a 'pluralistic security community' (Deutsch 1957) at its core. This is the most significant development in the Westphalian states' system since its appearance in the mid-seventeenth century, and is central to the analysis developed in this book.

Stanley Hoffmann has suggested that Europe, 'thanks to a combination of democratic regimes, diffuse threats, and extensive institutionalization, may be on the threshold of a new kind of politics that goes beyond such traditional categories as balancing alliances or alignments, loose cooperative concerts, or junglelike anarchy'. He goes on to note that whether Europe will cross this threshold depends on 'the chief actors inside and outside the continent, but ultimately on the United States and Germany above all' (Hoffmann 1995: 281). This book considers whether post-unification German foreign policy is contributing to the emergence of a 'new kind of politics'. It seeks to identify elements of continuity and change in German grand strategy, focusing on German policy towards the institutional adaptation and enlargement of Euro-Atlantic structures. Its geopolitical focus is Central and Eastern Europe, rather than Western Europe. In terms of policy issues, therefore, it is primarily concerned with the process of NATO and EU enlargement, rather than EMU – the other major project championed by Germany for transforming the economic and political contours of late modern Europe.

Theoretical approach

Germany's 'grand strategy'

This book is centrally concerned with Germany's grand strategy towards post-cold war Europe. This begs the question: what is meant by 'grand strategy'.

The concept of 'grand strategy' may sound indelibly realist and suggest an unfashionable preoccupation with the military dimension of security. Traditionally, this has indeed been the case. Liddel Hart, for example, famously defined strategy as 'the art of distributing and applying military means to fulfill the ends of policy' (quoted in Murray and Grimsley 1994: 1). However, the notion of 'grand strategy' has increasingly been used in foreign policy analysis to refer to a broader set of political, economic and cultural concerns which go beyond issues of war and peace. Grand strategy has an 'essentially political nature' (Kennedy 1991: 168). It addresses the question of a country's foreign and security aims, and how best to achieve them. Grand strategy is thus much more than 'the art of preparing for the armed conflicts in which a nation may become involved':

> It is also, in a broader sense, the modern equivalent of what was, in the seventeenth and eighteenth centuries, called *ragione di stato* or *raison d'état*. It is the rational determination of a nation's vital interests, the things that are essential to its security, its fundamental purposes in its relations with other nations, and its priorities with respect to goals. (Craig and Gilbert 1986: 869)

The crux of grand strategy thus lies in *policy*, and involves a 'balancing of ends and means' in order to preserve and enhance a nation's long-term interests. It is also closely bound up with issues of 'national morale and political culture', and assigns a vital role for diplomacy 'in improving a nation's position ... through gaining allies, winning the support of

neutrals, and reducing the number of one's enemies (or potential enemies)' (Kennedy 1991: 5). Moreover, in a globalised world characterised
by high levels of interdependence, the 'tools' of grand strategy are likely
to change. 'Economic, political, institutional and ideological sources of
power gain in importance at the expense of military sources'. Consequently grand strategy in the post-cold war era has been defined as '*a
state's theory about its international role and about how best to fulfill or
defend that role*' (Pedersen 1998: 18).

A nation's grand strategy is influenced by five key factors (see Murray
and Grimsley 1994). First, its geographical size and location. In the case
of Germany, its *Mittellage* is the decisive geographical factor shaping its
post-cold war grand strategy. Second, its historical experience which
'creates preconceptions about the nature of war and politics and may
generate irresistible strategic imperatives' (1994: 2). Third, its culture
and ideology, which 'shape the course of decision-makers and their societies in both conscious and unconscious ways' (1994: 2). These cultural
and normative factors rise to a distinctive identity and set of role conceptions, and provide a prism through which the 'national interest' is
formulated and conceived. Fourth, its economic resources, which can
shape both the goals and means of foreign policy. This factor is particularly pertinent in the case of the Federal Republic, given its identity as a
Handelsstaat (or 'trading nation') and its past penchant for 'cheque-
book' diplomacy. Finally, the nature of the regime and its system of government will determine its specific policy objectives and instruments.
One crucial factor explaining the diverse character of Germany's grand
strategy since 1871 has been the existence or otherwise of democratic
institutions and the rule of law. In the case of the Federal Republic, its
foreign and security policies are very much shaped by the decentralised
character of its political system, with a variety of competing bureaucratic
and institutional actors.

Foreign and security policy

The study of German grand strategy, by definition, entails an analysis of
its foreign and security policies. These two terms both require definition
because the way they are defined has implications for the research strategies designed to investigate them. As regards the term 'foreign policy', this
has been described as 'the attempt of a state to influence its international
environment in order to create good conditions for the realisation of its
own interests' (Lübkemeier 1998: ii). This definition implies that foreign
policy analysis must combine a study of both the power resources of the

state in question and the nature of the international environment. In other words, it involves a study of both agent and structure. For this reason, chapter 2 focuses on agent-level determinants of German foreign policy, whilst chapters 3 and 4 deal primarily with the changing nature of European international society. The question of the sources and dimensions of German power is considered in chapter 5, which also addresses the thorny issue of how to define the concept of 'national interests'.

The definition of 'security policy' is perhaps more problematical, given the 'essentially contested nature' of the concept of security. Barry Buzan has argued that security in general 'is about the pursuit of freedom from threat'. In the context of the international system, therefore, 'security is about the ability of states and societies to maintain their independent identity and their functional integrity. In seeking security, state and society are sometimes in harmony with each other, sometimes opposed. Its bottom line is about survival, but it also reasonably includes a substantial range of concerns about the conditions of existence' (Buzan 1991: 18–19). In terms of the making of security policy, it has been argued that security policy is formulated by policy-makers who 'define security on the basis of a set of assumptions regarding vital interests, plausible enemies, and possible scenarios, all of which grow, to a not-insignificant extent, out of the specific historical and social context of a particular country and some understanding of what is "out there"' (Lipschutz 1995: 10).

These definitions indicate that foreign and security policies cannot be understood by rationalist approaches that make a priori assumptions about interests as objectively determined and pre-given. Instead, they suggest that a state's behaviour can only be understood by an analytical framework that includes a study of two essential factors. First, the cognitive frameworks and normative assumptions of policy-makers. Foreign and security policies are 'socially constructed' within a specific set of discourses and discursive practices. These reflect the normative and historical context within which policy-makers operate. Second, whilst normative and ideational factors can help understand the broad strategic direction of a country's foreign and security policy – i.e., its 'grand strategy' – they cannot shed much light on specific policy decisions. For this reason, foreign and security policy analysis must consider the institutional context within which decisions are framed and implemented. This includes investigating not just the cocktail of ministries and government agencies that constitute the 'complex institutional ensemble' that is the modern state, but also the influence of non-governmental actors. These analytical observations are given more extensive elaboration in chapter two, which outlines a theoretical model for analysing German foreign policy based on three key concepts: interests, institutions and identity.

Germany as a 'situated actor'

'Grand strategy', Thomas Pedersen has written, 'could be argued to be the point where structural constraints and ideas intersect in a long-term plan of action. The choices on which grand strategies are based are influenced by causal beliefs shaped by a country's history' (Pedersen 1998: 18). The study of German grand strategy in relation to the reshaping of European order thus raises questions concerning Germany's ability to influence its external environment. Is the Federal Republic actively able to shape developments in post-cold war Europe, or are its policies simply determined by the political, economic and strategic context within which it is situated? In other words, to what extent is Germany the object rather than the subject of change in post-cold war Europe?

This takes us to the heart of what has been described as 'the central problem of social and political theory' (Carlsnaes 1992: 245) – the relationship between structure and agency. Stanley Hoffmann has argued that international politics 'is the interplay between the constraints and temptations "structure" provides and the ambitions or needs of the actors'. Structure 'limits, restrains, and creates both risks and opportunities for the policies of rational actors'. The crucial questions, however, are 'what *is* structure, and how does it affect state behaviour?' (Hoffmann 1995: 282–3). Addressing these questions takes us deep into a voluminous – and often somewhat esoteric – literature on the agent–structure problematique. Although it is not possible to do justice to the ontological, epistemological and methodological complexities of the agent–structure question, the approach adopted here will be briefly outlined.

A useful starting point is the work of Martin Hollis and Steve Smith (1990). They have argued that approaches that stress the primacy of agency and those that emphasise structure rest on 'incommensurable' ontological and epistemological foundations, and that consequently there are always 'two stories to tell' about international politics. Walter Carlsnaes, however, has argued that we can escape this harsh ontologically zero-sum perspective 'if we conceptualize the problem as having its roots essentially in the empirical rather than the philosophical domain'. He therefore suggests that we should focus on developing 'a *single integrative conceptual framework* in terms of which the *empirical interaction* of agential and structural factors in social behaviour can be properly analysed'. Our stories, he has argued, 'of whatever kind – are always about something', and if they 'do not mix well, so much the worse for our stories' (1994: 280).

Carlsnaes thus indicates the importance of studying the relative weight of agential and structural factors in different concrete instances of foreign policy behaviour. He emphasises the interaction over time between structure and agency, which allows this process to be 'penetrated analytically as a consequence of its essentially *sequential* thrust in societal transformation':

> In this perspective, actions thus not only are casually affected *by* structures, but in turn – in terms of both intended and unintended outcomes – subsequently affect them, and so forth, indicating the mutually dynamic relationship between the two over time as well as the inherently constraining *and* enabling character of the structural domain. In other words, to explain fully a policy action at a certain point in time, this conceptualization indicates the necessity of considering not only *its* underlying casual structures, but also previous actions and both the structural effects *and* structural antecedents of the latter. (Carlsnaes 1994: 284–5).

This perspective suggests that the *Bundesrepublik* is situated in a structured social context that defines its range of potential actions. At the same time, Germany's behaviour affects its external environment, thus transforming the structure within which it operates. This process of mutual constitution means that neither structure nor agency can be accorded ontological priority (McSweeney 1999). Germany can thus best be conceptualised as a 'situated actor' located in a structured social context. As Colin Hay has argued (1995: 205), this implies two avenues of investigation. The first is the 'contextualisation of agency'. This involves contextualising foreign policy behaviour within the structural context in which it takes place, and considering how developments in the wider Europe impact upon the context and strategies, intentions and actions, of the actors involved in German foreign policy. The second is the 'strategic selectivity of structure'. Germany is situated within institutional, normative and material structures that define the range of potential strategies and opportunities available to it. These structures can constrain Germany's freedom of manoeuvre, but can also provide resources for enabling action and amplifying its influence on European affairs (Hoffmann 1995: 282).

The relationship between Germany as agent and Europe as structure can thus best be understood as being mutually constitutive. This perspective owes much to social constructivist arguments that highlight 'the construction of social structures by agents as well as the way in which those structures, in turn, influence and reconstruct agency' (Finnemore 1996: 24). It also draws on critical realism, which emphasises the importance of 'strategic action' by intentional and knowledgeable actors operating within structural settings that are both materially and socially constructed (Hay 1995: 200–1). Critical realism highlights the way in which the structural context both disposes states to adopt certain grand strategies over others, and is in turn affected by the states' foreign policy behaviour. At the same time, states themselves are involved in a process of 'strategic learning' – or what Bill McSweeney calls 'seduction' (1999: 169–70) – which may result in changed conceptions of the structure and of the state itself. This means that state behaviour may alter the external environment, and thereby alter the state's normative understanding of itself and its structured context. As will be argued in the following chapter, these shifts in normative understanding are often manifested in changed identity and national role conceptions, which in turn will precipitate changes in foreign policy.

Power and agency in Europe

One final analytical consequence of the agency–structure problematic is its implications for the concept of power. The link between power and agency is evident from the shared etymological roots of *Macht* (power) and *machen* (to make, effect, do, or bring about). Power, Colin Hay has argued (1995: 191):

> is fundamentally bound up with the idea of the victory of the *agent* or *subject* over its other – *structure* or *object*. Power is a question of agency, of influencing or 'having an effect' upon the structures which set contexts and define the range of possibilities of others. This suggests the need for a *relational* conception of both structure and agency: one person's agency is another person's structure. Attributing agency is therefore attributing power (both causal and actual).

Germany's power as a 'situated actor' thus depends on its relative strength vis-à-vis other significant European and international actors (including multilateral organisations). As will be argued in chapter 5, power derives from both tangible and intangible resources (Stoessinger 1991), and can be both relational and structural (Strange 1988). It manifests itself in four dimensions: political, economic, military and normative. German power is distinctive in a number of respects because the Federal Republic is embedded in a series of multilateral structures that both constrain its range of foreign policy actions, and empower it to act in certain ways.

The question of the nature and extent of Germany's power in Europe remains under-theorised. Yet there is a substantial academic literature on the concept of power, although much of it is framed in a highly abstract and esoteric way.[10] This study has drawn upon part of this academic literature in order to define a concept of power with which to explore Germany's role in contemporary European affairs. In this way, it seeks to contribute to the more ambitious task of developing a set of sharper conceptual tools for analysing the complex nature of power in late modern Europe.

Theory and the study of German foreign policy

The aim of this book is to provide a theoretically informed and empirically grounded study of Germany's role in the reshaping of European order. Many excellent studies of German foreign policy in the 1990s have been written by political essayists or contemporary historians. These have provided some interesting narrative based accounts of German policy (Schwarz 1994; Rühl 1996; Baring 1994; Hacke 1997; Schöllgen 1993; Garton Ash 1994). However, there has been a lack of more analytically vigorous and theoretically informed studies of German foreign policy (Schneider 1997: 114). This book is a response to calls for a more 'systematically conceptualised, theoretically informed work on German foreign policy as a contribution to foreign policy analysis in general' (Peters 1997: 384). It seeks to fill a conceptual gap between international relations theory and foreign policy analysis, using Germany as a case study with which to investigate the role of Europe's central power in the reshaping of post-cold war European order.[11]

Some studies of foreign policy behaviour concentrate on presenting a wealth of empirical evidence and allowing the 'facts' to speak for themselves. However, as Ian Clark has argued (1989: 32), there are a number of methodological problems with 'such a simplistic empiricism'. To begin with, 'although the events of international life are real enough', they can only be described through language. Consequently 'linguistic clarification and systematisation is an inescapable task within the discipline'. Second, the terms we use in our analysis are contested not simply because of linguistic carelessness or imprecision 'but, more radically, because there is a lack of agreement about which empirical situations deserve to have these words attached to them'. Hence, our definitions inevitably involve normative judgements about values and principles. Third, the 'facts' are not neutral 'because they will themselves reflect the questions asked and the methodology employed'. Theoretical assumptions underpinning a research project inevitably direct the line of investigation and determine what counts as 'evidence': 'the types of empirical fish that are caught will depend critically on the nature of the methodological net that is used'. 'Studies of international order', he concludes, 'are peculiarly susceptible to his problem'.

Theory is thus essential in order to make sense of a complex world and to be able to sift through and understand an infinite mass of empirical data. As Morgenthau noted, theory is used to 'bring order and meaning to a mass of phenomena which without it would remain disconnected and unintelligible' (Morgenthau 1993 [1948]: 3). Theories thus function like 'conceptual maps', helping us to make sense of a complex reality and to classify information in manageable ways. 'Without a theory of some sort, we would forever be at the mercy of the immediate flow of events, unable either to formulate or to classify our needs and preferences' (Ashe *et al.* 1999: viii). In the study of international relations therefore, theory is essential in order to define what it is we wish to study and our purposes in studying it. Theory also provides a guide to the range of analytical tools that are appropriate to the study of the object in question.

In this study of Germany and European order, theory serves three purposes. First, it provides a framework within which to define key concepts and categories. It thus serves to establish 'taxonomies' with which to categorise data (Gaddis 1996). Second, it seeks to 'draw concepts together so as to outline perspectives or build up "maps" of the international arena' (Woods 1996a: 13). These maps do not provide a naturalistic depiction of a given terrain; rather, they simplify the terrain in order to highlight some features at the expense of others. In this sense, they 'construct' the terrain of international relations and provide 'abbreviations of reality' (Hanrieder 1989: x). Third, theories offer 'very different specifications of the *core actors* in international relations; how it is that core actors *formulate their preferences*; how it is that actors *interact*; and which *capabilities* affect the implementation and achievement of preferred outcomes' (Woods 1996a: 13).

Theories can, of course, serve a number of purposes and take a variety of different forms. One important distinction to make is between theories that seek to *understand* international developments, and those that aspire to *explain* them. These two terms derive from Max Weber, who distinguished between *Verstehen* (understanding) and *Erklärung* (explaining). Building upon Weber's work, Martin Hollis and Steve Smith (1990) have sought to clarify the difference between these two terms as follows: *Erklärung*, they argue, involves constructing formal theories in order to generate and test hypotheses designed to identify casual factors. Testing hypotheses involves studying a number of cases in order to identify the casual factors. It aspires to a 'scientific' methodology comparable to that of the natural sciences (particularly physics), and tends to use tools such as game theory and expected utility theory. Its perceived strength is that it allows one to identify general laws as in the natural sciences, thereby enabling prediction. This approach dominates US international relations and American social science in general, and not surprisingly is closely associated with structural realism (Guzzini 1998).

Verstehen, or 'understanding', on the other hand, is based on the belief that a scientific methodology modelled on that of the natural sciences is inappropriate for the study of human society. This is because international relations are conducted by

> conscious entities capable of reacting to, and often modifying, the variables and conditions they encounter. They can at times see the future taking shape; they can devise, within limits, measures to hasten, retard, or even reverse trends. If molecules had minds of their own, chemists would be much less successful in predicting their behaviour. It is no wonder that the effort to devise a "molecular" approach to the study of politics did not work out ... The simple persistence of *values* in politics ought to be another clue that one is dealing here with objects more complicated than billiard balls. (Gaddis 1992: 55)

Consequently, *Verstehen* employs a 'hermeneutic' (or 'interpretative') approach aimed at analysing the rules, conventions and normative contexts within which social action takes place. The hermeneutic approach stresses the importance of language and symbols, and emphasises the importance of ideas and perceptions in guiding human action. It draws on a range of methods, including discourse analysis, institutional analysis and the study of history. It does not aspire to formulate and test hypotheses in order to uncover the 'laws' of social development, but, rather, to understand the reasons and motivations underlying specific policy choices. Whereas *Erklärung* seeks to explain human behaviour in terms of law-like generalisations, *Verstehen* assumes that 'the focus of the social sciences should not be the explanation of behaviour from the external perspective of a rationally disengaged observer. The focus should instead be the interpretation of social meanings within a particular cultural context' (O'Neill 1999: 15).

In practice, the boundary between *Verstehen* and *Erklärung* in social and political analysis is blurred. Most of the social sciences employ a blend of the two. Weber himself complicated the situation by speaking of *erklärendes Verstehen*, or 'explanatory understanding'. The key point, however, is not to make an 'either-or' choice between the two, but to mix them in various quantities. In this study, the *Schwerpunkt*, or 'centre of gravity', falls is the hermeneutic tradition of *Verstehen*. In other words, it is primarily concerned to 'understand' Germany's role in Europe rather than to 'explain' it.[12] There are a number of reasons for this. To begin with, the 'explaining' approach so popular in US academia tends to rest on realist assumptions. It is also grounded in rationalist approaches that assume states are unitary actors and embody a priori assumptions about actors' preferences.

More importantly, the 'explaining' approach tends to be based on what Ekkehart Krippendorff has called 'an extremely limited and stunted concept of science'. This can lead political scientists to 'verbally box themselves into a conceptual fortress, from which reality can only be viewed through lookout slits, and thus appears in stunted, limited and simplified forms' (1999: 1,000). Krippendorff, one of the founders of peace studies in West Germany, has stressed the need for political science to concern itself more with the 'morality of politics' – 'It is either an ethics-based discipline, or none at all'. He has therefore urged political scientists to draw on the spirit of the Enlightenment humanism in order to preserve the democratic ethos and ethical foundations of politics which American 'political science' has cast aside with its emphasis on empiricism and positivism (1999: 992–9).

A hermeneutic approach which stresses understanding and shared meanings, and which opens spaces for a consideration of moral and ethical issues, I would suggest, is more appropriate for studying Germany and late modern European order than an 'explaining' approach which aspires to a 'scientific' methodology. This is because the study of European order inevitably raises moral and political questions that a preoccupation with 'relative power capabilities' and the structural dynamics of 'self-help' systems overlooks. Thus for example, the Kosovo war has raised sensitive questions – which have figured prominently in the German debate – about humanitarian intervention and the role of military force in reordering European security. More importantly, as Nobel Prize winner Günter Grass has argued (1990), 'anyone thinking about Germany these days and looking for an answer to the German Question must include Auschwitz in his thoughts'.

Theoretical diversity

The analysis developed in this book draws from a broad range of theoretical and conceptual sources. These include security studies and peace research, especially work on stable peace theory and security communities (Adler and Barnett 1998; Senghaas 1995 and 1997); the 'English school', above all, Hedley Bull; and the 'new institutionalism'. Most importantly, however it has been inspired by social constructivism and classical realism.

Social constructivism is based on the belief that 'individuals and society continuously constitute each other through the medium of rules, and that rules depend on the performative power of language. So conceived, constructivism complements the Enlightenment belief in the power of language to instantiate reason and qualifies the belief in the power of language to represent the world as it is' (Onuf 1998: 169). Constructivists thus stress the importance of ideas and communicative processes for understanding foreign policy behaviour and processes of interest and identity-formation. They maintain that 'material factors and conditions matter through cognitive and communicative processes, the "battle-ground of ideas", by which actors try to determine their identities and interests and to develop collective understandings of the situation in which they act and of the moral values and norms guiding their interactions' (Risse and Sikkink 1999: 7). In addition, constructivists tend to conceive of international politics in terms of an 'international society', constituted by rules and norms. These rules and norms provide the cognitive parameters within which interests and preferences are formulated. Constructivists are also more attuned to the blurring of domestic and international politics, and tend to postulate a wider range of possibilities for change and progress in world politics than those informed by rationalist and neo-realist perspectives.

Constructivism thus promises to open up new lines of enquiry, focusing in particular on the impact of identity and ideational factors on the process of interest formation. In this respect, it is an important advance on rationalist approaches to international relations, which tend to see states' interests and identities as a priori and exogenously given.[13] However, constructivism still needs to address some core problems, notably the causal relationship between the 'material' and 'interpretive' worlds.[14] In addition, the relative scarcity of constructivist-inspired empirical research suggests continuing problems in developing an operational methodology capable of guiding empirical analysis.[15]

Given continuing methodological and epistemological problems with constructivism, it is important not to ignore some of the interesting work produced by scholars working within other traditions and approaches. One example here is classical realism, which has enjoyed something of a renaissance over recent years. One need not accept classical realism's assumptions about the anarchic nature of the international system and the intractability of the 'security dilemma' to recognise that it has generated some useful insights into foreign policy behaviour. Classical realism's strengths are threefold: first, its attention to issues of power and politics in the international system; second, its recognition of the importance of history, culture and ideas for state behaviour; and third, its emphasis on agency rather than structure.

Of particular interest is the recent attempt to develop an 'ideational realism'. Although Thomas Pedersen has described this as a 'tentative concept describing a third realist position' (in addition to classical and neo-realism), its intellectual pedigree clearly lies with classical realism. 'While accepting the primacy of state actors', he argues, 'it leaves some scope for state learning and innovation. It differs somewhat from classical realism in that it focuses on coherent sets of ideas shaped by historical learning and constrained by systemic factors'. At the same time, 'ideational realism accords strategy greater importance than does structural realism and is more optimistic as regards the possibility of cooperation in international relations'. Although international structures constrain state behaviour, 'statesmen and decision-makers at large possess a considerable freedom of action'. Pedersen thus argues that what 'structuralist realists like Waltz fail to explain satisfactorily is the element of learning and innovation in international relations'. Consequently, he places considerable analytical weight on the importance of ideas in international relations: 'At a fundamental level, the new interest in the role of ideas reflects a rediscovery of classical realism with its emphasis on agency and the historically generated particularities of states' (1998: 16–17).

As shall be argued in the following chapter, those working in the social constructivist and classical realist traditions would both benefit from a closer engagement with each other's ideas. In terms of the theoretical analysis developed here, it must be recognised that there are problems involved in drawing on a wide range of different approaches and traditions. Such theoretical eclecticism raises questions about the epistemological and ontological commensurability of different approaches. On the other hand, however, theoretical diversity 'is a strength, not a weakness of international relations' (Halliday 1994: 1). It also reflects a belief that 'truth is not an attribute of any one tradition but of the dialogue between them' (Smith 1995: 13).

A primary concern of this study of Germany and European order is develop a new model of foreign policy analysis informed by social constructivism and classical realism. It questions a number of traditional approaches to the study of state behaviour and foreign policy change, and seeks to sharpen some of the conceptual tools employed by foreign policy analysts. In particular, it seeks to go beyond the limitations of neorealist and rationalist accounts of state behaviour. In doing so, it identifies with the 'emerging synthesis' in the study of world politics. This seeks 'to link the international and the domestic, the societal and the transnational in a way that incorporates some of the elements of traditional Realism' (Bowker and Brown 1993: 2). As Gunther Hellmann has argued (1996: 29), 'we need to broaden the theoretical horizon in the analysis of foreign policy strategies beyond the narrow range considered currently among U.S. security experts'. Given their structuralist assumptions concerning 'the logic of anarchy and self-help, realists see balancing and bandwagoning as the main possibilities for states'. The case of Germany, however, provides 'a prominent reminder that the spectrum of possible state strategies is broader than that suggested by recent studies based on realist concepts'.

Notes

1 Speech to the House of Commons on 9 February 1870. Quoted in Auffermann and Visuri (1995: 170).
2 These were the 'national characteristics' ascribed to the Germans in the confidential Whitehall memorandum drawn up by Prime Minister Thatcher's private secretary Charles Powell after an informal seminar at Chequers on Sunday, 24 March 1990. The seminar was attended by Mrs Thatcher and a number of British and American 'experts' on Germany, and the memo was leaked and published in the *Independent on Sunday* on 15 July 1990. Margaret Thatcher's prejudices about Germany and the Germans are openly displayed in her memoirs. She ascribed the 'German problem' in no small part to the 'national character' of the Germans, who have 'veered unpredictably between aggression and self-doubt'. This has been evident to many Germans themselves, and thus 'the true origin of German *angst* is the agony of self-knowledge'. She argued that 'a reunited Germany is simply too big and powerful to be just another player within Europe', and 'is thus by its very nature a destabilizing rather than a stabilizing force in Europe'. Reunification has thus witnessed the return of 'another familiar bogey from the past – the German

Question'. It has 'created a German state so large and dominant that it cannot be easily fitted into the new architecture of Europe', and is therefore prone to act as a 'destabilizing influence/over-mighty subject/bull in a china shop' (Thatcher 1993: 769, 791, 813–14).

3 Multilateralism is a form of institutionalised cooperation that 'coordinates relations among three or more states on the basis of generalized principles of conduct'. These generalised principles of conduct 'logically entail an indivisibility among the members of a collectivity with respect to the range of behaviour in question', and successful multilateralism generates 'expectations of diffuse reciprocity' among members (Ruggie 1993: 11).

4 The decision to transfer the seat of government to Berlin, it has been argued, is 'also a decision – perhaps an unconscious one – for the North: Berlin is only two hours drive from the Baltic Sea, a one hour flight from Copenhagen, and an hour-and-a-half by air from Stockholm' (Steinfeld 1996: 25).

5 'Unilateralism', it has been argued, 'is more than any orientation that maximises self-interest, it is a principle for action aimed at limiting commitment while maintaining autonomy of action.' This can take two forms, an active or passive unilateralism. The former former involves 'the pursuit of one's own interests with no consideration or only a minimal consideration for the interests of others. Such insistence on pursuing one's own agenda often goes hand in hand with domination over others, even if done with good intentions. It rests on a "fait accompli" backed by superior power.' Passive unilateralism, on the other hand, manifests itself in a disinterest in external developments, which if taken to the extreme, can assume 'the form of isolationism, that is, the renunciation of all international relations' (Bertele and Mey 1998: 198–200).

6 'Im Mittelpunkt dieser Debatte stand (und steht noch immer) die Frage, ob das vereinigte Deutschland in seiner Außenpolitik künftig mehr Machtpolitik betreiben wird, ob es weiterhin und in verstärkem Maße in erster Linie ökonomische Eigeninteressen verfolgen oder ob es seinen vergrößerten Handlungsspielraum nutzen wird, um eine stärker werteorientierte Außenpolitik mit dem Ziel einer Zivilisierung der internationalen Politik zu betreibe' (Schrade 1997: 255–6).

7 'Eine der zentralen Fragen ist dabei, ob Deutschlands Außenpolitik multilateral ausgerichtet und die institutionelle Einbindung – die Westbindung – erhalten bleibt. Alternativ dazu könnte das erstarkte Deutschland bestrebt sein, die Handlungsrestriktionen, die mit der multilateralen Einbindung verbunden sind, zu lockern oder zu beseitigen, und unilaterale Strategien multilateralen vorzuziehen' (Peters 1997: 362).

8 'Man könnte sagen, daß im Jahre 1990 das Weltstaatensystem als ein ramponierter Phoenix etwa so aus der Asche gestiegen ist, wie es im Jahre 1910 bestand ... Ins Auge springt, daß die "Großmächte" weitgehend dieselben geblieben sind und nicht einmal ihre Rangfolge untereinander, wenn man sich auf diese Fußballmentalität einlassen will, sich wesentlich geändert hat' (von Alten 1994: 306).

9 Nicholas Onuf has noted that there are two camps in social theory. 'One is late-modern. It takes the Enlightenment project of universal reason, individual moral autonomy, representative political institutions, technical rationalization and material progress as flawed, egregiously perhaps, but not beyond the possibility of reconstruction. The other camp is post-modern. It takes the Enlightenment project as misconceived, terminally flawed, unworthy of redemption and perhaps already ended.' In the late-modern perspective, he argues, 'the ground is shifting beneath the edifice of modernity, but ground there is. Social construction always proceeds, like *bricolage*, with the linguistic materials at hand'. Post-modernists, on the other hand, reject any sense of a secure ground on which to base our knowledge and understanding of the social world. They seek to invent a 'new, allegedly post-modern language' with which to 'dismantle modernity by rescinding its terms of reference. Yet modernity is not so easily dispatched. Post-modern critique becomes a modern fashion, its vocabulary vulgarized, its promise betrayed, its imaginative poverty confirmed' (1998: 169, 133).

10 Defining power is a major academic industry in its own right. Garton Ash lists three 'dimensions of power – the military, the economic and the social' (Garton Ash 1996: 81–2). Similarly Knutsen defines power as 'a composite of military, economic and normative capabilities' (1999: 2). Others distinguish between 'command' or 'cooptive' power (Nye 1990: 31), between 'hard' and 'soft' power (Katzenstein 1997: 3; Anderson 1997: 80), and between 'relational' and 'structural' power (Strange 1988). Another interesting approach to the study of the 'faces' of power is provided by Simon Bulmer (1997), who draws from the work of Steven Lukes and Stefano Guzzini. Of particular utility is the work of Stoessinger (1991), who distinguishes between tangible and intangible power resources. All of these approaches contain valuable insights, but none succeed in capturing the richness and complexity of contemporary German power in Europe.

11 There are, of course, pitfalls involved in seeking to generalise from one case-study. As Steve Smith notes, there are serious questions involved in using single case-studies in order to construct a general theory of foreign policy, 'given the variety of states involved, the very different situational contexts, and the varying salience for these actors and contexts of the components of foreign policy' (Smith 1989: 378). Clearly, this study of Germany's role in reshaping European order can only provide for contingent generalisations. Nonetheless, the theoretical approach and analytical framework outlined here might be of some interest and relevance to others foreign policy scholars. For an excellent discussion of the utility of the single case-study method in international relations theory see Karen Aggestam (1999: 9–11).

12 A good example of the rationalist 'explaining' approach is Andrew Moravcsik's monumental study *The Choice for Europe* (1998). See also Baumann, Rittberger and Wagner (1999) and Hasenclever, Mayer and Rittberger (1997).

13 Both neo-realism and liberal institutionalism – the two main schools of

thought within rationalism – make two assumptions which do not accord with the German experience: first, that the environment of states can be conceived solely in terms of physical capabilities; second, that institutions and structures only constrain the behaviour of states with fixed interests (see Checkel 1998: 333).

14 John Ruggie, whose own writings have contributed to the emergence of the 'constructivist' approach to international relations, has further suggested that constructivism lacks rigour and specification. In contrast to neo-realism and liberal institutionalism (which he defines as 'neo-utilitarian' approaches), he argues that constructivism 'rests on a deeper and broader ontology, thereby providing a richer understanding of some phenomena and shedding light on other aspects of international life that, quite literally, do not exist within the neo-utilitarian rendering of the world polity. At the same time, it lacks rigor and specification – in fact, it is still relatively poor at specifying its own scope and conditions, the contexts within which its explanatory features can be expected to make much difference. Improvements are inevitable as work in the constructivist vein continues to expand, but given the nature of the beast there are inherent limits to the endeavour' (Ruggie 1998: 37).

15 Adler notes that despite a burgeoning constructivist literature, there is still a 'relative scarcity of early constructivist empirical research' (1997: 320). Checkel also notes that constructivist approaches still need to 'explain important international puzzles and phenomena and thereby demonstrate the empirical value of their research' (1998: 328).

2

Analysing
German foreign policy

Great changes in the way a nation thinks of itself, and acts, come like a tide. They come gradually, almost imperceptibly, in a series of surges and recessions, unevenly, like the waves on a shore. But they come steadily and surely, so that if one fixes one's attention on a landmark upon the shoreline one can measure the advance in the course of time .

(Robert Osgood, quoted in Pritzel 1998: 36–7)

Understanding Germany's role in the reshaping of European order requires a distinct set of analytical tools. Foreign policy change 'is the result of a complex interplay of stimuli from the external environment and domestic-level cognitive, institutional and political variables' (Checkel 1993: 297). The aim of this chapter is to outline an analytical framework with which to explore the complex interplay of factors affecting German foreign and security policy. It is based on three main concepts – interests, institutions and identities – and departs in two crucial respects from neorealist and rationalist models of foreign policy analysis. First, it stresses that 'institutions matter', and second, it views interests not as a given but as contingent on norms, beliefs and values (Schaber and Ulbert 1994). It also draws attention to the importance of foreign policy culture as 'a set of attitudes, beliefs, and sentiments which give order to the foreign policy process and which provide the underlying assumptions and rules that govern behaviour in the international system' (Maull and Kirste 1997: 284). Only by taking cognisance of the reflexivity inherent in the relationship between interests, institutions and identity, the argument runs, is it possible to understand the evolution of post-cold war German grand strategy.

Foreign policy analysis and the end of the cold war
The peeling back of cold war bipolarity has revealed the extent to which underlying processes of societal transformation have changed the

structural dynamics of international society in late modern Europe (as we shall see in chapter 4). These transformations have been concentrated in Western Europe, but their impact has also been felt in Central and Eastern Europe. Of particular significance has been the emergence of a zone of stable peace, with the transatlantic security community at its core. This has helped erode some of the main pillars of the Westphalian states' system, and reduced the prevalence of balance of power and *Realpolitik* considerations in European order. Given that much traditional analysis of foreign policy has been grounded on realist assumptions about international anarchy and the state as 'coherent units' (Keohane and Nye 1977: 24), there is a pressing need for conceptual and theoretical innovation in this field.

New conceptual tools are particularly needed for analysing the foreign policy behaviour of mature liberal-democracies embedded in pluralistic security communities. Neo-realism offers little of value in this endeavour. For neo-realists like Kenneth Waltz (1979) and John Mearsheimer (1990), the behaviour of a state is determined, first and foremost, by its relative power capabilities and its structural position in the anarchical states' system.[1] This dictates an endless struggle for power and survival, in which states seek to cope with an intractable security dilemma through a balance of power. The decisions of states 'are shaped by the very presence of other states as well as by interactions with them'. It is the 'situation in which they act and interact' which 'constrains them from some actions, disposes them towards others, and affects the outcomes of their interactions' (Waltz 1979: 65).

The problems with neo-realist explanations of state behaviour in late modern Europe are threefold. First, neo-realism's paradigmatic assumptions are no longer appropriate to twenty-first century Europe. The pursuit of parsimonious theory leads neo-realists to ignore historical, political and societal change. Key neo-realist concepts such as 'anarchy' and 'multipolarity' are too ahistorical to offer much insight into contemporary European international politics. Neo-realist theory is unable to account for change or the enormous variation in state behaviour within 'anarchic' and 'multipolar' systems,[2] and overlooks the socially textured nature of European international society in the late modern era.

Second, 'the refusal to consider what goes on within states is perhaps the most serious flaw of neorealism' (Hoffmann 1995: 283). Because of the overarching explanatory weight neo-realists attach to structural factors such as 'anarchy', they overlook the importance of domestic factors for foreign policy behaviour. The case of Germany illustrates how absurd this is. Germany's relative power capabilities and geographical location in the international system has changed little over the course of the last hundred years or so. German policy towards its neighbours in *Mitteleuropa*, however, has exhibited enormous variation – from *Vernichtungskrieg* ('war of extermination') to Willy Brandt's famous *Kniefall* in Warsaw.[3] Such wide variations in state behaviour cannot be understood without reference to domestic factors.

Finally, neo-realism underestimates the effects of economic interdependence and the impact of international organisations on state behaviour.[4] In addition to its more general weaknesses, Thomas Pedersen notes (1998: 30), 'structural realism has some particularly weak spots, the case of European integration being one'. Neo-realism's pessimistic assumptions about the possibilities of cooperation means that it is hard pressed to account for the extent to which multilateral integration has developed in Europe. Neo-realism's crucial weakness is thus 'its inability to provide an explanation of the high degree of institutionalization and notably its durability in the European region'.

In contrast to neo-realism's privileging of the structural determinants of state behaviour (which is shared by some versions of social constructivism),[5] the analytical framework outlined below considers both actor-level and structural determinants of foreign policy behaviour. The analysis itself draws on a number of sources. First, some of the more innovative approaches within the field of foreign policy analysis ('FPA'), particularly those associated with so-called 'second generation' theorists (Neack, Hey and Haney 1995). Work in this field has focused, *inter alia*, on the institutional processes involved in foreign policy decision-making, and on the cultural and societal context within which policy options are considered.

Second, the insights of social constructivists such as Emmanuel Adler (1997) and Jeff Checkel (1997, 1998), who have sought to carve out an analytically robust 'middle ground' between rationalists and reflectivists. Constructivism's most important insight is that 'the manner in which the material world shapes and is shaped by human action and interaction depends on dynamic normative and epistemic interpretations of the material world' (Adler 1997: 322).

Third, what has been termed 'neo-classical realism' (Rose 1998; Schweller 1996; Snyder 1996). Scholars working in the classical realist tradition continue to place emphasis on the importance of material power capabilities of a state in relation to the wider international system as a dominant factor shaping broad patterns of foreign policy over time.

However, they also recognise that there is no direct transition belt linking material capabilities to foreign policy behaviour, and acknowledge the importance of both elite concepts of national role and identity, and the institutional policy-making process. In this way, neo-classical realists 'open spaces for conversations, perhaps even mutually profitable sharing of insights', involving 'constructivists of various stripes (including the English School)' (Donnelly 1998: 403; see also Dunne 1995, and Williams 1997: 300).

Interests

Defining the 'national interest'

Understanding the behaviour of states in international society is impossible without some notion of their interests, i.e., their preferences and concerns. The concept of 'interests' has long been central to political analysis, yet substantial methodological and epistemological difficulties remain in defining collective 'interests'. This is particularly the case with the concept of 'national interests'.[6] However, if 'society as a whole is granted a reality other than that of the sum of its contending parts, then it becomes difficult to deny that the group defined by the society has its "interests" just as the smaller, more particular groups have theirs' (Clinton 1991: 49).

The central problem in defining the 'national interest' is how to distinguish between the interests of the political community as a whole and more particularist interests of specific groups within it.[7] Once one discards neo-realist assumptions about states as rational utility maximisers in favour of a conception of the state as a 'complex institutional ensemble', then the national interest can only be seen the outcome of a complex political process.[8] The main actors involved in this political process are public opinion, parliament and government (Hacke 1997: 511). The analysis of a country's 'national interest' thus involves consideration of both the political discourse surrounding foreign policy role conceptions and of the institutional policy-making process.

The 'national interest' of a country defines the parameters of its strategic goals and orientations – in other words, its 'grand strategy'. In a democracy, the 'national interest' is defined through a political process of interest articulation and integration. As David Clinton notes (1991: 50–1), the 'national interest' should embody a society's sense of its 'overall common good', and is 'that which makes the state better able to fulfil its obligation of protecting and promoting the good of society'. In the context of international society, 'this includes the ability both to protect the society from outside threats and to engage in mutually beneficial cooperation with other societies':

> The national interest, as it relates to foreign policy, is the end of maintaining the capacity of the state – that entity delegated to speak and act for the society in matters of diplomacy – to protect the society while it continues its search for its shared good. (Clinton 1991: 50)

Germany's 'national situation'

How a political community defines its 'national interest' depends on objective, material factors (such as geography, size and wealth), but also on range of subjective, normative considerations (Hacke 1997: 510–11). These include the identity of a community, its political culture, dominant moral and ethical values, sense of justice and conception of the common good, and its belief in what makes it distinctive as a national community. In Germany's case, it has 'a general national interest in peaceful international relations governed by sets of rules of international law, preventive crisis management, arms control and effective international institutions' (Gillessen 1994: 32). Germany also has a strong national interest in multilateral integration and pan-European cooperation.

German grand strategy (and the definition of the national interest upon which it rests) is thus the product of what Stanley Hoffmann called its 'national situation'. This refers to both the domestic characteristics of a state and its people, and to its position in international society. 'It is a composite of objective data (social structure and political system, geography, formal commitments to other nations) and subjective factors (values, prejudices, opinions, reflexes, traditions toward and assessments of others, and others' attitudes and approaches)'. This national situation is not a 'given' that dictates policy, but it does 'set up complicated limits that affect freedom of choice' (1995: 75–6).

Hoffmann's concept of the 'national situation' provides a much richer approach to the study of state behaviour than that of neo-realism, which focuses almost exclusively on material power capabilities. John Mearsheimer, for example, emphasises that state behaviour 'is largely shaped by the *material* structure of the international system', and it is the 'distribution of material capabilities among states' that provides 'the key factor for understanding world politics' (1995: 91). This assumption of the 'objectivity' of interests is shared by structural marxists who emphasise the centrality of economically determined class interests, and by neoliberal institutionalists who 'continue to treat actor identities

and interests themselves as preexisting and fixed' (Kowert and Legro
1996: 458).

However, the problem with rationalist approaches is that '(m)aterial
capabilities *as such* explain nothing; their effects presuppose structures of
shared knowledge, which vary and are not reducible to capabilities'
(Wendt 1995: 73). 'The inescapable fact seems to be that this type of
analysis stressing strategic and geopolitical factors is badly flawed'
(Hilsman 1990: 30). The importance of normative and epistemic interpretations of the material world was evident to an earlier generation of
classical realists. Hans Morgenthau, for example (1993: 11), quoted
Weber to the effect that 'Interests (material and ideal), not ideas, dominate directly the actions of men.' However, he went on to observe that 'the
"images of the world" created by these ideas have very often served as
switches determining the tracks on which the dynamism of interests kept
actions moving'. Morgenthau thus concluded that 'the kind of interest
determining political action in a particular period of history depends on
the political and cultural context within which foreign policy is formulated'. Consequently, '(t)he goals that might be pursued by nations in
their foreign policy can run the whole gamut of objectives any nation has
ever pursued or might possibly pursue' (1993: 11).

A central concern of contemporary foreign policy analysis is thus to
explore the 'national situation' within which states as 'situated actors'
find themselves. Material factors are important in setting the broad parameters within which German statecraft operates. However, the study of
these material factors is not sufficient to indicate the course and objectives of Germany's grand strategy. Understanding this involves considering two other factors: institutions and identities.

Institutions

Institutional analysis provides the second leg of the foreign policy model
presented here. As we have seen, whilst the systemic distribution of
material capabilities establishes the broad parameters of foreign policy
behaviour over time, specific foreign policy decisions result from a complex process of institutional policy-making. Institutional structures are
therefore a decisive factor in determining what has been called 'the capacity for collective action', in other words, the ability of a state to extract and
utilise resources for foreign policy goals (Hoffmann 1995: 268).

The assumption underpinning this leg of the conceptual model is 'that
institutions sometimes matter, and that it is a worthy task of social

science to discover how, and under what conditions, this is the case' (Keohane and Martin 1995: 40). Institutions 'do not merely reflect the preferences and power of the units constituting them; the institutions themselves shape those preferences and that power' (Keohane 1988: 382). They can do this by altering 'the calculations of interest by assigning property rights, providing information, and altering patterns of transaction costs' (Keohane 1993a: 29). Over time, commonly agreed and jointly observed principles and norms become internalised by the actors involved, thereby reshaping the perception of interests (Rittberger 1993: 19).

The important point to note about institutions is that they do not simply facilitate the bargaining process between political actors by reducing transaction costs and reducing uncertainty, as liberal institutionalists suggest. More importantly, institutions play a key role in the process of interest and identity formation. This has been one of the most important insights of both social constructivism and the 'new institutionalism'. Institutions 'offer a normative context that constitutes actors and provides a set of norms in which the reputation of actors acquires meaning and value' (Katzenstein 1997: 12–13). International institutions and multilateral structures thus facilitate the emergence of a sense of *Gemeinschaft* (community) based on shared interests, trust and a common identity.

Institutional analysis and German foreign policy

Institutions play a constitutive role in defining Germany's interests and identity at two levels – domestic and international. At the domestic level, a number of institutional structures have played a pivotal role in defining post-war German identity. These were largely imposed on West Germany from outside by the victorious Western Allies, but have been widely accepted as legitimate by most Germans (Duffield 1994: 179). These institutions include the constitution (the *Grundgesetz*), which has generated a sense of *Verfassungspatriotismus* (or 'constitutional patriotism'); the Deutschmark; and Germany's social market economy (*soziale Marktwirtschaft*). This last factor has been important in linking concepts of national identity and citizenship with the idea of comprehensive welfare provision.[9] More generally it was suggested, a *Staatsbürgernation* ('citizens' nation') had evolved in the Federal Republic that had defined 'the construction of identity through the civil rights and the constitutional order of the Federal Republic' (Lepsius 1990: 244–5).

At the international level, institutions again play a key role in shaping

Germany's interests, identity and foreign policy role conceptions. From its very earliest days, the BRD was embedded in a network of Western multilateral institutions, the most important being the EEC, NATO and the Council of Europe.[10] The multilateralism of German foreign policy has meant that the *Bundesrepublik* 'has never conducted a sovereign foreign policy, never a truly national, never even a largely autonomous foreign policy' (Rühl 1992: 741).

Germany's *Westbindung* (its institutional embeddedness in the West) has shaped Germany's perception of its 'national' interests, generated a distinctively 'Europeanised' national identity, and generated a very 'postmodern concept of sovereignty' (Anderson and Goodman 1993: 62). Indeed, the 'Europeanisation of the German state', Klaus Goetz argues (1996: 40), 'makes the search for the national, as opposed to the European interest, a fruitless task. The national and the European interest have become fused to a degree which makes their separate consideration increasingly impossible'.

At the domestic level, German foreign policy-making is the result of a complex interplay between a plethora of institutional and societal actors. Studying this policy-making process is necessarily complex and involved, given that Germany has more institutional actors involved in its European policy-making than most other states (Bulmer and Paterson: 1987: 18–21). This is partly a function of its federal system, and partly a function of specific constitutional arrangements, notably Article 65 of the *Grundgesetz* ('Basic Law' or constitution). This assigns the Chancellor the competence 'to determine and be responsible for the general policy guidelines' (the *Richtlinienkompetenz*). 'Within the limits set by these guidelines', however, individual ministers are given the authority to 'conduct the affairs of his department autonomously and on his own responsibility' (*Ressortprinzip*). Given a written constitution and the nature of post-war West German political culture, many policy discussions are framed in terms of their *Rechtsstaatlichkeit* (their constitutionality).

The most important governmental actors involved in policy-making towards Europe are the Federal Chancellor's Office (*Bundeskanzleramt*), Foreign Office (*Auswärtiges Amt*), the Economics Ministry (*Bundeswirtschaftsministerium* (BMWi)) and the Defence Ministry (*Verteidigungsministerium* (BMVg)) (see Siwert-Probst 1998; Andreae and Kaiser 1998; and Hoyer 1998). Following the administrative reforms introduced at the end of 1998, some of the European responsibilities of the Ministry of Economics were transferring to the Finance Ministry (*Bundesfinanzministerium* (BFM)), adding to the problems of coordinating German *Europapolitik*. In addition, the Federal Ministry for Food,

Agriculture and Forestry (*Bundesministerium für Ernährung, Land-wirtschaft und Forsten* (BML)) is closely involved in pillar one issues. As the EU expands its competencies in the fields of pillar two (CFSP) and pillar three (JHA), the Defence Ministry, the Interior Ministry and the Justice Ministry will all be increasingly drawn into EU governance – adding to the complexities of the German foreign and security policy-making process.

In addition to these governmental actors, a number of other institutional actors are involved in foreign policy-making. Both the Bundestag and the Bundesrat help shape German policy, particularly given their traditions of power sharing, coalition building, compromise and consensus (Krause 1998). Political parties also help shape European and foreign policy, not least through the work of the party Foundations (Bartsch 1998a; and Bartsch 1998b). Given the federal structure of the German states, the European Ministers' Conference of the German Länder (*Europaminis-terkonferenz* (EMK), established in October 1992) has an input into policy towards the European Union (Knodt 1998).[11] To add to this already complex picture, the Federal Constitutional Court (*Bundesverfassungs-gericht* (BVG)) has a role in European policy, as its landmark ruling on the Maastricht Treaty of European Union exemplified (Herdegen 1994).

One final point to note is that in addition to the formal institutional structures of decision-making, foreign policy is also shaped by a range of other societal actors (Bühl 1994; Milner 1998). Structuralist accounts of international relations fail to accord sufficient weight to 'the importance of domestic factors in understanding foreign policy' and overlook the significance of relations between 'what is often called "civil society" and the state' (Hoffmann 1995: 270). In this respect, one feature of the German political system which should not be ignored is its highly corporatist nature. Both the trades unions (*Deutscher Gewerkschaftsbund* (DGB)) and corporate business organisations such as the *Bundesverband der Deutschen Industrie* (BDI) and the *Bundesvereinigung der Deutschen Arbeitgeberverbände* (BDA) have a keen interest in European policy making. Thus a wide range of actors are involved in shaping German policy towards Europe: state and non-governmental actors, political parties and their foundations, organised labour, and business and financial organisations (Holst 1998; Hartmann 1998; Brettschneider 1998).

The result of the institutional polyphony that characterises the German political system is that the making and execution of German *Europapolitik* is marked by a high degree of sectorisation. Policy emerges from the interaction of a plethora of institutional actors, each of which operates on the basis of their own distinctive 'organisational routines' and 'standard operating procedures'. Some ministries may be more concerned with their bureaucratic priorities than with meeting the strategic aims of the government. Others, like the Transport or Construction Ministries, often act as tribunes for powerful domestic lobbies. The result is that the policies pursued by individual ministries may not be congruent with the government's grand strategy (Goldberger 1993: 289–93). For this reason, institutional analysis is an indispensable tool in understanding state behaviour that complements analysis of systemic and ideational factors.

Organisational process and bureaucratic politics

The seminal text for understanding the role of institutional actors in the foreign policy-making process is Graham Allison's classic work, *Essence of Decision* – 'one of the few genuine classics of modern International Relations' (Brown 1997: 75). Allison outlined three models of foreign policy decision-making: the *rational actor model* (RAM), the *organisational process* model, and the *bureaucratic politics* model. The rational actor model assumes that foreign policy decisions are rational responses to a particular situation, formulated by a single unitary state actor operating on the basis of perceived national interests. The problem with the RAM approach is that states are not unitary actors, and that interests are not endogenously given.

Allison's other two models are of more use in understanding the institutional dimension of German foreign policy. His second model (organisational process) takes as its point of departure the institutional pluralism of modern states and focuses on intra-organisational factors. It posits that policy outcomes result from the interaction of multiple organisations, each of which has distinctive ways of making policy decisions – *organisational routines* and *standard operating procedures*. These organisations are highly resistant to attempts at centralised control and coordination. Whilst Allison's model was based on the US experience, it is also relevant to Germany – another Federal system – which, as we have seen, has more institutional actors involved in European policy-making than most other states.

Allison's third model (bureaucratic politics) focuses on inter-organisational factors. Whilst the two previous models suggest that foreign policy decisions will be taken on foreign policy grounds, the bureaucratic politics model suggests that this is not necessarily so. Political, economic and other factors external to the specific foreign policy issue being considered may affect decision-making. In particular, bureaucracies have their own specific interests and concerns to defend (budgets, resources, influence), and may therefore propose policy options that enhance their position within the overall policy-making process. Allison's third model thus stresses that bureaucracies make decisions on the basis of their own specific organisational interests – in a nut-shell, 'where you sit determines where you stand'.

As Allison argued, the three different models each have a certain explanatory power, and need to be integrated rather than segregated. The biggest lacuna in Allison's work, and in the literature on 'institutional pluralism' more generally, is an insufficient account of the cognitive and ideational dimension of decision-making. This has been an area of considerable theoretical innovation over recent years, although many questions remain to be addressed. The ideational or socio-cognitive dimension thus constitutes the third leg of analytical framework employed in this book.

Identity

The 'cognitive revolution'

Whilst an analysis of institutional policy-making processes can provide valuable insights into the making of German foreign policy, it can only reveal part of the picture. One of the important developments in the field of foreign policy analysis since Allison's path-breaking study has been the increased awareness accorded to cognitive and psychological influences on policy-making. This has been part and parcel of what has come to be known as the 'cognitive revolution'. The central insight of the cognitive revolution is that 'structural factors – such as institutions, bureaucracies, international regimes, the state of the economy, geopolitical emplacement, etc. – are *cognitively* mediated by the actors in question rather than affecting policy actions directly' (Carlsnaes 1994: 284). 'Thinking about foreign affairs', one British diplomat has written, ' – like any other kind of thinking – requires a conceptual map which, as maps do, simplifies the landscape and focuses on the main features' (Cooper 1996: 8).

The cognitive revolution has further eroded rationalist assumptions about the pre-given and objectively determined character of interests. The central argument of the cognitive revolution has been that rationality is *bounded*. Actors 'satisfice' rather than optimise. They do not have access to all relevant information, nor do they seek it. They process information differently in times of stress than under routine conditions. They act on the basis of hidden agendas, such as their specific institutional or bureaucratic concerns. Above all, historical precedents, cultural values, normative beliefs and other socio-pyschological factors influence the perception of interests. Consequently 'images of other states are difficult to alter. Perceptions are not responsive to new information about the other side; small changes are not likely to be detected. Once a statesman thinks he knows whether the other needs to be deterred and what kind of strategy is appropriate, only the most dramatic events will shake him' (Jervis 1983: 25–6).

In an important study of the impact of ideas on foreign policy, Judith Goldstein and Robert Keohane (1993) have proposed a three-fold categorisation of ideas or beliefs. First, 'world views': these are embedded in the symbolism of a culture and entwined with identity-conceptions. Second, 'principled beliefs': these are normative ideas for distinguishing between right or wrong. Third, 'causal beliefs': these are beliefs about cause–effect relationships which provide guides as to how to achieve a given policy objective.

They go on to suggest that ideas can influence foreign policy behaviour in three ways. First, they can serve as 'road maps', guiding actors' preferences and indicating ways of achieving them. Second, they can act as a 'focal point' for actors in the absence of compromise or cooperation. Third, they can become 'institutionalised', i.e., embedded in the operation of institutions and social practices. Their argument is that 'ideas influence policy when the principled or casual beliefs they embody provide road maps that increase actor's clarity about goals or end–means relationships, when they affect outcomes of strategic situations in which there is no unique equilibrium, and when they become embedded in political institutions'. In contrast to many social constructivists, however, they do not argue that it is ideas rather than interests that 'move the world'. Rather, they follow a Weberian approach in arguing that 'ideas *as well as* interests have causal weight in explanations of human action' (Goldstein and Keohane 1993: 3–4).

This study is sympathetic to Goldstein and Keohane's Weberian assumptions that both ideas and material interests shape foreign policy behaviour, although it does not adopt their approach. Subsequent chapters will examine German discourses on Europe in order to uncover the ideas and cultural assumptions that influence policy debates. The aim is to explore the impact on German policy of underlying sets of cultural norms and values, understood as 'social knowledge structures that define collective expectations of appropriate action' (K. Aggestam 1999: 36).

This assumes that states act according to the 'logic of appropriateness' rather than the 'logic of expected consequences' (March and Olsen 1998: 8–11).[12] German grand strategy can thus only be fully understood by considering the cultural determinants which shape it, and which provide:

> a framework for organizing the world, for locating the self and others in it, for making sense of the actions and interpreting the motives of others, for grounding an analysis of interests, for linking collective identities to political action, and for motivating people and groups toward some actions and away from others. (Ross 1997: 42)

Identity and foreign policy

One of the most important areas of theoretical innovation in foreign policy analysis over recent years has been the growing awareness that identities matter in international relations. Identities shape the definition of state and national interests, and thereby constitute an important influence on foreign policy behaviour. National identity 'serves not only as the primary link between the individual and society, but between a society and the world' (Pritzel 1998: 19). 'Effective foreign policy', it has been said, 'rests upon a shared sense of national identity, of a nation-state's "place in the world", its friends and enemies, its interests and aspirations. These underlying assumptions are embedded in national history and myth, changing slowly over time as political leaders reinterpret them and external and internal developments reshape them' (Hill and Wallace 1996: 8).

Identity becomes an essential object of foreign policy analysis once one discards the assumptions of structural realism. Structural realism homogenises unit level characteristics, thereby tending to equate statehood and identity. The state is seen as a 'national-territorial totality', which comprises 'in conceptual form what is denoted visually on a political map – viz. the country as a whole and all that is within it: territory, government, people, society' (Halliday 1994: 78). However, in this study the state is conceptualised as a 'complex institutional ensemble' that comprises a variety of administrative structures and practices. This means that the constitution of societal identity is not simply assumed as a function of statehood, but is revealed as a problematical area, requiring study in its own right.[13] In this study, identities are conceptualised as expressions of a group's shared sense of itself and its place in the social world. Identities define the primary values of the group, and ascribe standards of appropriate behaviour (Katzenstein 1996; Preston 1997).

National identity helps shape the broad directions of foreign policy (i.e., a nation's grand strategy) by providing cognitive lenses for policy makers, based on political judgements about the 'national interest'. Analyses of official discourses on national identity can only explain the grand schemes of diplomacy. They cannot provide explanations of discrete foreign policy behaviour or the nuances of negotiating positions on specific policy issues. They cannot, for example, shed significant light on Germany's negotiations on beef sales within the European Union, or on specific arms procurement decisions. These are determined by a political process involving the relevant ministries, other political actors and private sector interests. Conceptions of the national interest only affect this political process indirectly, by establishing the broad cultural parameters within which competing policy options are considered. National identity thus provides the ideational framework within which a nation's grand strategy is formulated. This can be illustrated by reference to the development of post-war West Germany identity.

German identity
Historically the Germans have conceptualised the relationship between state and nation in 'ethnic' rather than 'civic' terms. In contrast to their French neighbours, for example, whose idea of nationhood is founded on a notion of popular sovereignty and citizenship, the Germans have conceived of the nation in terms of its history, language and culture – the *Volksgeist* or spirit of its people (Kohn 1944: 45–7; Dyson 1980: 157–83). This ethnic conception of German nationalism fueled both territorial irredentia and an intolerant and exclusionist concept of *das Volk*.

Such conceptions of German identity were profoundly shaken by the experience of defeat in war and subsequent revelations about the Holocaust. Indeed, the crushing of the Third Reich in war constitutes one of those 'teachable moments' when rapid changes in internal and external environments spawn new definitions of self and the reordering of priorities, with far-reaching consequences for foreign policy (Pritzel 1998: 2). 'The political identity of the Germans', one commentator has noted, 'will in future continue to be defined only by reference to 1945 as the symbolic date for war and genocide' (Münkler 1998: 13). Since the late 1960s, a 'post-Holocaust' identity has developed in West Germany as a result of two institutional changes: the integration of the *Bundesrepublik* within Euro-Atlantic structures, and the gradual democratisation of West German politics and society. This post-Holocaust identity is grounded on 'Western' concepts of citizenship and a commitment to democratic values and human rights.

One distinctive feature of post-war German identity is its 'significant Other'. All identities are constructed in terms of a 'significant Other'. For most nation-states, this is usually another country or people, and is usually conflictual. In the case of contemporary Germany, however, its most significant defining 'Other' has been the Germany of Hitler and National Socialism. German identity has been reconstructed in opposition to the excessive nationalism of the past and the militarisation of German patriotism that it involved. As Ulrich Herbert (one of the new generation of German historians), has argued, the *Judenmord* (the Holocaust) has become for modern Germany 'the core event of the century'. 'Despite many other problems', he argues, 'one of the most significant and positive features of the political culture of the Federal Republic of Germany is that the debate on National Socialism has become a central point for the constitution of the identity of this republic' (Herbert 1998: 9).

Germany's evolving foreign policy identity

Germany's post-Holocaust identity, constructed around democratic domestic institutions and multilateral integration, has taken deep roots in the Federal Republic. Yet identities 'are neither permanent nor immutable'. Over time polities 'adapt to new circumstances, develop new mythologies, and recast themselves'. New identities can emerge that 'can result in different concepts of the national interest and therefore new foreign policies' (Pritzel 1998: 427).

Not surprisingly, unification and the end of the cold war have acted as a catalyst for debates about German identity. 'Unified Germany', Peter Pulzer has written, 'is looking for a role and seeking an identity' (1995: 13). Germans have again had to ask themselves: who are we?; what sort of a country are we, and what sort of a country do we wish to become?; where do we fit in Europe?; are we West European or Central European?; do we have national interests, and if so, what are they? This questioning has raised concerns in France, Germany's closest European partner, that unification may weaken Germany's civic nationalism and rekindle older, more ethnic and *Volkist* notions (Hopmann 1994: 79).[14]

These concerns have been fuelled by some of the writings of Germany's new nationalist right, who repudiate important elements of post-war Germany's political identity (see for example Schwilk and Schlacht 1994, and Zitelmann, Weissmann and Grossheim 1993). These 'normalisation-nationalists', as they have been dubbed (Hellmann 1996: 16–19), regard the *Bundesrepublik* as a victim of ideological terror on the part of the victorious Western Allies. German national identity, they argue, was

effectively eradicated by a policy of enforced Westernisation. As a consequence, Germans were forced to 'lose their historical identity, and with
that their sense of community and self-respect' (Klaus Rainer Röhl in
Schwilk and Schlacht 1994: 94). They also reiterate themes previously
aired in the *Historikerstreit* ('historians dispute') of the 1980s, which
sought to relativise the Holocaust and downplay the unique horror of
Auschwitz.[15]

Despite the notoriety surrounding these 'normalisation-nationalists',
their views have received little public echo. This indicates that Germany's
post-Holocaust identity has struck deep roots, and that the rejection of
National Socialism remains a 'central point for the constitution of the
identity' of the Federal Republic. This was demonstrated by the overwhelming public interest which greeted Daniel Goldhagen's controversial
study, *Hitler's Willing Executioners: Ordinary Germans and the Holocaust*
(1996). Goldhagen's central thesis is that an 'eliminationist anti-semi-
tism' was pervasive in late nineteenth- and early twentieth-century Germany that turned 'annihilationist' under the Nazis. Despite stringent
academic criticism of his research methodology, Goldhagen's book was
widely read and discussed by a German public thirsty for knowledge and
understanding of the horrors of the Holocaust (Joffe 1996). In contrast to
both Austria and Japan (Buruma 1994), therefore, Germany has engaged
seriously with a process of *Vergangenheitsbewältigung* ('overcoming the
past'). This has involved confronting the horrors of National Socialism
and trying to think through its consequences, rather than simply repress-
ing or denying it. One indication of this is that in a public opinion poll
conducted in Germany in 1995, four-fifths of those asked defined 8 May
1945 as a 'day of liberation' rather than defeat (Müller 1999: 167).

While there are few indications that Germany is seeking to shed its
post-Holocaust identity, there are intimations of other subtle but significant shifts in its political identity. Given the magnitude of the changes
that have transformed Germany and its external environment since 1989,
it would indeed be remarkable if German identity were to remain
untouched. Four factors in particular have contributed to a subtle refor-
mulation of aspects of German identity.

The first is associated with the end of cold war bipolarity, which has
again revealed the importance of Germany's central geographical location, its *Mittellage*. This has already affected discussions about Germany's
role in Europe, and the balance between its *Westbindung* and *Ostpolitik*
(Zimmer 1997). In addition, it has led some Germans to ask whether they
are West Europeans or Central Europeans, and what this means for their

national interests (Garton Ash 1994: 381). Second, unification has posed Germany with the classic problem of nation-building, and shifted its centre of gravity towards the north east. This is symbolised by the move of the capital and seat of government from provincial, Rhineland Bonn to the cosmopolitan metropolis of Berlin. Third, EMU will inevitably have implications for German identity, given the role the Deutsche Mark played in rebuilding the self-esteem of post-war West Germans. Finally, Germany is experiencing an important generational change (Schissler 1997). As a result of the September 1998 Bundestag elections, the generation with direct experience of the war and its immediate aftermath – the generation of Helmut Kohl and Helmut Schmidt – is finally leaving the political stage. It is being replaced by the post-war generation of 'sixty-eighters', epitomised by Joschka Fischer, Gerhard Schröder and Otto Schilly.

This last factor has already had an impact on German foreign policy. In an interview in *Spiegel* magazine, the new *Bundeskanzler*, Gerhard Schröder, emphasised the importance of the generational change. His generation and the successor generation, he argued, had 'grown up in and been politically socialised by a democratic Germany, which had always conceived of itself as a natural part of Europe'. Consequently his concept of a 'European identity' was different from that of his predecessor, Helmut Kohl:

> The generation of Helmut Kohl thought that we Germans must be European because otherwise the fear of the '*Furor teutonicus*' would re-appear. His words 'Europe is a question of war and peace' could only be understood in this way. I argue that we must also be European, but regard this as a natural fact of life which we have freely chosen, rather than as a question of historical duty. The advantage of this is that one can then be less taciturn about pursuing ones' interests than was the case in the past.

This generational change has had three initial foreign policy consequences. These will be considered at greater length in subsequent chapters, but can be briefly summarised as follows: first, human rights have become central to foreign policy discourse. This can be seen from discussions surrounding arms exports to Turkey and elsewhere, but was exemplified by the discourse surrounding the Kosovo war (Hyde-Price 1999). This portrayed the campaign as the archetype of a 'new moral crusade', with humanitarian intervention as a new moral and political 'categorical imperative' leading to a Kantian peace order. Second, the notion of 'enlightened self-interest' (*aufgeklärtes Eigeninteresse*) has emerged as a leitmotif of Schröder's *Europapolitik* (Schwarz 1999: 5). This marks a break with the rhetoric surrounding Kohl's *Europapolitik*, although its practical consequences are still relatively small.

Third, it has become more common in official circles to speak of Germany, not as 'great power' (*Großmacht*), but as 'large power' (*großer Macht*). This semantic nuance is meant to avoid unfortunate associations with Germany's past, but the practical difference between the two concepts remains unclear. According to Wolfgang Ischinger (State Secretary in the Foreign Office), as a *großer Macht* Germany must live up to the responsibilities appropriate to its 'weight, role, economic position and military structure' (Vernet 1999: 16). This reflects a switch away from the *Bescheidenheit* (modesty) and *Zurückhaltung* (reserve) which characterised the Bonn Republic to the greater confidence and self-assurance of the Berlin Republic. The Berlin Republic, it has been suggested, is becoming more *Unbefangen* (unselfconscious) and *gelassen* (relaxed) (Korte 1998).

Role theory

As a result of the cognitive revolution, it was increasingly recognised in foreign policy analysis circles that perceptions were vital in the policy-making process. Perceptions provided a means of intercepting, classifying and interpreting information in terms of pre-established beliefs. These beliefs, it was suggested, were organised into structured systems that set cognitive limits to rational decision-making. However 'most of the studies which focus on decision-makers' perceptions include only perceptions of the external environment, especially enemy characteristics and actions, and very few investigate decision-makers' perceptions of their own nations' (Wish quoted in Jönsson 1984: 3). One notable exception to this was the research tradition on national role conceptions.

Role theory was first introduced to foreign policy analysis by Kalevi Holsti in a seminal article originally published in 1970. He drew on sociological interpretations of role in order to suggest how perceptions may structure and guide foreign policy-making. He argued that a state's foreign policy is influenced by its 'national role conception'. This is a product of a nation's socialisation process and influenced by its history, culture and societal characteristics. 'A *national role conception*', he argued, 'includes the policy-makers' own definitions of the general kinds of decisions, commitments, rules, and actions suitable to their state, and of the functions, if any, their state should perform on a continuing basis in the international system or in subordinate regional systems,

(Holsti 1987: 12). His methodology involved analysing elite perceptions of national role, and initiated a research tradition focused on role conceptions (see for example Walker 1979; Wish 1980; Jönsson and Westerlund 1982). This approach has been relatively neglected for many years, although more recently it has received growing academic interest (see for example L. Aggestam 1999; Kirste and Maull 1996; Tewes 1998).

'Why the new interest in role conceptions?', Hudson and Vore ask (1995: 226). The answer, they suggest, is that national role conceptions provide 'one of the few conceptual tools we have for the study of how society and culture serve as a context for a nation's foreign policy'. Role theory thus 'allows one to bridge the conceptual gap between the general beliefs held in a society and the beliefs of foreign policy decision makers'. Defining a foreign policy role and having it accepted by others is one of the basic objectives of a state. As Le Prestre notes (1997: 5–6), a role concept 'reflects a claim on the international system, a recognition by international actors, and a conception of national identity'. Consequently, foreign policy change 'must rest on a redefinition of a role and on the role's congruence with politics'. Moreover, 'contrary to what structual realists would assert, capacities alone do not define a role'. Thus he argues that role theory 'can help explain the general direction of foreign policy choices':

> The articulation of national role betrays preferences, operationalizes an image of the world, triggers expectations, and influences the definition of the situation and the available options. It imposes obligations and affects the definition of risks. Focusing on this concept, therefore, allows one to go beyond the traditional explanation of foreign policy, which is based on security or on the national interest defined as the prudent search for power. Roles help define national interests and divorce them from power. (Le Prestre 1997: 5–6)

A state's grand strategy is, with rare exceptions, based on set of role conceptions, rather than just one or two. This means that the success or otherwise of a state's foreign policy depends on its ability to combine its 'role set' into a coherent programme of action. Sometimes states pursue contradictory objectives. The former Soviet Union, for example, conceived of itself as a bastion of 'peace' and 'socialism'. However, these different role conceptions generated very different foreign policy strategies – one concerned with *détente* and 'peaceful coexistence', the other with revolutionary class struggle. This role conflict at the heart of Soviet foreign policy eventually led to Gorbachev's *novoe Myshlenie* ('new thinking'), which amounted to a radical attempt to resolve the intractable dilemmas which were undermining the international credibility of the USSR (Shenfield 1987).

An additional complication is that different foreign policy actors within a country may favour competing role conceptions. Foreign and defence ministries, for example, may be more concerned with international status and alliance commitments, and regard higher defence expenditure and foreign aid as an acceptable price to be paid. Economic or finance ministries, on the other hand, may be more interested in the nation's international economic competitiveness and its potency as a *Handelsstaat* ('trading nation'). Similarly, the national role conceptions of political elites may not be shared by the wider public. In democratic states, this can cause paralysis or incoherence in foreign policy. The obvious examples here are the Maastricht Treaty on European Union, and the resistance of Swiss citizens to their political leaders attempts to involve their country more closely in international organisations (Goetschel 1999).

The ability of a state to execute its grand strategy thus depends in the first instance on the coherence or otherwise of its role set. All states, especially large states, need to pursue a range of foreign policy objectives and aspirations. Combining a range of role conceptions inevitably entails compromises and ambiguities. Timothy Garton Ash calls this ability to balance competing expectations and cultivate ties with a range of different states 'Genscherism', the hard core of which, he notes, is 'fudge' (1996: 85). To some extent, all states need to 'genscher'. The danger, however, is that some roles are incompatible, and that by attempting to do everything, one can end up achieving nothing. Only states that are able to reconcile the competing demands of their national role conceptions will therefore achieve the goals of their grand strategy.

Germany's foreign policy roles

Germany's foreign policy roles derive from its 'national situation' and the combination of objective and subjective factors shaping perceptions of its 'national interest'. More specifically, Germany's national role conceptions reflect its economic interests, geopolitical location, size, national identity, multilateral commitments and democratic institutions. Christian Hacke (Hacke 1997: 521–40) has suggested that the Federal Republic has six *Schlüsselrolle* ('key roles'). These are as follows:

1 Germany as a *'civilian power'* (*Zivilmacht*) with a particular responsibility for international peace and cooperation. This role conception developed as a reaction against the militaristic and aggressive tendencies

in German foreign policy, often associated with its Prussian heritage, which reached their apogee in Hitler's *Vernichtungskrieg* in the East. The perceived role of a civilian power is to facilitate the 'civilianisation' of international relations by strengthening international cooperation and the peaceful resolution of disputes. This finds its expression in commitment to multilateralism and the promotion of human rights norms.

2 Germany as a *'trading nation'* (*Handelsstaat*) and global economic power. 'Trading nations' are expected to concentrate on cultivating their economic, commercial and financial interests in order to boost the prosperity of their subjects, rather than concerning themselves with diplomatic status, global power projection or human rights norms. This role reflects the fact that Germany is deeply integrated in European and global markets, and is the second largest trading nation in the world. Its currency has an international reputation, and its legitimacy of its post-war political institutions has been closely bound up with the success of its social market economy.

3 Germany as the *'motor of European integration'*. Since the earliest days of the European integration process, Germany has championed deeper integration. This role has been closely linked to Germany's strategic partnership with France, and was evident most recently during the debate on EMU. This role has been accorded primary importance by the German political class, and has taken deep roots in the political culture and identity of the *Bundesrepublik*.

4 Germany as a *'loyal transatlantic partner'*. Post-war West Germany was not only dependent on the NATO alliance and the US nuclear guarantees it embodied for its very existence, it was also exposed to the pervasive influence of American culture and values (Pommerin 1995). This provided the basis for a German role conception of itself as the faithful ally and junior partner of the USA, which an influential part of the German political class remains eager to preserve.

5 Germany as an advocate of *'pan-European cooperation'*. From the late 1960s and early 1970s onwards, the Federal Republic acquired the reputation for being a 'leading advocate of *détente*' (or *Entspannungsvormacht*). This was important in changing popular attitudes towards Germany in Central and Eastern Europe, and came to form a significant dimension of Germany's foreign policy culture and identity. With the end of the cold war, this role conception has come to be associated with the commitment to strengthen the authority of the OSCE, cultivate a strategic partnership with Russia and foster new forms of pan-European cooperative security governance.

6. Germany as *'mediator between East and West'*. With the end of the cold war, Germany's central location has given it an important new role – one that builds on the traditions of Ostpolitik, but which demands new thinking and considerable ingenuity. Germany is securely anchored in Western institutions: its main partners are France and the USA, and its economic interests are overwhelmingly in Western Europe. Yet, important new economic opportunities, along with potential security risks, lie to Germany's east (Seidelmann 1996). Germany thus has a new role to play as 'mediator' or 'bridge' between East and West. This involves developing a strategic partnership with Poland and rapprochement with its immediate neighbours in *Mitteleuropa*. It also entails acting as the 'tribune' or 'advocate' for the interests of the new democracies inside NATO and the EU. This role has increasingly come to be associated with a commitment to the dual enlargement process, and reflects the view that 'the main responsibility for a future integrated Europe lies above all with Germany' (Hacke 1997: 537).

These six role conceptions are not exhaustive of Germany's foreign policy options, but provide a summary of the main roles at work within German grand strategy. As we have seen, a country's national role conceptions are not always in harmony. Indeed, one of the central concerns of role theory is to investigate the role conflicts within a country's foreign policy, because these often constitute an important determinant of foreign policy change. In the case of post-war West Germany, there were a number of important role conflicts at work at different times. For example, during the early 1980s, Bonn's role as 'loyal transatlantic partner' conflicted with its role as an advocate of *détente*. There was also a long-running tension between Germany's commitment to West European integration and the transatlantic alliance, which was evident during discussions on European Political Cooperation (EPC) and the function of the Western European Union (WEU). Broadly speaking, however, Germany's ability to 'genscher' prevented these from generating intractable difficulties.

The end of the cold war has changed the character and relative importance of these role conflicts, and generated new ones. The role conflicts inherent within united Germany's post-cold war grand strategy will be analysed in the course of this book. Briefly, however, there have been three principal role conflicts in the 1990s: deepening the integration process versus institutional enlargement; *Zivilmacht* versus alliance commitments; and European integration versus transatlantic relations. In addition, there have been tensions between Germany's roles as civilian power, *Handelsstaat* and loyal NATO ally. These have focused on the question of arms sales to states with dubious human rights records, in particular, Turkey (one of Germany's NATO allies).

Conclusion

The aim of this chapter has been to outline a conceptual framework for understanding the evolution and adaptation of German grand strategy in the decade since unification. This analytical model rests on three 'legs' – interests, institutions and identity. A constant theme throughout has been the limitations of the dominant neo-realist approach to foreign policy analysis, and the need to consider both the material and ideational factors defining Germany's 'national situation'. Attention has been drawn both to the role of institutional politics in shaping policy outcomes, and to the importance of culture and identity for foreign policy behaviour. Finally, the utility of role theory as a conceptual tool for operationalising the study of culture and identity on foreign policy has been underlined.

In the previous chapter, Germany was described as a 'situated actor'. The purpose of employing this term was to underline the importance of considering both structure and agency when assessing Germany's role in the reshaping of European order. In this chapter, we have concentrated on analysing Germany as agent. In the next two chapters, we shall consider the situational context within which German grand strategy unfolds. This involves, first, defining the meaning of 'European order', and, second, exploring the historical evolution of the Westphalian states' system and Germany's pivotal role within it.

Notes

1 State behaviour, Mearsheimer has asserted, 'is largely shaped by the *material* structure of the international system. The distribution of material capabilities among states is the key factor for understanding world politics. For realists, some level of security competition among great powers is inevitable because of the material structure of the international system' (1995: 91).

2 One important attempt to redress the obvious limitations of mainstream realism's obsession with material structures and relative power capabilities is Stephen Walt's influential work, *The Origins of Alliances* (1987). Walt seeks to modify Kenneth Waltz's structural realist approach by suggesting that states balance not against power *per se* but rather against *threats*. Anarchy and the distribution of power alone are unable to predict which states will be identified as threats. Walt argues that threats derive from a combination of

geostrategic and military factors and 'aggressive intentions', in other words, of capabilities and intentions (1987: 22–6). He therefore offers a 'balance-of-threats' approach in place of the traditional realist 'balance of power' concept.

Walt's approach is clearly a major advance on mainstream structural realism. The problem, however, is that his key concept of 'intentions' is left under-specified and under-theorised. Whilst he provides ample evidence that it is ideational rather than material forces which drive alliance formation (at least in the Middle East, his chosen empirical focus), he fails to establish a causal relationship between anarchy and the balance of power on the one hand, and intentions on the other. His theory is also unable to account for the divergent behaviour of France and the United Kingdom towards NATO in the 1960s. Both perceived the same threat (the USSR) and disposed of roughly equally relative power capabilities, and yet their policies towards the Atlantic Alliance diverged sharply after 1966 (see Spirtas 1996: 393–4). Walt's attempt to address the limitations and inconsistencies of neo-realist structural theory are thus ultimately unconvincing, reflecting the weakness of its underlying paradigmatic assumptions. In his critique of Walt, Michael Barnett suggests that '(i)t is the politics of identity rather than the logic of anarchy that often provides a better understanding of which states are viewed as a potential or immediate threat to the state's security' (Barnett 1996: 401).

3 On 7 December 1970, during his visit to Warsaw to sign the Eastern Treaty with Poland, Chancellor Willy Brandt knelt before the Warsaw Getto Memorial, head bowed. With this act, Brandt acknowledged the guilt of the Germans for the crimes done to Jews and other Poles during the Second World War. The picture of Brandt knealing before the Warsaw Ghetto memorial flashed around the world, and seemed to symbolise a new Germany. 'For a moment', Peter Bender commented, 'morality became a political force' (Bender 1996: 182).

4 Neo-realism has signally failed to develop an adequate model of the origins and effectiveness of institutions. John Mearsheimer (1994: 7, 24, 47) simply dismisses institutions as having 'no independent effect on states behaviour'. Institutions, he asserts, 'matter only on the margins'. They 'have minimal influence on state behaviour, and thus hold little promise for promoting stability in the post-Cold War world'. 'What is impressive about institutions', he insists, 'is how little independent effect they seem to have had on state behaviour'. Such dogmatic assertions effectively close off investigation of a key feature of late twentieth-century European international politics and underline the limitations of neo-realism. Joseph Grieco has made a valiant attempt to develop a neo-realist theory of institutional cooperation (1996), but his efforts are ultimately unconvincing (Spirtas 1996: 402–4). Neo-realism's analytical blind-spot when it comes to institutions has been an important catalyst in the current intellectual movement away from the barren parsimony of neo-realism to the 'richer analytical framework of traditional realism' (Schweller and Priess 1997: 23).

5 'Constructivism', according to Alexander Wendt, 'is a structural theory of the international system which makes the following core claims (1) states are the principal units of analysis for international political theory; (2) the key structures in the states system are intersubjective, rather than material; and (3) state identities and interests are in important part constructed by these social structures, rather than given exogenously to the system by human nature or domestic politics' (Wendt 1994: 385). This structural definition of constructivism is problematic in a number of respects. A better definition of constructivism as the 'middle ground' is provided by Emmanual Adler (1997).

6 Positing the 'state' as an actor is clearly problematical, given that it can be disaggregated down into different departments and even individuals. However, 'to disaggregate everything into individuals is not very helpful, because much of social life is understandable only when collectivities are seen as more than the sum of their "members" and are treated as social realities (methodological collectivism)' (Buzan *et al.* 1998: 40).

7 Writing from the perspective of the 'second generation' of American foreign policy analysts, Hudson and Vore suggest that 'for scholars involved in FPA, "the national interest", a concept which lies at the heart of the realist analysis of IR, is more productively viewed as the interests of various players – not all of which may coincide, and not all of which are coherently related to anything resembling an objective national interest' (Hudson and Vore 1995: 210).

8 'State interests do not exist to be "discovered" by self-interested, rational actors. Interests are constructed through a process of social interaction' (Katzenstein 1996: 2). See also Helen Milner (1998: 772).

9 This pride could take unpleasant and distasteful forms, as was demonstrated by the leader of the right-wing Bavarian Christian Social Union, Franz Josef Strauss. 'A people who have achieved such economic performances', he declared in 1969, 'have the right not to have to hear any more about Auschwitz' (quoted in Judt 1996: 36).

10 Article 23 of the Constitution explicitly commits the Federal Republic to the goal of European integration.

11 Articles 30, 70 (1) and 83 deal with the foreign and European competences of the Länder.

12 The 'logic of expected consequences' assumes that states act as rational utility maximisers on the basis of stable consistent and exogenously determined preferences. One example would be the work of Andrew Moravcsik on European integration (1998). The problem with the 'logic of expected consequences', however, is that 'it seems to ignore the substantial role of identities, rules, and institutions in shaping human behaviour' (March and Olsen 1998: 11). The 'logic of appropriateness', on the other hand, underlines norms and identities as the basis for action. 'Within the tradition of a logic of appropriateness', March and Olsen argue, 'actions are seen as rule-based. Human actors are imagined to follow rules that associate identities to particular situations, approaching individual opportunities for action by assessing similarities

between current identities and choice dilemmas and more general concepts of self and situations. Action involves evoking an identity or role and matching the obligations of that identity or role to a specific situation. The pursuit of purpose is associated with identities more than with interests; and with the selection of roles more than with individual rational expectations'.

13 A similar move has been made by the Copenhagen school of security studies: they have posited the existence of societal security alongside that of state security, rather than simply assuming a confluence of state and society as traditional realism has tended to do (Huysmans 1998).

14 In his analysis of French perspectives on international relations, Terrence Hopmann writes that the 'major issue for the future of Franco-German relations' is whether Germany 'can accept its (transformed post-war) identity as a state like others, with fixed boundaries and with sovereignty extending only over the people residing within those boundaries, or whether it will pursue past irredentist efforts to reunify the German Volk in one extended empire'. French writers like Dominique Moïsi and Jacques Rupnik, he notes, argue that it is essential 'to preserve the gains of recent decades in which many Germans have been resocialized to think of themselves as Europeans as well as Germans' by integrating Germany 'more strongly than ever within the framework of European economic, political, and military institutions' (Hopmann 1994: 79).

15 'The mention of the name "Auschwitz" has the function in post-war Germany of bringing to an immediate standstill any free movement of thought in this connection ... The ritual repetition of the word "unique" in connection with Nazi crimes is valuable above all in exposing the user's lack of education ... and is highly valuable for pressing certain interests' (Reinhard Mauer in Schwilk and Schlacht 1994: 77). On the *Historikerstreit* see Piper (1987) and Wehler (1988).

3
Conceptualising European order

We, in the ages lying
In the buried past of the earth,
Built Nineveh with our sighing,
And Babel itself with our mirth;
And o'erthrew them with prohesying
To the old of the new world's worth;
For each age is a dream that is dying,
Or one that is coming to birth.

(Arthur O'Shaughnessy, 'The Music-Makers')

The aim of the next two chapters is explore the structures of European order within which Germany frames and conducts its foreign policy. The specific concern of this chapter is to explore the meaning of the term 'European order'. The concept of 'order' is one that is constitutive of international relations as a discipline. Some commentators have worried that international relations 'lacks clear-cut boundaries with other social sciences', and 'has neither an obvious subject-matter of its own, nor a method specific to it' (Guzzini 1998: 2). Yet if there is one concern that lies at the heart of international relations, and provides it coherence as a discipline, it is the search for the origins, nature and implications of order in the international system. All disciplines must be 'about' something, and as Iver Neumann has argued, 'Order in world society is an "about" which must remain constitutive of the discipline of IR' (Neumann and Waever 1997: 368).

The argument developed in this chapter is that European order is more than simply a function of relations between sovereign territorial states. Inter-state relations are clearly an important element of international order because the state 'has been the key institution through which Western societies have regulated their population, their relations with each other and their interaction with non-European peoples' (Knutsen 1999: 5). International relations thus remain a 'state-dominated field' (Buzan *et al.* 1998: 37). However, the problem of order in contemporary international society cannot be reduced to the logic of inter-state relations. Order arises in the context of a socially constructed and textured international system comprising a whole corpus of institutions, regimes and governing arrangements. States do not simply balance each other in the bleak, featureless wasteland of the neo-realist imagination. Rather, they interact in a society of states constituted by multilateral institutions, socio-economic transactions, novel forms of multi-level governance and shared norms, rules and codes of behaviour. Conceptualising European order in these terms is essential if we are to understand the role of Germany in contemporary European affairs.

Defining Europe

Europe: unity and diversity

The first task in defining the concept of 'European order' is to specify what is meant by the term 'Europe'. 'He who speaks of Europe', Otto Von Bismarck is reputed to have said, 'is mistaken; it is only a geographical expression'. Geographically, Europe constitutes the north-western peninsula of the Asian landmass. The problem, however, is that 'the eastern boundaries of the European continent are fuzzy, shading into western Asia across a broad and topographically indefinite terrain' (Judt 1996: 45). The Austrian Chancellor Metternich once declared that immediately across the Rennweg (the street that runs right through Vienna), one is already in the Balkans, and in Asia (Magris 1990: 241). More usually, the boundaries of Europe are located at the Ural Mountains or on the Bosphorus, thereby posing the question of whether Russia or Turkey are 'European'. Definitions of Europe are thus inevitably political, and carry important policy implications in terms of institutional membership, political behaviour and bilateral relations.[1] This suggests that there are 'many "Europes", all with some legitimate claim to the title, none with a monopoly' (Judt 1996: 60).

Fernand Braudel has suggested one way of capturing both the diversity and similarities which characterise contemporary Europe. Writing about fifteenth century Italy, which was little more than a collection of small states and principalities, he described it as 'a representation of a historical entity within which events had similar repercussions and effects, and were indeed in a sense imprisoned' (Braudel 1975: 164). This phrase is very suggestive about contemporary Europe, and as J.M. Roberts has written (1996: 670), 'recognises enduring constraints within a framework which is nonetheless not a strait-jacket, and it indicates, above all, a theatre where a certain history unrolled'.

This sense of Europe as a theatre where a certain history unrolls has been expressed in social science terms by Barry Buzan (1991: 188–90). He has proposed the concept of a 'regional security complex' as a way of filling the gap between system and state levels by focusing on regional dynamics of amity and enmity. 'In security terms', Buzan argues, '"region" means that a distinct and significant subsystem of security relations exists among a set of states whose fate is that they have been locked into geographical proximity with each other.' A regional security complex is thus 'a group of states whose primary security concerns link together sufficiently closely that their national securities cannot realistically be considered apart from one another'.

Europe from the Atlantic to the Urals forms a regional security complex. However, this security complex is fractured into three broad zones. These three zones are not sharply delineated from each other, but nonetheless are distinguished by distinctive patterns of amity and enmity. They are defined by the nature of their political systems; the degree of institutionalised integration and multilateral cooperation; their economic performance and social structures; and their political culture. These political, economic and social characteristics echo deeper historical, cultural and religious cleavages within European civilisation, arising from the uneven impact of the Renaissance, the Reformation, the Enlightenment and the Industrial Revolution.[2] Broadly speaking, therefore, the contemporary European security complex exhibits the legacy of its 'three historic zones' (Szücs 1988) – Western, Central and Eastern Europe:

> As a result of innumerable geo-economic, geopolitical and cultural-religious developments, some of which can be traced far back into past millennia, while others are of more recent origin, many internal divisions have come into existence creating a multiplicity and diversity of culture in the Europe geographically defined above. Perceptibly the most obvious is the 'dividing line' separating western Europe from what, geographically at least, is called eastern Europe; this 'line', actually a wide transitional zone, sometimes called 'central Europe', stretches from the Baltic to the Balkans and roughly coincides with the present-day states of Poland, the Czech and Slovak Republics and Hungary. (Rietbergen 1998: xx)

Post-cold war Europe thus constitutes a regional security complex fractured into three broad zones. These zones correspond loosely with

Europe's 'three historical regions', but in the age of late modernity they
are defined less by cultural and religious characteristics, and more by
political, societal and economic criteria. One development which is of
particular significant for European order is the emergence in the post-
war era of a 'pluralistic security community' (Deutsch 1957) in Western
Europe. Germany currently constitutes the eastern bulwark of this security community, and it is this fact more than any other that drives the
grand strategy of united Germany.

Order

Defining 'order'

If defining 'Europe' is difficult, defining 'order' is even more problematic.
Although – or perhaps because – the concept is constitutive of international relations as a discipline, it is also one of those 'essentially contested
concepts' that pervade the social sciences. Attempts to define order
inevitably raise complex moral and ethical issues, not least because order
is 'not normatively neutral: it carries with it certain connotations and
these may not be acceptable to all people' (Clark 1989: 13). One person's
'order' may be another's tyranny. As Tacitus noted, the *Pax Romana* was
experienced by Rome's enemies not as 'peace' but as tyranny. He quoted
the words of the British General Calgacus: 'To robbery, butchery and rap-
ine, they give the lying name of "government"; they create a desolation
and call it peace.' Order is thus 'a term that carries normative and ideological connotations, as it bears particular conceptions about how social,
political, and economic systems are and ought to be structured' (Paul and
Hall 1999: 2; see also Rengger 2000).

One point to note at the outset is that order is not the only – or necessarily the most important – value in international politics. There are
other values such as justice, liberty and freedom, which some might
regard more highly than order. As Hedley Bull argued, 'order is not the
only value in relation to which international conduct may be shaped, and
is not necessarily an overriding value' (1977: xvi). The cold war, it is commonly argued, provided order but not justice for Europe (especially for
those in Central and Eastern Europe).[3] On the other hand, the search for
justice or freedom can be disruptive of orderly and established relationships. The tension between order and justice has recently been illustrated
in the case of Bosnia. On the one hand, the prosecution of those responsible for war crimes by the International Tribunal is an intrinsic part of
the search for justice in Bosnia. However, a peace accord could only be

achieved by negotiating with some of those responsible for ordering war crimes.

Nonetheless, a stable international order 'is a prerequisite for an international community that widens the moral opportunity of its participants, permitting their policy to move beyond the pure self-interest of Machiavelli to a self-interest softened by the obligations imposed by membership in a community' (Clinton 1991: 57). In the words of Hedley Bull:

> Order in social life is desirable because it is the condition of the realisation of other values. Unless there is a pattern of human activities that sustains elementary, primary and universal goals of social life, it will not be possible to achieve or preserve objectives that are advanced, secondary or the special goals of particular societies. International order, or order within the society of states, is the condition of justice or equality among states or nations; except in a context of international order there can be no such thing as the equal rights of states to independence or of nations to govern themselves. (Bull 1977: 93)

Stability and order

One further initial observation about the concept of order is that it does not imply an unchanging preservation of the status quo. On the contrary: the long-term stability of European order requires an ability to adapt and evolve in order to release the tensions generated by a constantly evolving environment (Hassner 1968). Without a continual process of organic change, any domestic or international arrangement will ultimately prove fragile. The USSR and *real existierender Sozialismus* are a case in point: their authoritarian inflexibility and unresponsive planning mechanisms 'became so many fetters' to further social progress that – in the words of *The Communist Manifesto* – 'They had to be burst asunder; they were burst asunder' (Marx and Engels 1968: 40).

Order thus requires a delicate balance of structural solidity on the one hand, and flexibility on the other. It must be robust enough to contain and channel disruptive forces, whilst flexible enough to facilitate peaceful and organic change. In the 1952 film *Scaramouche*, the fencing master says to his pupil 'the rapier is like a bird. Grasp it too loosely and it well fly away, too tight and you will crush it' (Robert Cooper 1996: 18). This is a perfect image for the concept of European order: it must be solid enough to resist disruptive pressures, but not so solid that it crushes organic development. Thus 'the success of international order is predicated on the extent to which it can accommodate change without violence' (Paul and Hall 1999: 2).

This, however, touches on one of the central problems facing European international society. Change in Europe and the wider international system has historically always resulted from war or violent revolution. As Trotsky once remarked, war has been 'the locomotive of history'. The problem is that the international system 'has as yet not managed to devise a universally acceptable means for the peaceful resolution of conflict brought about by change within the system' (Clark 1989: 28). This, however, might be changing, as the manner in which the East–West conflict ended suggests. For the first time in European history, far-reaching change occurred without widespread violence and disorder. The challenge for the future is how to shape a post-cold war system of European order that permits peaceful change, but prevents threats to the 'elementary or primary goals of social, political and economic life among the peoples of Europe'. This is a challenge with which the Germans, given their central geographical location, are particularly concerned.

Hedley Bull's definition of 'order'

The most important contribution to our understanding of the nature of 'order' in international politics is Hedley Bull's influential work, *The Anarchical Society: A Study of Order in World Politics* (1977). Whilst some of his arguments now appear dated, his overall contribution to our understanding of international relations remains seminal (Vincent and Miller 1990). *The Anarchical Society* thus offers an ideal point of departure for thinking conceptually about the changing nature of European order.

Hedley Bull began his analysis by defining 'order' in social life as 'a pattern of human activity that sustains elementary, primary or universal goals of social life'. These elementary, primary or universal goals he summarised as security from violence, the honouring of agreements and the stability of possessions. The 'fulfilment in some measure' of these goals, he reasoned, 'is a condition not merely of this or that sort of social life, but of social life as such' (1977: 4).

He went on to distinguish between 'world order' and 'international order'. *World order* he defined as 'those patterns or dispositions of human activity that sustain the elementary or primary goals of social life among mankind as a whole' (1977: 19). *International order*, on the other hand, he defined as 'a pattern of activity that sustains the elementary or primary goals of the society of states, or international society' (1977: 8). Most importantly, he stressed that '[o]rder among mankind as a whole is something wider than order among states; something more fundamental and primordial than it; and also, I should argue, something morally prior to it' (1977: 22).

This distinction between 'international order' and 'world order' is crucial to Hedley Bull's analysis. The key difference is the referent object of 'order'; in other words, to whom or to what does it apply? Whilst 'international order' takes as its referent object the 'society of states', the concept of 'world order' is far wider in scope, embracing as it does 'social life among mankind as a whole'. These two conceptions of order rest on different philosophical and political assumptions. International order draws its underlying assumptions from 'communitarian' or 'Hegelian' conceptions that conceive of political life as resting on discrete political communities. 'The root notion of communitarian thought', it has been argued, 'is that value stems from the community, that the individual finds meaning in life by virtue of his or her membership of a political community' (Brown 1992: 55). As the embodiment of discrete political communities, states have an intrinsic moral and political value. Consequently, 'international order' involving the 'society of states' is a politically legitimate and morally defensible goal for international society.

World order, on the other hand, is rests on 'cosmoplitan' or 'Kantian' conceptions that refuse 'to regard existing political structures as the source of ultimate value' (Brown 1992: 24). For cosmopolitans, the legitimacy of existing states is at best contingent and provisional. Moral and political value attaches to individuals, not political structures, and thus cosmopolitan 'world order' should take priority over 'international order' between discrete political communities.

The antinomies of European order

Hedley Bull's distinction between international order and world order serves to illustrate the different ways that the problem of order in international society has been addressed. In late modern Europe, however, the distinction between 'international' and 'world' order is beginning to dissolve. Order no longer unequivocally rests on the principle of territorial sovereignty as it did for much of the last three and a half centuries. The main reason for this is that the principle of state sovereignty has been increasingly qualified by normative concerns for human rights.

This means that there is now a series of unresolved tensions and ambiguities at the heart of late modern European order 'in which state and individual coexist uneasily with each other in our intellectual and legal frameworks' (Clark 1989: 44). The *Gretchenfrage* or key question of contemporary European order is whether individuals enjoy legal and political rights as citizens of an organised political community, or as human beings who are members of an extant or incipient cosmopolitan community of humankind. Historically, the Westphalian system has been grounded on a notion of 'international order' between states, which stressed the principle of non-intervention in the internal affairs of sovereign states. Since the Second World War, this principle has been steadily weakened. The Nuremberg trials represented one of the first attempts to highlight the importance of human rights and to enshrine them in international law. The CSCE Helsinki Final Act both reaffirmed the principle of non-intervention in internal affairs of states, and at the same time made respect for human rights a legitimate concern of the international community.

More recently, developments in Iraq (with the Kurds) and in former Yugoslavia questioned the right of states to enjoy sovereignty if they are guilty of gross violations of human rights. This has been accompanied by discussions about whether a new principle of international law is emerging – the right to humanitarian intervention (Habermas 1999).[4] Ulrich Beck has also suggested that traditionally accepted distinctions between war and peace, domestic and international politics – upon which order in the international system has been based until now – have broken apart. This, he argues, is the lesson of the Kosovo war – the first 'postnational war' in the age of globalisation (Beck 1999: 984–6). Reflecting on his experience of Kosovo, Defence Minister Rudolf Scharping has written that 'a new balance between two principles of international law, namely state sovereignty and the universal validity of human rights, now needs to be worked out. The conflict around Kosovo, the intervention against genocide and terrible crimes against humankind is hopefully the beginning of such an international learning process' (1999: 222).

European order: a definition

Given the antinomies of international law in late modern Europe, 'European order' needs to be defined in terms that transcend the dichotomy between 'international' and 'world' order. Consequently European order will be defined here as *those patterns or dispositions of human activity that sustain the elementary or primary goals of social, political and economic life among the peoples of Europe*. Following Bull, these elementary or primary goals are defined in terms of 'three basic values of all social life – sometimes called those of life, truth and property' (1977: 5). These three basic values are *limiting violence, keeping promises and safeguarding property*.

The concept of 'European order' is thus concerned with 'patterned behaviour' in international society. It involves the search for regulatory mechanisms and institutions which can provide a framework for what Martin Wight called the 'habitual intercourse of independent communities' (1966: 96–7). Order thus emerges in the context of 'a rudimentary society which cannot be reduced to military or economic interaction, but which must be understood in terms of rules, norms and values'. These rules, norms and values provide evidence of the existence of an international society, and are formalised to some extent in international law. 'Although all states do not obey international law all the time, they obey it often enough for law to constitute an important formative fact in modern international relations' (Knutsen 1999: 2; see also Byers 1999).

The emergence of patterned behaviour consistent with sustaining the 'elementary goals of social, political and economic life among the peoples of Europe' has four aspects. First, formal multilateral institutions. The plethora of international organisations that make up the complex architecture of European multilateralism is a relatively new feature of European international society, and constitutes an important bastion of late modern European order. Second, various forms of international governance, which underpin and nourish Europe's institutional architecture. Governance involves a wide range of policy networks and more specialised international regimes, and facilitates regularised patterns of behaviour even in the absence of formal rule-making structures. Governance is thus 'a system of rule that is as dependent on intersubjective meanings as on formally sanctioned constitutions and charters' (Rosenau and Czempiel 1992: 4).

Both these formal institutional structures and governance systems are embedded within a thick-woven web of informal transnational socio-economic exchanges and transactions which criss-cross Europe's territorially organised political structures. These forms of 'informal integration' constitute the third aspect of European order. Informal integration can be defined as 'those intense patterns of interaction which develop without the impetus of deliberate political decisions, following the dynamics of markets, technology, communications networks and social change' (Wallace 1990: 9).

The final aspect of the patterned behaviour which constitutes European order is its normative component, or what Robert Cox has called its 'reigning ideas' (Cox 1986). Order among European states has been generated not only by states, institutions, governance and law, but by norms, values and shared understandings too. Norms provide 'collective expectations for the proper behaviour of actors with a given identity' (Katzenstein 1996: 5), and are inter-subjectively constituted through a process of communicative action. These norms operate not only at the international level, but also at the domestic level (Neumann and Welsch 1991: 328). They are nearly always contested and ambiguous. Nonetheless, they provide a normative context within which international actors operate, establishing the boundaries of acceptable international behaviour (Checkel 1998; Wendt 1999).

Europe's society of states

European order and international society

The concept of European order implies that Europe is more than the sum of its constituent parts, i.e., more than just the aggregate of its many peoples, states and institutions. Europe's political communities do not relate to each other randomly or haphazardly, within some sort of anarchic 'state of nature'. Instead, their interactions form patterns of relationships that provide Europe with a degree of predictability and relative stability, at least in terms of its core relationships. The notion of European order thus highlights the elements of cooperation and regulated intercourse within Europe – in other words, the elements of 'sociability' within the European society of states.

This conception of European order departs sharply from the neo-realist paradigm. Neo-realists conceive of international relations as a self-help system occupied by rational utility-maximising unitary actors, whose interaction with each other resembles balls on a billiard table. Such theoretical parsimony, however, overlooks a primary feature of contemporary Europe – the socially textured and historically evolving nature of Europe's society of states. In contrast to neo-realism, therefore, European order is conceptualised here in terms of an intricately textured fabric, composed of a myriad of inter-connections and institutionalised relations.[5] 'International relations', it has been suggested, 'like all social relations, exhibit *some* degree of institutionalization: at minimum, a mutual intelligibility of behavior together with the communicative mechanisms and organizational routines which make that possible' (Ruggie 1998: 2). Even in the absence of a pan-European authority, able to enforce compliance and generate legally binding decisions, European order has developed into much more than an anarchic system dominated by sovereign states striving for power and security.

European order is thus best conceptualised in terms of a 'society of states' or 'international society'. Hedley Bull, one of the doyens of the

English school, argued that a 'society of states (or international society) exists when a group of states, conscious of certain common interests and common values, form a society in the sense that they conceive themselves to be bound by a common set of rules in their relations with one another, and share in the workings of common institutions' (1977: 13). The origins of the international society approach lie with the Grotian tradition of international relations theory, which argued that international anarchy was mitigated by institutional arrangements that facilitated international cooperation and understanding. In the modern period, the Grotian tradition has been exemplified by the 'English School' of international relations (see Dunne 1998; and Roberson 1998).[6] In contrast to neo-realism's focus on the distribution of relative power capabilities within the international system, the adherents of the English School focus on the historical emergence and development of the institutions of international society.

The great strength of this approach (which shares certain assumptions with classical realism) is its recognition of the importance of history and culture in generating shared norms, values and understandings. As David Armstrong has argued, international society 'is not just a juridical association but a framework within which multifaceted social interaction among states takes place – most intensively among the major liberal democracies'. In the course of such interaction, he argues, 'states are subject to a constant process of socialization in which they internalize each others' policies and practices across a wide spectrum, including economic, financial, educational and social policies (Armstrong 1999: 560).

European order and the 'new institutionalism'

One approach that has contributed to the study of the socially textured nature of European order is 'new institutionalism'. This has been particularly influential in economics and sociology, and in political science, it has led to greater awareness of the effect of social and political structures on political behaviour and decision-making (March and Olsen 1989). It has also served to increase cross-fertilisation between domestic, comparative and international politics (Milner 1998: 760). The renaissance of institutionalism reflects a backlash against the behaviouralism, which tended to view institutions as epiphenomenal – in other words, little more than the sum of individual decisions and actions (Powell and DiMaggio 1991: 2). This perspective has become untenable in a world in which 'social, political, and economic institutions have become larger, considerably more complex and resourceful, and prima facie more important to collective life' (March and Olsen 1984: 734).

Although the new institutionalism in political science has sometimes been associated simply with 'bring the state back in' (Skocpol 1985), its implications are more far-reaching than that. This is because it defines 'institutions' in a much broader and differentiated way than usual. Institutions, it is argued, can take three forms: *organisations*, which are established structures with a bureaucratic apparatus, a physical location and formalised decision-making processes; *regimes* or systems of governance, based on explicit rules and regulations; and *conventions*, based on implicit rules and understandings, and involving norms, habits, and routinised patterns of behaviour. Organisations are embedded in broader structures of institutionalisation and draw much of their strength and effectiveness from these wider networks of institutions.[7] The EU, for example, derives its effectiveness not simply from its formal decision-making capacities and powers of compliance, but rather from the wider forms of governance and accepted codes of behaviour between member states upon which it is based.[8]

Within international relations, the new institutionalism has been part of a more general assault on the discipline's dominant realist paradigm. In a way analogous to the methodological individualism of behaviouralism, structural realism assumed that states operated in a largely featureless self-help system. The new institutionalism has challenged this assumption and focused attention on the impact of institutions –broadly defined[9] – on state behaviour. It has stimulated interest in the broader issue of 'governance without government' in international society (Rosenau and Czempiel 1992), and on the nature of international order in an anarchical system (Young 1994).

Above all, however, the new internationalism has been most closely associated with regime theory (Rittberger 1993). The classic definition of regimes is 'sets of implicit or explicit principles, norms, rules, and decision-making procedures around which actors' expectations converge in a given area of international relations' (Krasner 1983: 2). Like the international society approach of the 'English School', regime theory draws attention to the institutional context within which states define their identities and pursue their interests (Evans and Wilson 1992; Hurrell 1993). In particular, it highlights the importance of norms, networks and patterns of behaviour which facilitate coordination and cooperation for mutual benefit – a dimension of international life overlooked in structural realism's drive for parsimonious theory.[10]

The Grotian tradition, the English School and the new institutionalism share a common concern with the regulatory mechanisms that constitute international order. These regulatory mechanisms derive not simply from international law or formal international organisations – important although these are for international order – but from inter-subjectively constituted norms of behaviour, communicative mechanisms, organisational routines and unwritten rules (Byers 1999). All three approaches thus contribute to our understanding of the socially textured nature of European order.

Order as 'process' or 'substance'

An important theme in discussions of order in international society is whether it involves 'process' or 'substance'. According to the former view, order simply involves a framework for managing disputes peacefully, and does not stipulate the ends served by this process of peaceful conflict resolution. The latter view, by contrast, suggests that order can only arise if certain substantive social, economic and political conditions are met. Focusing exclusively on the process of conflict management, the argument runs, ignores the goals served by this institutional framework (Clark 1989: 3–4).

This distinction between order as process and substance corresponds to Hedley Bull's distinction between 'minimum' and 'optimum' international order (Bull 1977: 90). The former embodies a more conservative or traditionalist perspective, which assumes an inherent tension between order and justice in world politics, and believes that the best that can be hoped for is a minimum of coexistence based on agreed rules and procedures. The latter view regards justice as an essential precondition for order, even if, in the short term, demands for justice might unsettle established regulatory mechanisms and international institutions.

Historically, discussion about the nature of order in Europe has concentrated on process rather than substance. The primary concern has been with the regulatory mechanisms underpinning order, not substantive questions about political values, social justice and economic prosperity. In late modern Europe, however, the distinction between process and substance is breaking down, as two developments demonstrate. First, the increased importance attached to human rights and democracy as the basis for a durable peace order (Risse *et al.* 1999). This has been codified in the UN Charter, the Helsinki Final Act and the 1990 'Paris Charter for a New Europe' (Hanson 1993). It has also been reflected in the work of the Council of Europe and the OSCE (particularly the

Office of Democratic Institutions and Human Rights [ODIHR] and the High Commissioner on National Minorities [HCNM]). These developments demonstrate an increasing concern with the 'substance' of European order rather than simply its regulatory processes.

Second, efforts to address the economic and social dimensions of security. It has been increasingly recognised that poverty, homelessness and unemployment breed insecurity, and provide the conditions in which demagogues and unscrupulous populists can incite inter-communal hatred. This has become an almost constant refrain of official German statements on international security. It also provided the rationale for the Stability Pact for Southeast Europe, which the German government played a pivotal role in devising (see Hombach 1999; and Ehrhart 1999). In late modern Europe, therefore, European order has both procedural and substantive dimensions.

War and order

European order was defined above as 'those patterns or dispositions of human activity that sustain the elementary or primary goals of social, political and economic life among the peoples of Europe'. The first – and arguably most important – of these 'elementary or primary goals' is 'limiting violence'. This raises a difficult moral and ethical question: does order involve the complete absence of violence, or is the use of violence sometimes a necessary precondition for order? This question has proven particularly troubling for post-war Germany, given its identity as a *Zivilmacht* and its distinctive foreign policy culture.

In general, peace is of course an essential precondition for order, because without it, individuals and political communities will find it much harder to achieve their other goals and values – be they economic prosperity, social justice, democratic government or the rule of law. However, 'the importance of peace is, in the ultimate analysis, *derivative*. Taken to its deepest roots, peace is important because "the dignity and worth of the human person" are important' (Ali Mazrui quoted in Bull 1977: 93–4). This implies that the use of military force may sometimes be necessary in order to prevent a greater injustice. It may be required in order to prevent gross violations to 'the dignity and worth of the human person'. In the face of genocide or gross human rights violations, for example, military force may offer the only way to safeguard the 'three basic values of all social life' – life, truth and property. This is most clearly demonstrated by the Holocaust, which was only brought to an end by the Allied victory in 1945.

The debate on the question of war and order in post-war Germany has, not unexpectedly, taken the Holocaust as its point of departure. During the wars in Bosnia and Kosovo, the question of whether there was a legitimate right to humanitarian intervention was frequently posed in terms of *Nie wieder Krieg* ('no more war') or *Nie wieder Auschwitz* ('no more Auschwitz'). In the face of growing evidence of widespread brutality and ethnic cleansing, pacifist sentiments – prevalent amongst the German left throughout the cold war – were increasingly questioned on moral and ethical grounds (Scharping 1999: 137). '*Nie wieder Krieg*' (the former rallying cry of the peace movement) was challenged by a new moral imperative – '*Nie wieder Auschwitz*'. During the cold war, many on the German left assumed that these two moral imperatives were two sides of the same coin. The deepening tragedy in the Balkans, however, made many aware of the tension between the two, and forced them to confront the moral choices involved in shaping European order.

On deeper reflection, therefore, the concept of European order implies a more paradoxical relationship between order and military force than simply the absence of war. Reshaping post-cold war European order will pose complex moral and ethical dilemmas about the legitimate use of military force – dilemmas which the Kosovo campaign has highlighted, and which have preoccupied the Germans more than many other nation in Europe.

Spontaneous, imposed and negotiated order

Much of the discussion of European order in this chapter has focused on the various elements involved in order, i.e., states, institutions, governance, socio-economic transactions and norms. Another perspective can be gained from considering how it is established and maintained. In this respect, Oran Young's distinction between 'spontaneous', 'imposed' and 'negotiated order' is of particular interest (Young 1989: 86–7).

Spontaneous or *self-generating* systems of order are not the product of human design, but emerge through the operation of the 'hidden hand' of international anarchy. They 'are distinguished by the facts that they do not involve conscious coordination among participants, do not require explicit consent on the part of subjects or prospective subjects, and are highly resistant to efforts at social engineering' (Young 1989: 85). In international society, spontaneous order primarily takes the form of the balance of power.

Imposed order is 'fostered deliberately by dominant powers or consortia of dominant powers', and is exemplified by classical feudal arrangements as well as imperial systems. They involve the deployment of hard power resources in order to compel subordinate actors to conform if necessary. 'In short', Young argues, 'imposed regimes are established deliberately by dominant actors who succeed in getting others to conform to the requirements of these arrangements through some combination of coercion, cooptation, and the manipulation of incentives' (1989: 88). A modern example of imposed order would be the 'socialist commonwealth' which the USSR established in post-war Eastern Europe.

Negotiated order, on the other hand, is characterised by bargaining, consensus and the search for legitimate forms of international regulation. Systems of negotiated order involve 'conscious efforts to agree on their major provisions, explicit consent on the part of individual participants, and formal expression of the results'. Young distinguishes between 'comprehensive negotiated regimes' arising from careful and orderly negotiations, and 'those that can be described as partial or piecemeal'. 'Given the conflicts of interest prevalent in international society, however, it is to be expected that negotiated arrangements will often exhibit a piecemeal quality, leaving many issues to be settled through practice and precedent'. The primary example of negotiated order is post-war Western Europe, particularly the EEC/EU.

These three forms of order represent ideal-types. Historically, European order has consisted of elements of all three. The interesting question to consider is how they have been combined, and which of the three has predominated – if any. In this respect, Ian Clark has offered a complementary approach to the study of European order, based on two distinct processes of resolving conflicts of interests. These are the *power model* (which corresponds to Young's notion of imposed order) and the *authority model* (which corresponds to negotiated order):

> The first can be described as the unbridled interplay of opposing forces in which the capabilities of the contestants will determine the outcome. The second can be characterised as the pursuit of decision-making procedures, the legitimacy of which would be recognised by each of the constituent units. All international political practice can be encompassed within these two extremes and a major point of interest for the student of international politics is, which tendency is uppermost or, historically speaking, how have the two tendencies been combined? (Clark 1989: 14–15)

The power model includes a continuum of practices 'that begins with diplomacy and bargaining and ends with outright violence'. It also includes the 'many decisions, or non-decisions, that are made by those more powerful parties who do not actually have to employ their force but can keep it tacitly in the background'. The authority model, on the other hand, 'entails the whole history of efforts to establish norms, procedures, techniques and institutions that might compensate for the absence of a supreme decision-making body within the international system'. Clark argues that historically, forms of international order have not corresponded directly to either of these two extremes. Rather, elements from both have been combined to a greater or lesser extent. 'It is the tension, the conflict, the uneasy harmony between the power and the authority models of politics that provide the fascination in the study of international relations' (Clark 1989: 15–16).

In the next chapter, we shall consider the 'tension, the conflict, the uneasy harmony between the power and authority models' in contemporary Europe. The purpose of doing so is to explore the defining characteristics and structural dynamics of European order in the age of late modernity. This can best be done by situating recent developments in their historical context. The task of the following chapter is thus to explore the rise – and possible fall – of the Westphalian states' system, and Germany's pivotal place within it.

Notes

1 For a discussion of different concepts of 'Europe', see Kumar (1992).
2 'European civilisation is not of one piece', Krishan Kumar notes. 'More than with other civilisations, its strength and vitality come from the diversity of strands that make up its fabric.' He goes on to argue that 'Russian culture has, for more than a thousand years, contributed one of those strands', and has been 'a powerful and creative element in European life.' This means that 'the choice is not between one thing or the other, "east" or "west": Europe includes both "east" and "west", and individual European countries, especially those in the "lands in between", are likely to find elements of both in their make-up' (Kumar 1992: 458–9).
3 Anton Deporte argued in 1978 that 'the postwar system, built over a decade or more of acute tensions sometimes threatening war, can yet be given high marks for providing stability, even if in a sense inadvertently, and at least fair marks for the kind of stability'. This post-war security order, he argued, 'like all that prove viable, has been well rooted in power realities' and 'if not an inevitable outcome of history, it was at least a natural one'. Unfortunately, his subsequent comments, although understandable given the times in which he was writing, illustrate the dangers that lie in wait for academics when they attempt to predict the future; 'I suggest', he concluded, 'that the system which

has lasted from 1955 until today – 1978 – may well last as long again, that is, until 2001' (Deporte 1979: xii–xiii)

4 In many respects this 'new' development represents a return to the natural law principles of medieval Christendom (Clark 1989: 43–5; and Brown 1992: 132–3).

5 It is worth noting that in contrast to structural (or neo-) realists like Waltz or Mearsheimer, classical realists were much more attuned to the socially textured character of international politics. 'Nothwithstanding Morgenthau's emphasis on power as the driving force', John Ruggie notes, 'he saw the world of international politics in socially textured terms.' He recognised, for example, that shared values and universal standards of action could affect the operation of the balance of power, and also acknowledged a role – albeit limited – for law and organisations (Ruggie 1998: 5).

6 Interest in the English School has been steadily growing over recent years. As Ole Waever notes, the English School is 'a respectable, traditional approach which includes quasi-philosophical and historical reflection. It also cross-examines deep institutions in the system, and can relatively easily be linked to postmodernist notions, an emphasis on the cultural colouring of international systems, and especially the general "radical" interest in thinking the basic categories of the international system instead of taking them as mechanical givens. At the same time, the classics of the English School, especially Bull's *Anarchical Society*, offer a comprehensible, seemingly straightforward discussion of the actual system with relatively clear, operational concepts. Thus, the American mainstream can find a moderate and not too dangerous way to extend its institutionalism by using Bull (and reading him almost as a regime theorist or neo-liberal institutionalist). The new wave of English School enthusiasm thus ties in with the attempted rapprochement between reflectivists and rationalists, with the de-radicalization of reflectivism, and the rephilosophization of the rationalists' (Waever 1997: 25).

7 Oran Young distinguishes between institutions and organisations. Institutions he defines as 'sets of rules of the game or codes of conduct that serve to define social practices, assign roles to the participants in these practices, and guide the interactions among occupants of these roles'. Organisations, on the other hand, are 'material entities possessing offices, personnel, budgets, equipement, and, more often than not, legal personality. Put another way, organisations are actors in social practices. Institutions affect the behaviour of these actors by defining social practices and spelling out codes of conduct appropriate to them, but they are not actors in their own right' (Young 1994: 3–4).

8 'Formal organizations may represent the concrete locus at which the other forms of institutionalization can be most clearly aggregate and transformed into more conventional manifestations of power … Organizations are not powerful in themselves, but only in so far as they are constituted within the other elements so far described. Only so far as they can generate, maintain and deploy the social capital upon which they are based – and can continue to do

so in ways which accord with the desires of their members – can they maintain themselves as powerful and socially effective actors' (Williams 1997: 299–300).

9 Keohane defines institutions as 'persistent and connected sets of rules (formal and informal) that prescribe behavioral roles, constrain activity, and shape expectations' (Keohane 1989: 3).

10 In this respect, it is interesting to note that there are a number of close conceptual and theoretical links between regime theory and the international society approach (see Evans and Wilson 1992; Hurrell 1993).

4

Germany and
the Westphalian states' system

In the affairs of a nation and in the relations between states, as in the life of the individual, the present always has a past dimension, which it is better to acknowledge than to ignore or deny. And even if we can see the present only in it's own surface terms, we still have available to us what may be the greatest value history has to offer: its ability, by clarifying and making some sense of the past, to help us think about the present and the future.

(Paret 1986: 8)

The nature of contemporary European order can only be properly under-stood by situating it in its broader historical context. The aim of this chapter is thus to provide a brief historical outline of the Westphalian states' system and Germany's pivotal role within it. The purpose of this historical exegesis is to explore the changing structural dynamics of Euro-pean order, thereby identifying the elements of continuity and change in Germany's external environment.

The argument advanced here is that in late modern Europe, the central pillars of the Westphalian system are being ineluctably eroded. Germany thus finds itself at the heart of a continent being reshaped by four distinct but inter-related processes: the end of cold war bipolarity, the develop-ment of multilateral forms of institutionalised cooperation, globalisation and the 'triple transformation' of Central and Eastern Europe. These processes of change have contributed to the partial erosion of key pillars of the Westphalian states' system and the emergence of elements of a 'neo-medieval' system of European order. Late modern European order is thus characterised by a mix of old and new. 'The emerging state system in Europe and the world at large', Wolfram Hanrieder has written (1989: 375), 'is a peculiar amalgam of the past and the present, moving towards an uncertain future. It is multidimensional, contradictory, and in transition.'

The most important development in the history of the Westphalian states' system has been the emergence of a 'pluralistic security community' or Kantian *foedus pacificum* ('Pacific Union') in Western Europe and the wider transatlantic area. This has transformed the structural dynamics of contemporary European order, and laid the foundations for a durable peace order in the wider continent. The key to the future of European order, and to the prospects of building a durable pan-European cooperative security system, is thus the relationship between this Euro-Atlantic security community and the countries of Central and Eastern Europe. Germany is firmly embedded in this Euro-Atlantic security community. Its eastern neighbours, however, are engaged in a demanding and potentially destabilising process of political and economic transformation. Germany thus has a pivotal role to play in the new Europe as the mediator and bridge between West and East. 'The main responsibility for a future integrated Europe lies above all with Germany' (Hacke 1997: 537). It is in this context that the dual enlargement process assumes such historic importance, both for Germany and for Europe as a whole.

The Europes of Westphalia, Versailles and Yalta

The 'Europe of Westphalia'

The 1648 Treaty of Westphalia is generally regarded as marking the birth of the modern states' system. This treaty not only ended the Thirty Years War – a brutal conflict which brought appalling human suffering and material devastation to vast swathes of what is now Germany[1] – it also created a new diplomatic order based on legally sovereign states. Although states had existed in medieval Christendom, they operated in a very different legal, diplomatic and political context than that created by the Treaty of Westphalia.

In medieval Christendom, power relations were not organised vertically into separate states with clearly defined geographical borders, but horizontally across the whole of Christendom on a functional basis. In this medieval system, the Latin church exercised a universal spiritual role that also affected the exercise of power by the secular authorities. Lay authority was vested primarily in the hands of kings, princes and nobles, although townspeople and merchants enjoyed considerable autonomy in the management of their own affairs. In addition, the Holy Roman Empire provided an overarching political structure that encompassed much of Central Europe. Order in medieval Christendom thus rested on a complex normative and institutional structure characterised by an overlapping and interlocking system of lay and religious authorities, and multiple identities. Although this system of medieval order proved 'exceptionally turbulent, dynamic and enterprising', it was also prone to occasional outbursts of violence, and the breakdown of social order was an ever-present threat (Bull and Watson 1984: 13).

This medieval order was eroded from within by a series of deep-seated social, economic and cultural trends. Existing political structures were increasingly questioned as a consequence of the Renaissance, which stimulated an interest in classical models of statehood, particularly the political philosophy of Graeco-Roman civilisation, with its concern for the *polis* (the self-governing city-state). In its turn, the Reformation broke the authority of the Catholic church and hastened the growth of secular forms of collective identity. Finally, the wars of religion of the sixteenth and seventeenth centuries led many Protestants and humanists to develop arguments in favour of state sovereignty independent from any external authority.

From the fourteenth century to the mid-seventeenth century, therefore, a growing number of Europeans saw their main political task as building sovereign states capable of providing domestic stability and security from external threats. This led to a rejection of feudal obligations and the claims to universal authority by both the Catholic church and the Holy Roman Empire. Beginning in Italy and spreading throughout area of medieval Christendom, 'the complex horizontal structure of feudal society crystallised into a vertical pattern of territorial states, each with increasing authority inside defined geographical borders' (Bull and Watson 1984: 15). By the mid-seventeenth century, the hegemonic authority of both the Pope and the Holy Roman Emperor had collapsed. It was in this context that the emergence of a new system of international order was given legal expression by the 1648 Treaty of Westphalia.

'The Treaty of Westphalia', Kalevi Holsti has argued, 'organized Europe on the basis of particularism. It represented a new diplomatic arrangement – an order created by states, for states – and replaced most of the legal vestiges of hierarchy, at the pinnacle of which were the Pope and the Holy Roman Emperor'. Westphalia created 'a pan-European diplomatic system based on the new principles of sovereignty and the legal equality [of states]'. It thus 'paved the way for a system of states to replace a hierarchical system under the leadership of the Pope and the Habsburg family complex that linked the Holy Roman and Spanish Empires' (Holsti 1991: 25–6).

'Like all such historical benchmarks', it has been argued, 'Westphalia is in some respects more a convenient reference point than the source of a fully formed new normative system'. Nevertheless, 'the Peace of Westphalia created at least the foundations of a new European system – one that would not become truly a world system until the second half of the twentieth century – out of the ruins of the political structures and idealized rationale for them that had existed more or less unchanged in Europe for the preceding thousand years' (Miller 1994: 20).

Westphalian order and the 'German problem'

The key feature of the Westphalian states' system was the existence of legally sovereign states functioning without a higher source of legitimate political authority. In this 'anarchic' international system, states struggled to preserve their sovereignty in the face of threats both internal and external. Given the absence of an overarching source of authority (such as the universal church and the Holy Roman Empire), states needed to devise other means to regulate their conflicts and maintain the stability of the international system. They did so by creating five 'institutions' or mechanisms: the balance of power, diplomacy, international law, the management role of the great powers and war. The emergence and strengthening of these institutions meant that the modern international system was increasingly characterised by elements of cooperation and regulated intercourse, rather than simply struggle and competition between states. Thus as Hedley Bull argued, the Westphalian states' system was not just an international 'system', it was increasingly an international 'society'. He therefore spoke of the emergence of an 'society of states' (or 'international society') within the Westphalian states' system (Bull 1977).

Throughout much of the history of the Westphalian states' system, the primary ordering mechanism for regulating European international society was the balance of power. This was the principle that no one state should dominate the European continent. From the mid-seventeenth century until the start of the twentieth century, European order rested on a balance of power that was regulated by a mix of diplomacy and periodic wars. With the exception of the Napoleonic era, these wars were usually of a 'limited' nature. Following the 1815 Treaty of Vienna, the principle of the balance of power was coupled to another key mechanism – a 'Concert' of the European great powers. By the late nineteenth century, therefore, the balance of power and the concert of the great powers had emerged as the key mechanisms for regulating European order.

At the heart of this Westphalian states' system was Germany – 'the central capstone of the European system' (Geiss 1997: 16). Germany has long

been central to European order – either as the 'hammer' or the 'anvil' of
European power politics, in the words of Bernhard von Bülow. Since the
Treaty of Westphalia, Germany has been the pivot around which the
European balance of power has revolved. For much of this time, 'Germany' was a weak and fragmented collection of small and medium-sized
states, loosely bound together in the 'Holy Roman Empire'. It was therefore all too often the victim of great power machinations.[2] However, Germany's role as the weak centre – or 'anvil' – of the Westphalian states'
system was fundamentally to change in 1871 with the creation – through
'blood and iron' – of a Prussian-dominated *Kleindeutschland* ('small Germany'). This new German Reich was soon to become Europe's 'hammer'.

Unification in 1871 transformed Germany 'from a potential victim of
aggression to a threat to the European equilibrium' (Kissinger 1994: 134).
The emergence of a new military and economic great power in the centre
of the continent proved highly destabilising to the European balance of
power (Deporte 1979: 116). Thus was born the contemporary 'German
problem': the problem, in other words, of how to integrate – or at least
contain – the prodigious economic strength and military potential of a
unified German state, situated at the heart of Europe. Charles de Gaulle
famously spoke of the German problem as 'indeed the European problem' par excellence, because the question of Germany's place and role in
Europe concerned all of its many neighbours in Europe.[3] The failure to
resolve the conundrum of Germany's place in Europe was to contribute
to two world wars, and ultimately to the division of Germany in the context of a bipolar Europe.

Many analyses of the 'German problem', and of Germany's role in late
nineteenth and twentieth century Europe more broadly, focus on Germany's size and its central geographical location – its *Mittellage*. 'What is
wrong with Germany', A.J.P. Taylor once wrote, 'is that there is too much
of it' (Taylor 1967: 21). Germany's *Mittellage* has amplified German influence on European affairs, thereby contributing to the fears of its many
neighbours. This has led to suggestions that the German problem 'does
not somehow emanate from some special German "character"', but from
its geography':

> Unlike Britain, Russia, or the United States, the Germans lacked the space to
> work out their abundant vitality. Moreover, because of geography, Ger-
> many's vitality was an immediate threat to the rest of Europe. Modern Ger-
> many was born encircled. Under the circumstances, whatever the lesson of
> the wars between Germany and its neighbours, it cannot be found merely
> by analysing the faults of the Germans. (Calleo 1978: 206)

Yet, the 'German problem' was not simply a function of Germany's size or structural location in the Westphalian states' system. The decisive factors were the political character of the German state and the different grand strategies pursued by its ruling elite. As regards the latter factor: Bismarck's cautious diplomacy epitomised a sophisticated *Realpolitik* that sought to reassure the other European powers that the Reich was a satisfied power willing and able to play the role of Europe's 'honest broker'. After 1890, however, Wilhelmine Germany engaged in a more aggressive diplomacy that antagonised Russia and challenged the British Empire – with disastrous results. This represents a change from a grand strategy informed by the 'sophisticated realism' of Bismarck to the 'hard realism' of the Wilhelmine Reich.[4] Of greater importance than the choice of grand strategy, however, was the authoritarian and militarist character of the state Bismarck founded in 1871, which was to find its most extreme expression in the National Socialist regime of Adolf Hitler. As Konrad Adenauer wrote in his memoirs, 'The German people in all walks of life suffered for decades from a false concept of state, power, and the relation of the individual to the state' (Adenauer 1965: 44). The fundamental cause of the 'German problem' does not therefore lie with its size, its *Mittellage* or its economic potency, but rather with its authoritarian politics and its pursuit of an aggressive grand strategy. This was recognised by Czech President Vaclav Havel who declared, 'Germany can be as large as she wants to, as long as she stays democratic' (quoted in Hauner 1993: 252).

The 'Europe of Versailles'

The Great War of 1914–18 marked a decisive watershed in modern European history. The 'war to end all wars', as it was known, led to a major reshaping of the map of Europe, as four multinational empires (the Habsburg, Ottoman, Russian and German) collapsed amidst a wave of revolution and violence. Throughout vast swathes of Central and Eastern Europe and the Balkans new states sprang up, many of whom found themselves embroiled in violent conflicts with their erstwhile neighbours. 'The war of giants has ended', wrote Winston Churchill, 'the wars of the pygmies begin' (quoted in Davies 1996: 926).

The peacemakers who gathered in Paris in 1919 wanted to create a new system of international order that would transcend the balance of power and *Machtpolitik* more generally. President Woodrow Wilson set the tone in his famous fourteen points speech to the American Congress. His radical aim was to forge a 'peace without victory', combining order with justice. The central notion was that, 'no nation should seek to extend its polity over any other nation or people, but that every people should be left free to determine its own polity, its own way of development, unhindered, unthreatened, unafraid, the little along with the great and powerful' (quoted in Holsti 1991: 177). This belief in the right of nations to self-determination was the dominant principle governing the reordering of Europe that followed the 1919 Treaty of Versailles. The 'Europe of Versailles' was thus characterised by the creation of a number of new territorial nation-states on the ruins of once-mighty multinational empires.

Despite the best intentions of its creators, however, the 'Europe of Versailles' was to prove inherently unstable. The territorial settlement of 1919 generated manifold new grievances and nationalist irredentia. At the same time, the mechanisms for conflict resolution created by the League of Nations were ineffective, whilst economic recession undermined the already weak democratic polities of Central and Eastern Europe. To make matters worse, several of Europe's traditional great powers (notably Weimar Germany, Soviet Russia and Fascist Italy) were implacably hostile to the new international order. Not surprisingly, therefore, the fragile peace of Versailles collapsed in 1939 as another round of world war broke out.

The 'Europe of Yalta'

The Second World War once again led to a profound reshaping of Europe. Although there was no formal peace settlement, the foundations for a new post-war order were laid at a series of summit meetings between the wartime allies. The most famous – or perhaps infamous – of these was the Yalta summit of February 1945. This summit has subsequently acquired enormous political symbolism. In popular mythology, it is now seen as a grand exercise in great power geopolitical engineering.[5] This is not historically justified.[6] Nonetheless, the 'Europe of Yalta' does provide a convenient shorthand to categorise post-war Europe's bipolar order.

The 'Europe of Yalta' was distinguished by five unique characteristics: the decisive role of the superpowers in European affairs; the creation of two military-political alliance systems (NATO/EEC on the one hand and the Warsaw Pact/CMEA on the other); the division of Germany; nuclear deterrence; and the existence of a small group of neutral and non-aligned countries (Hyde-Price 1991: 47–9). This structure of power relations was to define European order for four decades. It was an arrangement that brought stability and order to much of Europe, but at a cost of much injustice – primarily in the Soviet bloc, but also in the West – as well as the ever-present threat of nuclear Armageddon.

At the heart of this bipolar system of European order were the two German states, each of which constituted the front line of their respective military-ideological blocs (Grewe 1986 and Wagenlehner 1988). The leaders of the old Federal Republic 'were always deeply conscious of Germany's Cold War position as the divided center of a divided Europe and Berlin's position as the divided center of the divided center' (Garton Ash 1996: 81). The fact that the division of Europe ran directly through the heart of Germany was of tremendous political and symbolic significance for the subsequent dynamics of the cold war. Divided Germany served as 'the permanent catalyst for change' (Brzezinski 1989: 291). It ensured that the division of Europe remained a live issue despite a stalemate of over four decades, in a way that it might not have, had the East–West divide run along the Rhine or the Oder-Neisse, rather than along the Elbe. The division of Germany gave the East–West conflict a national dimension, and therefore linked it to one of the most potent and enduring political forces in the modern age – nationalism. Moreover, it was the Promethean struggle over Germany which shaped the character of the two alliance systems, and through which the two sides reached some sort of implicit understanding about the means and limits of the East–West struggle. Through the conflict over Germany, therefore, both sides began to develop the unspoken rules of the cold war game (Hyde-Price 1991: 30).

For some in Europe, the division of Germany 'provided a solution, inadvertently, to the problem which the countries of Europe had faced and failed to master since 1870: the place of a too-powerful Germany in a European system which could not of itself preserve the independence of its members in the face of German strength' (Deporte 1979: 116). The creation of two separate German states, each integrated into opposed military-political blocs, and each with its own 'special relationship' to its superpower patron, provided an apparent solution to the perennial *deutsche Frage* ('German question'). Germany, some argued, had only been united in a single nation-state for a relatively brief period in its history, and the experience had not been a happy one – either for the German people themselves or the rest of Europe (Bertram 1988: 138). Many Germans suspected that, despite their formal commitment to unification, some of their Western allies shared the sentiments of François Mauriac, who famously said: 'I love Germany so much that I rejoice at the idea that today there are two of them' (quoted in Moreton 1987: 76). This suspicion was fuelled in 1984 when the then Italian Foreign Minister declared that 'one has to recognise that pan-Germanism is something that must be overcome. There are two German states and two German states they should remain'.[7]

The problem with the division of Germany, and with the bipolar model of European order more generally, was that it was not acceptable to those living in the East. The communist regimes imposed on Eastern Europe by the Red Army after the Second World War never succeeded in gaining the trust of their citizens. Their political illegitimacy was compounded by their comprehensive economic failure, and by the 1980s, pressures for far-reaching reform were becoming irresistible. With the coming to power of a reformist leadership around Mikhail Gorbachev in Moscow in 1985, the stage was set for the collapse of the 'Europe of Yalta' and an *Epochenwende* ('change of epochs') in European order.

Germany's response to the end of cold war bipolarity will be explored in the following chapter. Before considering the significance of the demise of the East–West conflict for European order, however, we need to examine in greater depth the changes that have taken place within post-war Western Europe. These changes are significant because they have led to the erosion of key pillars of the Westphalian states' system, thereby significantly affecting the structural dynamics of European order in the late modern era. The two most important changes are the (West) European integration process, and – more recently – globalisation, both of which have affected the nature of statehood in late modern Europe.

Integration and globalisation

Germany and the European integration process

The onset of the cold war thwarted aspirations for a new era of peaceful cooperation in Europe. However, whilst the bipolar division of Europe created a stark divide between East and West, it also stimulated a major process of multilateral integration and cooperation in Western Europe. The consequences of this were profound and far-reaching. By the time the cold war ended, it was evident that the West European integration process had had a dramatic impact on the structural dynamics of the Westphalian states' system and the constitution of European order. In doing so it provided the essential conditions for the resolution of the German problem – a fundamental cause of conflict in Europe from the late nineteenth century onwards.

The process of European integration dates back to April 1951, when the European Coal and Steel Community (ECSC) was created. The purpose of this organisation was to provide a supranational framework for integrating the coal and steel industries of the major West European economies – in particular, those of the French and West Germans. By meshing together under multilateral control what were the leading economic sectors of the time, it was hoped, war between member states would ultimately become structurally impossible (Adenauer 1965: 41). The ECSC was thus seen as a *de facto* peace project for Western Europe, designed to 'lay the foundations of a destiny henceforth shared' and to create 'a broader and deeper community among peoples long divided by bloody conflicts'. Moreover, from the start the ECSC was conceived as the kernel of a more inclusive process of pan-European cooperation and integration. 'This isn't just coal and steel', Jean Monnet remarked when the Treaty was signed. 'It is the beginning of a process – a dynamic process to build a great market for all the people of Europe' (quoted in Reinicke 1993: 11).

The signing of the Treaty of Rome in 1957 heralded a new stage in the European integration process. This created the European Economic Community (EEC), the forerunner of today's European Union. Again, this was presented as the core of an inclusive and comprehensive integration process leading to a cooperative European peace order. The signatories to the Treaty of Rome declared that they were 'determined to lay the foundations of an ever closer union among the peoples of Europe', and called upon 'the other peoples of Europe who share their ideal to join in their efforts'.

Given the subsequent importance and centrality of the EEC/EU to European affairs, it is easy to overlook the complexity and multi-faceted character of this integration process as a whole. As Helen Wallace has argued (1999: 2), 'we too easily exaggerate the simplicity of the transnational organisation of Western Europe' and overstate 'the role of the EU as the predominant transnational organisation and the coherence of west European integration and multilateralism'. Whilst the EEC/EU has played a pioneering role in the integration process, other organisations have played their part in promoting regional integration – for example, the European Free Trade Association (EFTA) and the Nordic Council. In addition, the process of West European integration has been 'nested' within a broader set of relationships (Katzenstein 1997: 303), the most important of which is the Atlantic Alliance. Finally, the whole complex architecture of European multilateralism has been underpinned by a thick web of socio-economic transactions and a series of interlocking bilateral relationships between neighbouring states – most importantly, that between France and Germany.

The relative socio-economic homogeneity and shared political values of West European societies meant that the integration process generated novel and extensive forms of multilateral cooperation. This involved not only functional multilateral cooperation institutionalised primarily – although not exclusively – in the EEC/EU, but also transnational security cooperation through NATO. In addition, it stimulated the emergence of multiple identities and criss-crossing patterns of political affiliation (William Wallace 1990: 33, 56). Post-war Western Europe therefore experienced what Helen Wallace has termed a process of 'deep integration' between a core of predominantly Rhineland, catholic countries (1999). Deepening economic interdependence and a strong normative consensus around core values and beliefs complemented the formal institution-building involved in this multilateral 'deep integration'. This process of deep integration provided the foundations for the emergence of a 'pluralistic security community' characterised by a growing 'sense of community'. This 'sense of community' was based on feelings of 'mutual sympathy and loyalties; of "we-feeling", trust, and mutual consideration; of partial identification in terms of self-images and interests; of mutually successful predictions of behaviour, and of cooperative action in accordance with it – in short, a matter of a perpetual dynamic process of mutual attention, communication, perception of needs, and responsiveness in the process of decision-making' (Deutsch: 1957: 36).

The post-war West European process of deep integration had two important consequences for the Westphalian states' system. First, it provided the multilateral framework for the resolution of the 'German problem'. As we have seen, the emergence of the Bismarckian *Kleindeutschland* in 1871 provided a major challenge to the European balance of power. The difficulties of accommodating this large and economically dynamic country at the heart of Europe were ultimately to precipitate a series of increasingly destructive wars. The cold war division of Germany seemed to offer one solution to this problem – albeit temporary. More importantly in the long run was the West European integration process. This provided a multilateral framework for integrating the *Bundesrepublik* into cooperative structures, thereby harnessing German economic power to broader European purposes. Together with the consolidation of democracy and the creation of a more decentralised, federal system of government, European integration provided the means for Germany to regain its sovereignty without arousing fears amongst its neighbours. It is for this reason that Helmut Kohl was frequently to refer to European integration and German *Westbindung* as a question of 'war and peace'.

The second important consequence of the integration process for the Westphalian system was that it led to the emergence of novel forms of pooled sovereignty and multi-level governance, which have significantly transformed the nature of statehood in late modern Europe. Whilst there is little agreement on the causes of the European integration process,[8] few would dispute that it has had a major impact on patterns of governance and decision-making amongst member states. The EU has developed a complex institutional architecture, combining elements of inter-govern-mentalism with supranationalism. Of particular importance are the elements of multi-level governance which have developed within the EU's 'combined polity'. These have eroded the distinction between domestic and international politics intrinsic to the Westphalian notion of sovereignty (William Wallace 1999: 504–5).

Multilevel governance has been defined as 'a system of continuous negotiation among nested governments at several territorial tiers – supranational, national, regional and local'. This comes about 'as the result of a broad process of institutional creation and decisional realloca-tion that has pulled some previously centralised functions of the state up to the supranational level and some down to the local/regional level' (Marks 1993: 392; see also Jachtenfuchs and Kohler-Koch 1996). The concept of multilevel governance draws attention both to the importance of different territorial levels in political processes, and to the distinctive nature of the political processes operating at and between these levels. The EU has developed into a 'highly interdependent system' charac-terised by 'the shift of allocative powers to different levels of policy-mak-ing depending on the issues at stake, the interpenetration of political processes, and the contingencies for political action beyond national boundaries' (Kohler-Koch 1996b: 360). The new governance mecha-nisms which are emerging within this multilevel system 'are reshaping statehood with regard to its societal function, its institutional structure and its activities at the policy formation level' (Heinelt 1996: 11).

The European integration process has accelerated a development that is evident throughout the wider international system, namely a marked blurring of the boundaries between domestic and international politics (Bühl 1997).[9] The disciplines of both international relations and com-parative public policy have been built on the assumption of different 'levels of analysis', each operating with their own logic, structural dynamics and explanatory variables. In contemporary Western Europe, this assumption is increasingly less tenable. The European integration process – both the informal integration of societies and economies, and the formal institutional integration associated primarily with the EU – has created new forms of multilevel governance and policy networks.

The consequent 'Europeanisation' of the nation-state is the product of the interplay between changes in relations *between* European states and changes *within* each state (Olsen 1996: 245). As a result of the 'particular combination of losing and pooling sovereignty in the European Union', a 'new mode of governance' has thus emerged with a 'multi-tier negotiating system' (Kohler-Koch 1996a: 170–1). The result is the emergence of a new type of governing – governing through networks. 'Networking is the main task, which means offering the institutional framework within which transaction costs can be reduced and successful self-regulation can be supported' (Kohler-Koch 1996b: 371). With its weak political core, overlapping and multi-tier structures of authoritative decision-making and many spatial locations, the EU is very much a 'post-modern' polity (Caporaso 1996), characterised by coalition-building and sectorial networks in which the Commission can play an influential role. Finally, the EU typifies a new form of governing – described as a transition from 'engineering to gardening' (March and Olsen quoted in Mörth 1998: 6) – given its primary focus on regulation rather than redistribution.

Contemporary Germany is thus embedded in multilateral structures created by the West European 'deep' integration process. This integration process has led to the gradual pooling of sovereignty and fostered new patterns of multi-level governance. It has also eroded the traditional importance of borders and boundaries, and blurred the distinction between domestic and European issues. In addition, it has stimulated the emergence of multiple forms of identity and political affiliation. In this way, the deep integration process has weakened one of the central pillars of the Westphalian states' system – the principle of state sovereignty. The Westphalian states' system has also been deeply affected by another key process, which in some respects has developed in tandem with the European integration process – namely, globalisation.

Globalisation and European order

Globalisation has come to occupy a central place in contemporary German political discourse – as it has in many other countries in Europe and beyond. The precise meaning and implications of globalisation are contested (Rosamond 1999). At its most basic, globalisation posits a significant intensification of global interconnectedness between geographically dispersed societies such that events in one part of the world have effects on peoples and societies far away. Over recent decades, the accelerating pace of technological innovation and global economic activity has intensified trends towards informal integration and complex interdependence. Improved communications and transport systems have facilitated the internationalisation of production, distribution and exchange, along with the globalisation of banking and financial services.

The increasing mobility of capital and the transnationalisation of production processes, suggests that shifting patterns of trade and technological innovation are together eradicating the constraints of physical distance to economic interaction. Some even speak of the 'end of geography', particularly as regards global financial markets. Consequently, major production and investment decisions are increasingly orientated towards international rather than domestic markets. At the same time, 'the revolution in communications and transport technologies has facilitated greatly the global interplay of cultures, values, ideas, knowledge, peoples, social networks, elites and social movements. That this is a highly uneven and differentiated process does not detract from the underlying message that societies can no longer be conceptualized as bounded systems, insulated from the outside world ... In modern society the local and the global have become intimately related' (McGrew 1992: 3).

One of the most important political consequences of globalisation has been to greatly intensify the dialectic between integration and fragmentation that has been evident throughout the twentieth century. A 'most fundamental paradox of our era', Kalevi Holsti has noted, is the 'intense trend toward political fragmentation within the context of a globalizing economy', as individuals search for a sense of community 'based on ethnicity, religion, language, and other primordial attributes' (Holsti 1993: 407). The *Bundesrepublik* thus finds itself at the heart of a Europe buffeted by conflicting pressures: integration, cooperation and convergence on the one hand, fragmentation, conflict and divergence on the other. As Ian Clark has argued, 'neither globalization nor fragmentation is likely ever to be the exclusive tendency within any one historical period: both will tend to occur simultaneously and often the international system will reflect the contradictory nature of their occurrence' (Clark 1997: 4).

Globalisation has contributed to the blurring of the international and domestic realms, and further eroded the foundations of the Westphalian system. The term 'plurilateralism' has been coined to refer to the increasing diffusion and decentralisation of power both upwards to the supranational and downwards to the sub-national level (Cerny 1993: 27). According to this perspective, complex globalisation has added a third level to 'two-level games' popularised by Robert Putnam (1988). Along with the domestic and international levels, a transnational level has emerged. This includes 'not only "firm-firm diplomacy" but also trans-governmental networks and policy communities, internationalised market structures, transnational cause groups and many other linked and interpenetrated markets, hierarchies and networks' (Cerny 1997: 270–1).

In a similar vein, Seyom Brown has argued that 'the world polity is ever more a *polyarchy* in which national states, subnational groups and transnational special interests and communities are vying for the support and loyalty of individuals'. In the context of this polyarchy, he argues, 'conflicts are prosecuted and resolved primarily on the basis of ad hoc power plays and bargaining among combinations of these groups – combinations that vary from issue to issue' (Brown 1995: 140). While 'nation-states are still the most powerful political entities in world society', they are being weakened by new 'subnational and transnational material and ideational forces'. 'The progressive erosion of the ability of national politics to retain sovereign control over conditions of their respective countries', he suggests, 'is a symptom of the expanding – and essentially irreversible – interdependence of peoples across national boundaries'. The increasing mobility of goods, persons, and information across national borders has created a dialectic between those who welcome and those that fear an expansion of contacts and competition. At the same time, it is producing 'a multiplicity of cross-cutting relationships at all levels of society – individual, group, national, transnational, and global'. Operating within the inherited structures of the traditional nation-state system, these developments 'are producing, on the whole, a global pattern in which the formal institutions of governance lack congruence with the loyalties and association of peoples' (Brown 1995: 2–8).

Globalisation and integration are sometimes presented as deterministic processes driven by impersonal economic, social and technological forces. This has led some to view the contemporary state as increasingly impotent and irrelevant. 'Wherever we look across the social sciences', it has been argued, 'the state is being weakened, hollowed out, carved up, toppled or buried. We have entered a new era of "state denial"' (Weiss 1998: 2). There is of course 'a basic and fundamental truth at the heart of the notion of globalisation, namely that states must live within a larger surrounding which pushes them to change and rationalize' (Paul and Hall 1999: 403). Economic, social and technological forces shape the broad parameters within which states are situated, thereby both constraining specific policy choices and facilitating others. Nonetheless, states are *situated actors*, in the sense outlined in chapter 1. They are not simply 'shaped and shoved' by globalisation and integration, but are able to facilitate, impede or channel the forces of economic and technological change they embody. For this reason, Linda Weiss has spoken of the 'myth of the powerless state', and has used the example of Germany to demonstrate that states with efficient and robust national institutions retain a significant ability to shape the 'rules of the game' (1998: 212). The key factor here is the size of the country concerned and the effectiveness of its national institutions and political leadership. 'Precisely how the balance between globalization and fragmentation will be adjusted', Ian Clark has argued, 'depends on the new role that states are able to forge for themselves, and how successfully they manage to mediate between increasingly potent international pressures and the heightened levels of domestic discontent that will inevitably be brought in their wake' (1997: 202).

The primary impact of globalising pressures on Germany has been to expose the exhaustion of the post-war *soziale Marktwirtschaft* (the social market economy). Perhaps the greatest achievement of the Bonn Republic has been to combine economic efficacy with a significant degree of social justice, within the framework of a democratic *Rechtstaat* (a government based on the rule of law). However, the continued viability of the social market model – *Model Deutschlands* – has been questioned by intensifying global economic competition. This manifests itself most clearly in cheap products from developing countries, the fluidity (and instability) of the world financial markets, cheap agricultural products from Poland and relatively low-cost skilled labour throughout East Central Europe. The search for continued economic success in the face of global competition thus threatens to erode the commitment to social justice – one of the key pillars of the social market system. For many Germans, the solution to globalisation is deeper EU integration, in order to reproduce at the European level the achievements of *Model Deutschlands*. How this is to be realised in an enlarged EU of twenty-five or more members, however, is not clear, and will constitute one of the key political issues on the German and European policy agenda in the early twenty-first century.

Statehood in late modern Europe

Globalisation and integration are steadily transforming the spatial and temporal contours of European order. State sovereignty – the defining principle of the Westphalian system – has been partially eroded from within by integration, and from without by globalisation. This has transformed the nature of statehood in late modern Europe.

In the nineteenth and early twentieth centuries, states had two primary responsibilities: external defence and diplomacy, and internal law and order. This gave rise to a relatively small state apparatus based on a hierarchically organised bureaucracy structured like a pyramid. With the dramatic growth in their responsibility for the management and regulation of complex, modern societies and economies in the twentieth century, modern liberal-democratic states have increasingly been characterised by a more dispersed network of ministries, agencies, executives and semi-state bodies. The modern state is thus best defined as a 'complex institutional ensemble' (see pp. 28, 37). These institutional ensembles operate in a multi-level and 'mixed actor' international system, in which a variety of non-governmental and transnational players interact with an array of disaggregated state actors. States in late modern Europe are thus not only structurally different from their nineteenth-century predecessors, they also interact in different ways. Rather than simply engaging in traditional state-to-state diplomacy, they now interact through a disaggregated set of transnational and trans-governmental linkages within a multi-level system.

Thus whilst the state may not be 'withering away' as Marx predicted or as some 'hyperglobalists' suggest (Mayall 1998: 248), it is no longer useful to conceptualise it in neo-realist terms as a rational unitary actor. As David Armstrong has argued (1999: 558–9), although the fundamental nature of international society has not changed as much as some radical theorists assert, 'neither is the society of states unchanged from its nineteenth century form. Globalization and other forces may well have created a structure of economic, social, political and cultural interactions that cannot fully be understood within a framework defined solely by the state and the relations among states, but they have not replaced that framework'. The key change they have affected is in 'what it means to be a state at the end of the millennium'. In turn, this has 'influenced the social interaction among states, including the processes by which international society arrives at its rules, and the nature of the rules themselves'.

'Less than one hundred years ago', Armstrong continues, 'all major states were in a posture of permanent readiness for war with each other' and 'dominated the rest of the world'. Today, however, 'both war among the major powers and straightforward colonial domination by them of other states look less and less plausible'. The main reasons for this are 'the increasing interdependence and multi-level interaction among the great powers, and the fact that all of them are subject to far greater degrees of popular scrutiny and accountability'. 'Today's liberal democracies', he suggests, 'are kinder, gentler things than they used to be, organised at least as much to provide justice as order or security' (1999: 559–60). Thus as Peter van Ham and Przemyslaw Grudzinski have noted (1999–2000: 84), although 'West European states still very much *look* like classical modern states, they are qualitatively different, most obviously because they emphasize wealth and welfare rather than warfare'.

One consequence of globalisation is that 'the major powers constantly watch each other, not, as in the past, out of fear of military threat but because they face the same kinds of economic, social and political problems and are interested in observing how others deal with them'. International society thus constitutes 'a framework within which multifaceted social interaction takes place', in the course of which, 'states are subject to a constant process of socialization in which they internalize each others' policies and practices across a wide spectrum, including economic, financial, educational and social policies. One consequence of this continuing process has been a redefinition in the West of collective understandings of what being a legitimate state entails'. International society thus 'remains a society of states, but one dominated by states that bear little resemblance to their imperial predecessors' (Armstrong 1999: 560).

The changing nature of statehood in late modern Europe is especially marked in the *Bundesrepublik*, given the rupture in its political development in 1945. The subsequent re-forging of a new democratic political order and a post-Holocaust national identity took place largely in tandem with the Federal Republic's integration into Euro-Atlantic structures. Consequently the 'Europeanisation' of the contemporary German state is particularly marked. The *Bundesrepublik* is undoubtedly a 'kinder, gentler thing' than its predecessors, and in a number of respects compares favourably with other West European liberal democracies. Moreover, with its *soziale Marktwirkschaft*, it has been 'organised at least as much to provide justice as order or security'. This has provided the domestic economic and social conditions for the emergence and consolidation of *Zivilmacht* Germany with a distinctive set of national role conceptions.

The Federal Republic has been variously described as a 'post-classical' or 'post-modern' nation-state, in recognition of its commitment to integration.[10] Given the problematic nature of the term 'post-modern', Germany is perhaps better described as a *late modern nation-state*, embodying as it does many of the ambiguities and uncertainties of the age. The Federal Republic retains an important role in the nation-state's 'identity-security interpretative system',[11] even though national identity coexists with other local, regional or European identities. Similarly the

German state is deeply embedded in Euro-Atlantic multilateral structures, whilst retaining a significant ability to shape aspects of its external
environment. In contrast to the nineteenth century, however, patterns of
economic activity and social interaction are no longer contained within
the borders of the nation-state, but are interwoven with their neighbours. Finally, late modern Germany is part of a larger normative
community of values, principles and beliefs which has shaped its foreign
policy behaviour.

Beyond Westphalia: neo-medievalism in Europe

The *annus mirabilis* of 1989 sounded the death-knell of the bipolar
'Europe of Yalta'. With the subsequent break-up the USSR, Czechoslovakia and Yugoslavia, much of the territorial settlement from the peace settlement of 1919 also began to unravel. Thus the early 1990s witnessed
both the end of Yalta and the decomposition of 'the order of Versailles
(the borders and states that emerged from the Ottoman and the Austro-
Hungarian empires)'.

What is particularly interesting, however, is that the 'order of Westphalia – the idea of a system based on territoriality and the sovereignty of
states – is also being called into question' (Hassner 1993: 53). The peeling
away of cold war bipolarity has revealed the extent to which the central
features and underlying structural dynamics of European international
society have been transformed during the post-war period. Although
these changes have been concentrated in Western Europe, their influence
has been felt throughout much of Central and Eastern Europe, lending
credibility to suggestions that the 'Europe of Westphalia' might itself be
facing a more fundamental challenge.

At the end of the twentieth century, therefore, Germany finds itself at
the centre of a continent being reshaped by four distinct but inter-related
processes of change: the end of bipolarity; globalisation; multilateral integration; and the 'triple transformation' of Central and Eastern Europe.
These processes of change have fostered new patterns of governance;
stimulated multiple forms of identity and affiliation; eroded the traditional importance of borders and boundaries; and transformed existing
forms of statehood and sovereignty. Contemporary European international society is thus characterised by a mix of old and new elements.
While the established Westphalian system has not been completely superseded, elements of a new pattern of European politics have emerged
which point to possibility of a post-Westphalian system of European
order in the twenty-first century.

This new, post-Westphalian pattern of international politics in Western Europe will resemble the 'new medievalism' described by Hedley Bull as 'a system of overlapping authority and multiple loyalty'. He suggested that if 'modern states were to come to share their authority over their citizens, and their ability to command their loyalties, on the one hand with regional and world authorities, and on the other hand with sub-state or sub-national authorities, to such an extent that the concept of sovereignty ceased to be applicable, then a neo-mediaeval form of universal political order might be said to have emerged' (Bull 1977: 254–5; see also Linklater 1998).

Although it is perhaps too early to consign the Westphalian states' system to the dustbin of history, European international society is undoubtedly in a process of change and transformation. Certainly in the Western half of Europe, patterns of political authority and affiliations do not fit easily within the formal structures of the Westphalian system. Established forms of sovereignty, national identity and political authority have been eroded by elements of pooled sovereignty, multi-level governance and transnational interaction. As William Wallace notes, the EU polity 'has moved far beyond traditional concepts of sovereignty without developing a consensus on what is emerging in its place' (1999: 517). Government in Europe is becoming a more stratified affair, as power, and a little identity, is shifted upwards to multilateral organisations, and identity, and a little power, is shifted downwards to local and regional authorities (Katzenstein 1997: 304). This may not be a fully fledged neo-medieval system: indeed, it may never develop fully into such a post-Westphalian system. Nevertheless, it has brought a new level of complexity to Europe's society of states, and is indicative of the deeper changes affecting European order.

Whatever the precise outcome of these processes of change and transformation, it is clear that late modern European order is much more multi-level, diffuse and multifaceted than previously. This has transformed the form and content of modern European diplomacy, particularly in Western Europe. In the time of Bismarck or Metternich, states were organisationally smaller and functionally less developed, and the international system was composed of a more limited range of actors and institutions. Consequently statecraft was a more discrete affair, and was largely conducted away from the glare of public opinion.

Today, however, diplomats operate alongside a range of transnational non-governmental actors in a diffuse range of policy sectors. The international system is increasingly multi-level and transnational, and constituted by a rich corpus of multilateral organisations, international regimes and governing arrangements. In addition, the normative dimension of international society now provides an important influence on state behaviour. Thus in late modern Europe, order is not constituted simply by relations between states, but involves a much wider range of international actors operating within the context of a plurilateral or polyarchic system. This polyarchic system is characterised by a dense institutional and normative matrix, which is both under-girded by complex patterns of socio-economic interdependence and embedded within an increasingly globalised economic and financial system.

The Euro-Atlantic security community and pan-European order

Post-war Western Europe: beyond Westphalia
The blurring of the boundaries of the domestic and international domains, and their fusion in a process of 'Europeanisation', points to the emergence of a new pattern of international relations in Western Europe. The Westphalian system was constructed around sovereign states operating within an anarchical framework. Within this anarchical system, international order was generated by a shifting balance of power regulated by diplomacy and periodic wars. However, a series of secular trends concentrated in West Europe in the last fifty years or so have significantly altered the structural dynamics of European order.

Most strikingly, the significance of two of the five institutions of international society identified by Hedley Bull – namely war and the balance of power – has been drastically reduced, if not eliminated.[12] At the same time, the importance of two other institutions – international law and a concert of the great powers – has increased, whilst the content and context of the fifth – diplomacy – has been significantly altered. Above all, the nature of the Westphalian states' system has been fundamentally transformed by the emergence of a pluralistic security community in Western Europe. This has had a profound and far-reaching impact on what has long been the defining feature of the Westphalian system for some three hundred and fifty years – the principle of state sovereignty.

The changes that have transformed West European international society, and which have eroded some of the key pillars of the Westphalian states' system, are associated with five underlying and interlocking processes. First, the spread and consolidation of democratic systems of government and the rule of law throughout Western Europe. Second, the development of comprehensive welfare systems and the emergence of what in Germany has been termed 'social market economics'. Third, the creation of institutionalised forms of multilateral cooperation, characterised by a significant pooling of sovereignty and innovative forms of multi-level governance.[13] This 'formal integration' consists of 'deliberate actions by authoritative policy-makers to create and adjust rules, to establish common institutions and to work with and through those institutions; to regulate, channel, redirect, encourage or inhibit social and economic flows, as well as to pursue common policies' (Wallace 1990: 54).

Fourth, an extensive and dense web of socio-economic interdependence, transnational exchanges and informal integration. This informal integration involves 'intense patterns of interaction which develop without the intervention of deliberate governmental decisions, following the dynamics of markets, technology, communications networks and social exchange', and is thus 'a matter of flows and exchanges, of the gradual growth of networks of interaction' (Wallace 1990: 54). Last but not least, the emergence of a normative consensus based on human rights, democratic values and non-violent forms of conflict resolution. This normative context is not simply an ideological superstructure reflecting the interests of states, but helps determine states' perceptions of their interests (Brock 1999: 337). In this manner, the emergence of a transatlantic security community represents the development of a distinctive 'sense of community' or 'we-feeling'.

The relative importance of these five factors for the transformation of post-war Western Europe is a matter of dispute. Advocates of 'democratic peace theory' tend to emphasise unit level factors, in other words, the domestic attributes of territorial states (in particular, the existence or otherwise of democratic forms of government). Others place more weight on the integration process and formal institution-building. The analytical problem for peace and conflict researchers is that the emergence of a new pattern of international relations in Western Europe has been 'over-determined', and cannot be reduced to any single casual factor.

One approach that is of particular analytical utility, and which fits well with the concept of European order outlined in chapter 3 (see pp. 58–60), is the 'cosmopolitan peace thesis' (Knutsen 1999: 296–7). This is a system-based approach that 'sees peace as an attribute of a system of open and strong states'. The cosmopolitan peace thesis conceptualises a security community as 'an expression of a growing community of states ... which has been formed through modern history by a succession of leading powers (or hegemons) whose promulgation of principles like openness, tolerance and self-determination facilitated their pursuit of national interests'. The cosmopolitan peace thesis emphasises the socially textured

nature of international society and the importance of transnational societal interaction, economic interdependence and the emergence of a new
cosmopolitan normative consensus within a distinct regional and historical context:

> In this perspective, peace is a syndrome rather than a simple effect. It
> augurs the evolution of a transnational *civic culture* which engenders
> mutual trust and legitimacy. It is an attribute of a (regionally concrete, civ-
> ilizationally specific and historically constructed) order secured by a com-
> plex, interactive web (rather than a simple bi-variate, unidirectional
> relationship). Democracy is certainly an important element in this order-
> ing web. However, the web also involves other important elements. It
> involves a common, historically based understanding as to the rules which
> govern the interaction among sovereign states. And it involves the regional
> evolution of an intersubjective, liberal identity whose common norms and
> values – social openness, pluralism and dialogue, natural law, individual
> and equal rights, representative political bodies of freedom of trade and
> possession – operate as identity markers and common indicators of recip-
> rocal peaceful intentions.
>
> The reason why no war has broken out among Western states, then, lies
> not primarily in the national make-up of individual Western states, but in
> an *inter*national (cosmopolitan) public sphere which sustains the develop-
> ment of a shared set of values and norms that transcend the cultural char-
> acteristics of individual states. (Knutsen 1999: 297)

Western Europe's zone of stable peace

Whatever its precise causes and determining factors, the essential point to
note is that a zone of 'stable peace' (Boulding 1978: 17; see also Singer and
Wildavsky 1996) has emerged in Western Europe and the wider transatlantic area, with a 'pluralistic security community' (Deutsch 1957: 5) at
its core.[14] The defining feature of this zone of stable peace is that the states
that constitute it no longer regard war, or the threat of war, as an acceptable means of resolving conflicts within the security community. Thus
the spirit of Kant ('perpetual peace') has replaced the spirit of Clausewitz
('war as a continuation of politics by other means'). International relations in Western Europe's *foedus pacificum* have become 'civilianised', and
states now operate with a broader range of considerations than the struggle for power, security and influence. Most importantly, they no longer
consider using military force or coercive diplomacy in their relations with
each other. This is of tremendous significance, for 'if physical violence is
no longer a serious option then in practice sovereignty has been seriously
weakened, whatever the legal position. In the absence of an effective right

to resort to force, sovereignty is, it seems, a very amorphous notion' (C. Brown 1995: 195).

The emergence of this transatlantic security community heralds a profound transformation in the structural dynamics of West European international society, one that has important and potentially far-reaching consequences for the Westphalian states' system in Europe as a whole. Up until the middle of the twentieth century, all European states were locked into a complex and shifting balance of power arrangement, with Germany at its core. These states jealously guarded their sovereignty, and engaged in power politics based on *Realpolitik* calculations. Within this *Realpolitik* mind-set, military assets constituted the key element in the assessment of relative power capabilities.

The emergence of a security community in the transatlantic area, however, has meant that West European states no longer view their neighbours within this security community as potential threats. Consequently neither the security dilemma nor the balance of power operate amongst states in Western Europe.[15] Instead, a process of deep integration has transformed Western Europe. Thus German interests 'are being advanced not in a balance of power clash, but in tedious bureaucratic manoeuvring in the confederation-plus of the EU and the confederation-minus of the transatlantic community' (Pond 1996: 36).

The limitations of neo-realism

The emergence of this security community means that realism – particularly in its structural and power politics variants – is of limited analytical utility in understanding the structural dynamics of the Euro-Atlantic security community. Realism can provide insights into the functioning of regional security complexes characterised by a high degree of conflict and mistrust, but it is not so useful for understanding international relations in a zone of stable peace.[16] This is because '*where common interests exist* realism is too pessimistic about the prospects for cooperation and the role of institutions' (Keohane 1993b: 277). Similarly, realists stress the importance of relative gains for states in a self-help system, but 'the concern about "relative gains", which is, in general, a consequence of anarchy, is far less among allies than it is between opponents' (Snyder 1996: 175). Thus 'the constraining effects of anarchy are felt less by liberal democracies enmeshed in complex cooperative networks'. The spread of globalisation and the emergence of 'post-modern states' must increase 'the relative importance of cooperation based on the soft power resources required in complex, plurilateralist networks, and decrease the relative importance of conflict based on more traditional forms of power, especially military power'. Consequently the 'latter form of power is less relevant for the creation of multi-level governance regulating increasingly globalized economies and societies' (Sørensen 1997: 268).

The emergence of the Euro-Atlantic security community does not mean that a harmony of interests exists in this region. The distinguishing feature of a zone of stable peace is that conflicts over resources and influence, which remain an indelible feature of international society, are resolved peacefully, without recourse to threats of violence. A 'durable peace' (*dauerhafter Frieden*), Dieter Senghaas has written, involves a structure or political order based upon 'peaceful coexistence and a political order characterised by reliable and civilised conflict-resolution' in which 'constructive conflictive resolution routinely, "unseen", silently and quite naturally takes place' (Senghaas: 1995 15). European international politics – like other politics – is about who governs and by what means, and it therefore raises questions about the process of acquiring, shaping, distributing and exercising power. However, the emergence of a security community changes the relative value of the currency of power. As Stanley Hoffmann notes,

> The structural theory [of neo-realism] was geared to a world in which states, as discrete actors, sought power or sought to balance power in a game that entailed the possible resort to war. This limited the importance of variations in state behaviour caused by each actors' domestic regime or politics. Remove that possibility of war or relax those constraints and the nature of the game changes. It is not that the actors will stop seeking power and influence, but rather that the way of acquiring gains, the nature of the desired gains, and the means of provoking international change all will change. In traditional politics, war provided the most visible and often the quickest instrument of change. If war is removed, change in international affairs, or in the pecking order of states, will tend to result either from revolutions or from domestically driven modifications in the goals or in the power of states. (Hoffmann 1995: 271)

Europe's three zones

The emergence of a pluralistic security community in Western Europe is without doubt the single most important development in the history of the Westphalian system. It has fundamentally transformed the structural dynamics of European order, and generated new patterns of international relations that bear little or no resemblance to those of Europe's past. More importantly for this study, it has transformed Germany's geopolitical situation in Europe. It has recast the dilemmas of Germany's *Mittellage*, and provided the context within which Germany has been able to define a new set of roles to play in European affairs (Rühl 1996: 112). Consequently the 'German question', in its traditional power political form, no longer dominates European security as it did for much of the late nineteenth and early twentieth centuries.

Yet whilst Western Europe has experienced the emergence of a zone of stable peace, developments elsewhere in the European 'regional security complex' (Buzan 1991: 188) have been less sanguine. The contrasts within Europe were symbolised in the early 1990s by two cities: Maastricht and Sarajevo. The aspiration towards an 'ever closer union among the peoples of Europe' came a step closer with the signing of the Maastricht Treaty of European Union in 1991, even though the subsequent problems of ratification were to demonstrate that nationalist sentiments remain a potent force within Western Europe. By way of contrast, Sarajevo – in 1914 the flashpoint of the first great conflagration of twentieth-century Europe – came to symbolise the bloody 'wars of Yugoslav succession', which produced a new euphemism for human evil: 'ethnic cleansing'.

Although the post-cold war situation in Europe was characterised by considerable complexity, ambiguity and contradiction, some broad trends and developments have emerged. Across the continent, the 'most fundamental paradox of our era' – the 'intense trend towards political fragmentation within the context of a globalizing economy' (Holsti 1993: 407) – is much in evidence. The paradoxical coexistence of integration, cooperation and homogenisation on the one hand, and fragmentation, conflict and diversity on the other, is apparent in contemporary Russia or Romania as well as in France or Portugal. Nonetheless, 'there are significant differences among groups of states as to the speed at which they are involved in this process of historical change' (Zacher 1992: 60). In contemporary Europe 'three contexts of European change' have emerged in the form of 'concentric circles radiating out from Brussels' (Goldmann 1997: 261, 266). These three zones are distinguished by the uneven impact of the manifold processes of change affecting late modern Europe. What is very striking is that these 'three contexts of change' bear a striking resemblance to the 'three historic regions' of Europe identified by Szücs (1988) – namely Western, Central and Eastern Europe (see also Kumar 1992 and Hupchick 1994).

The first of these three zones is the *core zone*. It consists of the mature democracies of Western Europe and North America, which together form a zone of stable peace, with a security community at its core. This core zone is characterised by responsible and representative government; a high degree of transnational socio-economic interdependence; relatively open and tolerant civil societies; a plethora of multilateral institutions; and a shared set of liberal-democratic norms and values. Nationalism in Western Europe has been 'tamed' and primarily takes the form of 'civic nationalism'. Moreover, national identity coexists alongside other forms of political affiliation, generating multiple forms of identity – national, local, regional, European, cosmopolitan. This core zone of Western Europe has witnessed the greatest erosion to the pillars of the Westphalian states' system and exhibits evidence of the emergence of elements of a post-Westphalian form of neo-medieval order.

The second zone is the *intermediate zone*, which is largely constituted by the countries in Central Europe. One of its defining features is the region's historic links with Western Christendom, its participation in many of the defining cultural and intellectual movements of Europe (such as the Renaissance and the Reformation) and the influence of German language, culture and economics. In some respects, this zone roughly corresponds to the historic lands of *Mitteleuropa*. However, the defining feature of this intermediate region is not geography or history, but rather the extent to which the 'triple transformation' process has impacted on the every-day life of these countries. In this intermediate zone, political democratisation is well advanced; civil society has developed; and political life is marked by the emergence of pluralist politics and a broad liberal-democratic consensus. Excessive nationalism has been partially tamed, and largely replaced by a 'new nationalist myth' which has encouraged the East Central Europeans to adopt 'European' norms with respect to individual and minority rights. This 'new nationalist myth' is the 'myth of belonging to European culture, the myth of return to real or imaginary European roots, the myth of normal development brutally interrupted by the Bolshevik experiment or the Russian aggression or both' (Zaslavsky 1992: 110). In the intermediate zone, the process of economic restructuring and marketisation is well developed; trade has been largely reoriented towards the EU – especially towards Germany; and levels of Foreign Direct Investment (FDI) are relatively high. Above all, this second region is characterised by an overwhelming desire to 'return to Europe'. This foreign policy commitment to join Western organisations and structures provides the key motor driving the domestic economic, political and societal reform process, and is widely accepted by dominant elite groups and public opinion in general.

The third distinct area within the European security complex is the *outer zone*. It consists of those countries furthest away (politically if not geographically) from the Euro-Atlantic security community. This outer zone, or periphery, is constituted by countries in Eastern Europe and the Balkans where the reform process is less advanced and the relationship with the West more problematical. In this zone, one-party rule has tended to given way to regimes characterised by a mix of authoritarian impulses and nascent democratic structures. Nationalist identity is primarily defined in terms of a 'blood and land' ethnicity, and is often intolerant of minority communities. The task of state- and nation-building remains central to the political agenda, and generates uncertainty and instability. Economic reform in this peripheral zone has generally been less thorough, and civil society is less developed. In many respects, this region resembles Giselher Wirsings's *Zwischeneuropa*, 'a zone, that is, of weak states, national prejudice, inequality, poverty, and *schlammessel*' (Garton Ash 1988: 56).

These three zones represent ideal-types rather than geographically delineated areas. The boundaries between them are not clear-cut, and it is particularly hard to distinguish between the second and third zones. This is because processes of economic, political, societal and foreign policy change are not coterminous, either temporally or spatially. Poland, the Czech Republic, Hungary and Slovenia are countries that clearly fall within the intermediate zone ('Central Europe'). Russia, Moldova, Serbia and Macedonia, on the other hand, are countries in the outer zone ('Eastern Europe' and the 'Balkans'). However, there are a number of post-communist countries that fall between the two ideal-types of the intermediate and outer zones (i.e., between 'Central' and 'Eastern' Europe). Estonia and Latvia, for example, are 'Central European' in terms of their economic development, their commitment to 'return to Europe' and their relationship to Euro-Atlantic structures. However, their political culture is marked by a pronounced ethnic nationalism, and their Western patrons have had to exert a great deal of pressure to ensure that they meet minimum standards of acceptable behaviour in their treatment of the Russian minority communities. Similarly Slovakia is 'Central European' by economic criteria, but politically, it still needs to demonstrate that it there will be no return to the intolerant nationalism and populist authoritarianism of the Mečiar years.

Clearly, these ideal-types cannot be defined by any single factor. Rather, they can best be distinguished in terms of Wittgenstein's notion of 'family resemblances'. Objects or practices can most appropriately be characterised, Wittgenstein argued, not by 'something that is common to them all' (a single defining feature), but by 'similarities, relationships, and a whole series of them at that'. He went on, 'I can think of no better expression to characterize these similarities than "family resemblance"; for the various resemblances between members of a family: build, features, colour of eyes, gait, temperament, etc., etc., overlap and criss-cross in the same way' (Wittgenstein 1953: 66–7). Europe's three zones or 'contexts of change' are thus not defined by any one factor, but through a series of overlapping and criss-crossing 'family resemblances'.

Conclusion

In this chapter, we have considered the historical evolution of the Westphalian states' system and Germany's role within it. The central argument developed above has been that the emergence of a pluralistic security community in Western Europe has fundamentally altered the structural dynamics of European order and contributed to the erosion of the defining features of the Westphalian system. The emergence of a *foedus pacificum* in Western Europe has also provided the international framework for the resolution of the 'German question'.

Europe, however, now faces a major new question – how to develop cooperation and integration on a pan-European basis in a continent no longer divided by the iron curtain and the Berlin Wall. As we have seen, the contemporary European 'regional security complex' has fractured into three broad zones. The decisive question for the future of European order is how these three zones will relate to each other. The balance of power no longer operates within the core zone, but this does not mean that it might not operate in relations between the core and outer zones, for example. The question of how Europe's three zones will relate to each other is one that affects Germany above all, given its *Mittellage* and its national role conception as a 'mediator' or 'bridge' between East and West. It is thus to Germany's response to the *Epochenwende* of 1989–91 that we now turn.

Notes

1 'The misery endured by the Germans throughout the hideous progression of campaigns and sieges, with the slaughter, plague and famine which followed in the train, cannot be denied; though perhaps it was not so widespread as was formerly believed. Certainly warfare was destructive, but it was not universal. Many towns never saw enemy troops more than once perhaps throughout the

whole war. The main fighting was limited to Bohemia and Austria, the Saxon plain, the Rhineland and the Black Forest, and the most intensive period of warfare for the German states was from 1632 to the Treaty of Prague in 1635' (Maland 1968: 138).

2 This was particularly evident during the later years of the Thirty Years War (from 1635 to 1648), when 'Germany was the victim of this European conflict. Foreign armies crossed her soil, but the causes for which they fought were not those of any German prince; and the history of these years can best be described in the relevant chapters on Spain, France and Sweden. Only when the powers outside the empire had finally reached stalemate could a general peace be made' (Maland 1968: 135).

3 At a press conference on 4 February 1965 (the twentieth anniversary of Yalta), De Gaulle spoke at length about the German problem. It derived, he suggested, from the German anguish 'created by its own uncertainty about its boundaries, its unity, its political system, its international role, so that the more its destiny remains undetermined, the more disturbing it always appears to the whole continent'. A solution to the 'German anomalies', he argued, would only come about as a result of the end of Soviet domination of Eastern Europe and the emergence of a more integrated European Community. Such a development, he argued, would leave Germany playing a major role in Europe 'from the Urals to the Atlantic' (*Europa Archiv* 20, 1965, p. 94).

4 'We place under hard realism realist theories that predict that states are predisposed to aggrandizement, and under sophisticated realism theories that expect agents to possess the capacity to make choices that avert self-destructive wars' (Paul and Hall 1999: 68).

5 'To find the main reason for today's threat of war, we must go back to the year 1945, to Yalta. It was there that a helpless Europe was divided; it was there that agreements were reached for military zones of occupation that would become spheres of interest as well. Yalta gave birth to a system of international relations based upon a state of rivalry and equilibrium between the Soviet Union and the United States. Whether the three old gentlemen who met there knew it or not, the idea of the Iron Curtain was born at Yalta' (Konrad 1984: 1).

6 'Contrary to Yalta's later reputation, an agreement to partition Europe was not reached there. It was rather the deplorable lack of any clear consensus on this and other matters that explains the summit's notoriety' (Masty 1988: 17).

7 'Most Europeans', the then West German President von Weizsäcker was subsequently to note, 'dislike the Wall about as much as they do the idea of a large German state in Central Europe' (Kiep 1985: 320).

8 For a representative sample on the causes and nature of European integration, see Diez (1998), Moravcsik (1998), Caporaso (1996), and Bulmer (1993) and Milward (1992).

9 'Aufgrund gesellschaftlicher, wirtschaftlicher und politischer transnationaler Verflechtungen ist die eindeutige Unterscheidung von "innen" und "außen"

angesichts bestehender Interdependenzen und Globalisierungstendenzen indessen kaum noch tragfähig' (Peters 1997: 372).

10 The description of the BRD as a 'post-classical nation-state' comes from Heinrich August Winkler (quoted in Schwarz 1994: 287). The notion of Germany as a 'post-modern nation-state' has been defined by Niedhart as follows: 'Der Postmoderne Nationalstaat hat seine autonome Handlungsfähigkeit aufgegeben bzw. eingebüßt. Er agiert in einem internationalen Geflecht, ist in internationale Regimes und in Europa auch supranationale Institutionen eingebunden und steht in Konkurrenz zu transnationalen Organisationen' (Niedhart 1997: 16).

11 William Bloom refers to the nation-states's 'identity-security interpretative system', and argues that 'If there has been a general identification made with the nation, then there is a behavioural tendency among the individuals who made this identification and who make up the mass national public to defend and to enhance the shared national identity' (Bloom 1990: 79).

12 Robert Cooper, a member of the British diplomatic service (although writing in a personal capacity) has declared that 'what happened in 1989 was not just the end of the Cold War, but also the end of the balance-of-power system in Europe' (Cooper 1996: 7). Similarly, US Secretary of Stat Madeline Albright has argued that 'Today in Bosnia, virtually every nation in Europe is working together to bring stability to a region where conflict earlier this century tore the continent apart. This reflects a sharp departure from the spheres of influence or balance of power diplomacy of the past, and an explicit rejection of the politics based on ethnic identification' (Albright 1997).

13 In an otherwise rather conservative assessment of the elements of continuity and discontinuity between the post-cold war era and the 'world of yesterday', Hans-Peter Schwarz emphasises the importance of international organisations and institutions as a new and hopeful element in late twentieth-century Europe (Schwarz 1995a: 30–1).

14 Deutsch and his colleagues defined the key terms involved in the concept of a 'security community' as follows:

'A SECURITY-COMMUNITY is a group of people which has become "integrated".

By INTEGRATION we mean the attainment, within a territory, of a "sense of community" and of institutions and practices strong enough and widespread enough to assure, for a "long" time, dependable expectations of "peaceful change" among its population.

By SENSE OF COMMUNITY we mean a belief on the part of individuals in a group that they have come to agreement on at least this one point: that common social problems must and can be resolved by processes of "peaceful change".

By PEACEFUL CHANGE we mean the resolution of social problems, normally by institutionalized procedures, without resort to large-scale physical force' (Deutsch 1957: 5).

15 Hedley Bull argued that international society rested on five key institutions: war, the balance of power, diplomacy, great power concert and international law. Karl Deutsch noted that 'One of our findings which challenges a prevailing notion is that a balance of power, designed to prevent any one unit from becoming much stronger than the others, did not have to be maintained among members of a large union or federation. Instead, the development of a strong core, or nucleus, seemed to promote integration if the core area had certain capabilities' (Deutsch 1957: 137–8).

16 Arnold Wolfers' metaphor of a burning house is instructive in this regard (1965: 13–19). He argued that in crisis situations, individual traits tend to be suppressed as actors respond to the imperatives of the moment. However, in more routine and low-pressure contexts, their individual identities and role conceptions become more idiosyncratic.

5

Epochenwende:
unification and German grand strategy

A statesman cannot create anything himself. He must wait and listen until
he hears the steps of God sounding through events; then leap up and grasp
the hem of his garment.

(Otto von Bismarck, quoted in Taylor 1955: 115)

For decades a thick closed blanket of clouds obscured the star of German
unity. Then for a short time the blanket of clouds parted, allowed the star to
become visible, and we grabbed for it.

(Hans-Dietrich Genscher, quoted in Zelikow and Rice 1995: ix)

The end of the 1980s witnessed one of those rare moments when the pace
of historical change sharply accelerated, and one epoch gave way to
another. The demise of cold war bipolarity and German unification were,
of course, the result of deeper, more subterranean processes of change
which had been undermining the foundations of post-war European
order for decades. Nonetheless, during the 329 days from the opening of
the Berlin Wall to the Day of German Unity, 'the whole map of Europe
was – or began to be – redrawn'. During this extraordinary period 'more
happened in ten months than usually does in ten years' (Garton Ash
1994: 343). The result was an *Epochenwende* (change of epochs) which
not only left the Federal Republic larger and fully sovereign, but also
transformed its geopolitical situation in Europe.

The aim of this chapter is to analyse Germany's response to the end of
the cold war, and to consider the influences on its post-unification grand
strategy. The two previous chapters have focused primarily on the historical and structural context within which Germany, as a 'situated actor',
operates. This chapter, by contrast, focuses on Germany itself, rather than
on the structures of European order. One of the distinctive features of the
new Europe is that the *Bundesrepublik* is destined to play a pivotal role in

European affairs, in a way it could not – and did not wish to – during the cold war. This chapter assesses the nature and extent of German power in Europe, and the implications of this for German foreign and security policy. It also considers Germany's response to the dilemmas of its *Mittellage*, and the debate in Germany on 'normalisation' and 'national interests'. It concludes by considering the factors which have led Germany to emphasise the importance of the dual enlargement of NATO and the EU for the reshaping of European order, and the questions this poses for Germany and Europe more widely.

United Germany's new *Mittellage*

Epochenwende

The events of 1989–91 constitute one of those intense, seminal moments when established political and institutional structures are shaken to their foundations, geostrategic arrangements recast, and long-cherished assumptions confounded – in short, when the existing order is overturned. During such moments of historic transformation, '[a]ll fixed, fast-frozen relations, with their train of ancient and venerable prejudices and opinions, are swept away, all new-formed ones become antiquated before they can ossify. All that is solid melts into air, all that is holy is profaned, and man is at last compelled to face with sober senses, his real conditions of life, and his relations with his kind' (Marx and Engels 1968 [1848], 38).

The hurley-burley of events that unfolded from late 1989 onwards with increasing pace and scope was one of those rare moments when 'all that is solid melts into air'. In this *annus mirabilis*, the very foundations of European order were shaken to the core by a geopolitical earthquake whose after-shocks continued to reverberate around the globe for many years afterwards. For the third time in the 'short twentieth century' (Hobsbawm 1994), European diplomats and statesmen found themselves grappling with the problem of re-establishing order and security in the continent.

The nature of the *Epochenwende* of 1989–91 was determined by five key events, the dates of which symbolise pivotal moments in the unfolding drama of Europe's 'gentle revolution':

- *10 September 1989*: the first crack in the 'iron curtain', as Hungary opened its border to allow East Germans to flee to the West. When informed of this decision by his Hungarian counterpart, the East

German Foreign Minister, Oskar Fischer, spluttered 'That is treason! Are you aware that you are leaving the GDR in the lurch and joining the other side! This will have grave consequences for you!' (Zelikow and Rice 1995: 68).

- *9 November 1989*: the opening of the Berlin Wall. Without prior warning or preparation, SED Politburo member Günter Schabowski announced that East Germans would be allowed to visit the West. The result was a spontaneous storming of the Wall, and a wave of popular jubilation, exhilaration and expectation which swept outwards from Berlin to engulf Europe.
- *3 October 1990*: the 'Day of German Unity'. In contrast to 1871, reunification in 1990 came about not through *Blut und Eisen* ('blood and iron'), but 'by telephone and checkbook' (Garton Ash 1996: 79).
- *1 July 1991*: the dissolution of the Warsaw Pact. This event signalled the end of Soviet domination of Central and Eastern Europe, and was followed by Soviet troop withdrawals from the region. In this way, the military and strategic contours of Europe were fundamentally – and peacefully – recast (Hyde-Price 1996: 232–34).
- *21 December 1991*: the USSR was formally dissolved and replaced by a 'Commonwealth of Independent States' (CIS). Almost without a shot being fired, a nuclear armed superpower passed into the dust-bin of history. Russia is back in the borders it had three centuries ago (before the 1654 Treaty of Union with Ukraine), and is both smaller than the former USSR and geographically more distant from Western and Central Europe. A pluralistic and diverse geopolitical space has emerged in Eastern Europe, in which Ukraine is an important new actor. Indeed, independence for Kiev has been described as 'the most significant geostrategic development in Europe since the end of the Second World War' (Allison 1993: 36).

The most astounding aspect of the *Epochenwende* of late twentieth-century Europe was its largely peaceful and democratic character. All previous moments of accelerated historical change have been associated with war or violent revolution – from the French Revolution of 1789 to the two world wars of this century. War, as Trotsky once noted, has been the locomotive of history. The end of the cold war, however, was different. In contrast to all previous periods of historical transformation, far-reaching political and geostrategic change came about without large-scale violence – something that bodes well for the future of Europe. 'Something profound in world affairs is surely under way when one superpower can abdicate without a shot being fired against it, and the other can elect a draft-dodger as its president and commander-in-chief. It is difficult to imagine any similar conjuction of events in any other period of international history' (Booth 1995: 343).

Germany and the end of the cold war

At the heart of a Europe in flux stood Germany – *die Zentralmacht Europas* ('Europe's central power'), in the words of Hans-Peter Schwarz (1994). The fall of the Berlin Wall and the collapse of communism created a historic opportunity to reunite the German people democratically and through international agreement. This was an opportunity which Chancellor Kohl and his long-serving Foreign Minister, Hans-Dietrich Genscher, moved swiftly and decisively to grab.

'The unification of Germany ended the post-war period and at the same time opened a long-term phase of exceptional demands for German foreign policy' (Schwarz 1991: 113). Unification was the last outstanding 'classical' diplomatic goal of the Federal Republic, and its achievement in 1990 led to the 'reshaping of inner-German, inner-European and transatlantic relations' (Hanrieder 1995: ix). Its success was not simply due to the efforts of Kohl and Genscher, but was a result of the trust and diplomatic capital built up over preceding decades. Unification was thus a vindication not only of Adenauer's policy of *Westbindung* and *Politik der Stärke* ('policy of strength'), which won the Federal Republic the trust of its Western Allies,[1] but also of Brandt's policy of *Ostpolitik*. *Ostpolitik*, which was begun by Brandt but continued by Schmidt and Kohl, made possible a process of rapprochement with the Central and East Europeans and helped assure them that Germany – and the Germans – had changed. Thus as Peter Bender notes, 'it is due to the Eastern and Western policies together that the second unification of Germany, unlike the first in 1870–1, took place in harmony with the rest of Europe' (Bender 1996: 278).

The newly united *Bundesrepublik* found itself in a radically changed geostrategic environment. It was no longer a frontline state between two hostile alliance systems, but a country at the heart of the continent aspiring to become 'whole and free'. In this brave new Europe, German policymakers faced new opportunities – and new problems. For the first time in its history, Germany was completely surrounded by friends and had no obvious enemies. In this new and apparently benign security environment, the prospects for building a stable and lasting peace order in Europe – with a democratic Germany at its core – looked highly promising. In addition, the dismantling of the iron curtain offered new business and investment opportunities in *Mitteleuropa*, and the promise of access to a huge new market in the wider Eastern Europe.

At the same time, however, it quickly became apparent that the 'triple transformation' of Central and Eastern Europe was proving a difficult and potentially destabilising process. New security 'risks and challenges' appeared, such as large-scale migration, transnational criminality and ethno-nationalist conflict. More serious, perhaps, was the concern that in the absence of a external threat, Western solidarity could dissolve, prompting a 'renationalisation' of foreign and security policy, and a return to the old 'nightmare of coalitions'. United Germany thus faced new opportunities, but also new dilemmas – dilemmas between *West-bindung* and *Ostpolitik*, and between *Kerneuropa* and *Mitteleuropa*. In short, united Germany was forced to confront, once again, the dilemmas of its *Mittellage*.

Return to the Mittellage

Unification and the demise of the East–West conflict left Germany 'larger, more powerful and more sovereign', and occupying 'a more central geopolitical position than the old Federal Republic' (Garton Ash 1996: 80). This last point is of particular importance. Once more, Germany is back in its central European location. As Lothar Rühl has written, 'with the reunification of Germany, the historical *Mittellage* has once again become the foundation of German politics' (Rühl 1996: 112).

Germany is, above all, a central European power. Together with Austria, it constitutes *west* central Europe. Not surprisingly perhaps, given its size and its *Mittellage*, Germany has more neighbours than any other European state. To the West, Germany borders on Holland, Belgium, Luxembourg and France; to the South, Switzerland and Austria; to the north, Denmark; and to the East, Poland and the Czech Republic. What happens in Germany, therefore, has ramifications for developments throughout the rest of Europe – for good or bad. Historically, Germany has stood at the juncture of many of Europe's primary trade routes and lines of communication. It has been the conduit for ideas, mainly from West to East, but also from East to West, and between the Scandinavian North and the Latin South. Today, Germany stands at the crossroads of cultures, peoples and security zones in Europe – in particular, between the transatlantic security community and the post-communist East.

Napoleon Bonaparte once declared that 'the policy of a state lies in its geography'. Geography, however, does not determine the fate of nations, even though Germany's *Mittellage* has clearly shaped its foreign and security policies. Geography undoubtedly has an influence on foreign policy, for the simple but often overlooked fact that states are fixed rather than mobile. Consequently each state faces 'a relatively stable salient environment consisting of the major units [i.e., states] in its geographical proximity (power waning with distance) (Mouritzen 1997: 80).[2] However, geographical location only influences state behaviour because of the way it is perceived and interpreted politically. This is a function of the cognitive and institutional factors shaping a state's foreign policy. As Sir Halford MacKinder (one of the founders of geopolitics as a discipline)[3] himself acknowledged, the 'influence of geographical conditions upon human activity has depended … not merely on the realities as we now know them to be and to have been, but in even greater degree on what men imagined in regard to them' (MacKinder 1942: 28).

Physical location does not therefore determine a state's foreign policy behaviour in the simplistic way suggested by cruder versions of geopolitics. Of far greater importance than physical geography are two other factors: the nature and structural dynamics of the regional security complex in question, and the defining political and societal characteristics of its key actors. Together, these constitute Germany's 'national situation' (see pp. 00–00). Although Germany is once again confronted by the dilemmas of the *Mittellage*, it is not simply 'back in the old *Mittellage* of the Bismarckian second Reich: that fateful monkey-in-the-middle situation to which a long line of conservative German historians have attributed the subsequent, erratic and finally aggressive foreign policy of the Reich' (Garton Ash 1996: 80).

The *Mittellage* to which Germany has returned is not that of Bismarck, Stresemann or Hitler. In late modern Europe, 'the understanding of the centre is today embedded in a context of international politics dramatically different from any previously'. Moreover 'Germany has become a "civilian power" with a strong tradition of multilateralism in its foreign policy' (Zimmer 1997: 33). The 'laws of geopolitics' – accorded so much weight by Germany's 'normalisation-nationalists' (Hellmann 1996: 18) – have been significantly altered by the emergence of a transatlantic security community based on multilateralism and institutionalised cooperation. The geopolitics of *Mitteleuropa* have thus been transformed by the proximity of Euro-Atlantic structures, of which Germany is an integral part (Rühl 1996: 112). In short, Germany in now back in what is best termed a '*multilateral Mittellage*'.

Germany's *Mittellage* is without doubt a major factor in its foreign and security policy. However, as Matthias Zimmer notes (1997: 35), the 'German *Mittellage* and the prominence of the centre in German foreign policy are not necessarily detrimental to European security, nor do they automatically lead back to the future, to a re-emergence of the spectres that have haunted Germany's neighbours in the past'. Germany today is mature liberal democracy deeply enmeshed within the multilateral structures of the Euro-Atlantic security community. During the cold war, it contributed to European order by providing the Eastern bulwark of the transatlantic community, thereby fulfilling a stabilising role along Europe's political-security dividing line. However, 'the new Europe demands a new definition of the *Mittellage*'. Germany now has a new 'stability-promoting role' – not as a Western bulwark 'along Europe's enduring dividing-line, but as a trans-european mediating power (*Vermittlungsmacht*) which can bridge this divide' (Hanrieder 1995: 447). The dilemmas of the '*multilateral Mittellage*' confronting the Berlin Republic in the twenty-first century are thus how to stabilise the lands to its East and develop pan-European cooperation, without thereby weakening the cohesion and stability of the Euro-Atlantic community. Although there are some faint echoes of earlier dilemmas between *Westbindung* and *Ostpolitik*, the end of cold war bipolarity has transformed their substance and content.

The sources and dimensions of German power in Europe

Germany's pivotal role in Europe

Putting to one side for a moment controversies over how much autonomous power European states have to shape their external environment in an age of globalisation and integration, there is one feature of the present historical conjuncture that is worthy of consideration. For the first time in its history, the *Bundesrepublik* will be a central actor – if not *the* central actor – in the shaping of European affairs.

Historically, German states like Prussia and Austria have long been influential players in the great game of European diplomacy. However, for four decades during the cold war, the *Bundesrepublik Deutschland* was a 'semi-sovereign' state (Katzenstein 1987). During this time, the BRD 'never conducted a sovereign foreign policy, never a truly national, never even a largely autonomous foreign policy' (Rühl 1992: 741). Throughout much of the cold war, it was the object, not subject, of change in Europe.[4] The fate of Germany and of Europe lay primarily in the hands of the two superpowers, with a lesser role for Europe's remaining middle powers,

Britain and France. The Federal Republic only formally gained sovereignty in 1955, and even then, it remained a 'penetrated system', exposed
to developments in the international system and the shifts in the policies
of its strategic partners.

The 'penetration' of the Federal Republic was in part a conscious policy of its first Chancellor, Konrad Adenauer (1965: 42). His foreign
policy strategy was presaged on making the BRD a reliable and predictable ally for its two most important strategic partners, the USA and
France. The Bonn political class also sought to embed the BRD firmly
within multilateral organisations, notably the EEC and NATO.[5] Only
with the *Ostpolitik* of Brandt and Scheele did the BRD seek to define and
pursue its own distinctive foreign policy interests.[6] Even then, German
Ostpolitik was firmly anchored within the framework of the Atlantic
Alliance, European Political Cooperation (EPC) and the CSCE (Conference on Security and Cooperation in Europe). Thus as Wolfgang Schäuble has written (1998: 42), during the post-war years, the responsibility
for German foreign policy 'lay with the allies, and later in part with the
EC and NATO. Our foreign policy was not grown-up, not mature, but
under guardianship. Since 3 October 1990, all this is different'.

With the 'Treaty on the Final Settlement with Respect to Germany'
(the 'Two plus Four' treaty) in October 1990, Germany has regained 'full
sovereignty over its internal and external affairs'. Not only has Germany
regained full sovereignty, its 'potential for power has increased', enabling
it to 'grow towards world-power status' (Hacke 1993: 564, 568). Thus
'Germany is back' in the words of Gregor Schöllgen (1994, 35); it has
returned 'to the world-stage' (Schwarz 1994). Once more, Germany is a
'European great power' (Schöllgen 1993: 31), with all the responsibilities
that entails.

There is therefore a new element at work in post-cold war European
international politics. The *Bundesrepublik Deutschlands* will henceforth
play a pivotal role in European order. It will play this pivotal role because
of its size, its central geographical location, its prodigious economy and
its influence in Euro-Atlantic institutions. How Germany copes with its
new responsibilities will be an important factor in determining the
prospects for security and cooperation in Europe. Yet Germany's power
to influence the course and direction of European affairs is not unlimited.
'Germany is now the most powerful country in Europe', Timothy Garton
Ash has noted (1996: 81–82), 'But it is not a superpower.' It has great
assets in each of the four main dimensions of power – the political, the
economic, the military and the normative. 'But it also has liabilities in

each department.' This poses a question central to understanding Germany's role in Europe – how much power does Germany have, and of what does its power consist?

Defining 'power'

Examining Germany's role in the reshaping of European order involves addressing one of the central issues of contemporary political analysis – the sources and dimensions of power. 'Power', as we have seen (pp. 14–15) 'is a question of agency, of influencing or "having an effect" upon the structures which set contexts and define the range of possibilities of others' (Hay 1995: 191). *Macht* (power) is a function of an agent's ability to *machen* (to do, make, have an effect upon). Germany's *Macht* is thus relational: it depends on both Germany's tangible and intangible resources and the structural attributes of European international society.

The study of power in international relations has been the primary concern of realism, in both its classical and structuralist (or neo-realist) variants (Guzzini 1998: 121). Most structural realists define power in terms of material capabilities, particularly economic and military power.[7] This parsimonious definition of power in terms of 'hard' power resources alone is of limited analytical utility in the context of a zone of stable peace, and would certainly give a very misleading picture of German power in Europe.

A more useful starting point for considering the nature of power is the classical realist tradition. Morgenthau famously advocated the study of international relations based on 'the concept of interest defined as power'. His concept of power revolved around notions of 'control' and 'domination', and emphasised the significance of historical, political and cultural factors:

> Its content and the manner of its use are determined by the political and cultural environment. Power may comprise anything that establishes and maintains the control of man over man. Thus power covers all social relationships which serve that end, from physical violence to the most subtle psychological ties by which one mind controls another. Power covers the domination of man by man, both when it is disciplined by moral ends and controlled by constitutional safeguards, as in Western democracies, and when it is that untamed and barbaric force which finds its laws in nothing but its own strength and its sole justification in its aggrandizement. (Morgenthau 1993: 11)

While Morgenthau's emphasis on the political and cultural environment is valuable (and a consideration largely excluded from more

'parsimonious' neo-realist accounts of international relations), his definition of power in terms of 'control' and 'domination' is more problematical. Torbjørn Knutsen offers a less loaded definition of power, which, he
suggests, is best conceived of in terms of 'influence' rather than 'control'.
Power, he argues, can be defined 'in the commonest of ways: as the
ability to influence others. This ability is commonly identified as a composite of military force, economic wealth and command over public
opinion' (Knutsen 1999: 2). A complementary approach is offered by
John Stoessinger (1991: 34), who defines power as follows: '*power in
international relations is the capacity of a nation to use its tangible and
intangible resources in such a way as to affect the behaviour of other nations*'
(original emphasis). Power is therefore more than just material capabilities, although it includes these capabilities. 'Most importantly, while
capabilities are objectively measurable, power must in every case be evaluated in more subtle psychological and relational terms.' Thus power 'can
no longer be calculated simply by adding up a nation's physical capabilities. Psychology and will must be given as much weight as resources and
hardware'.

More broadly in the social sciences, there is a wide consensus that
power derives from different sources and manifests itself in different
dimensions or forms. These sources of power are both tangible and
intangible. Tangible material resources include physical geography;
resource endowment, population, economic system, societal cohesion
and system of government. Geography is clearly an important factor,[8]
although perhaps in an age of globalisation, e-commerce and ballistic
missiles, not as decisive as it once was. Nonetheless, as we have already
seen, Germany's central geographical location (its *Mittellage*) remains a
significant explanatory factor for its influence on European developments. These tangible resources have both a quantitative and qualitative
aspect. Population is important not simply in terms of size, but increasingly in terms of its education, training and skills. Similarly possession of
natural resources is important, but so is the industrial and technological
capability to process and utilise them.

These 'objective bases of national power', Stoessinger argued, are
important, but they are 'by no means the whole story'. Of no less importance for a nation's 'power arsenal' are 'its image of itself and, perhaps
most crucial of all, the way it is viewed by other nations. To understand
the latter dimension of power we must consider chiefly the factors of
national character and morale, ideology, and national leadership' (1991:
31). These factors – national character and morale, ideology and national

leadership – constitute important 'intangible' power resources for a state. In addition, the degree of trust and social capital a country enjoys from others, and its influence in multilateral institutions, is a major intangible power resource. 'Finally', Stoessinger suggests,

> the quality of nation's *leadership* and the image which it projects upon the world are important sources of power. If leadership is defective, all other resources may be to no avail. No amount of manpower or industrial and military potential will make a nation powerful unless its leadership *uses* these resources with maximum effect on the international scene. If the tangible resources are the body of power, and the national character its soul, leadership is its brains. (Stoessinger 1991: 34)

The four dimensions of German power

Unification increased the population of the Federal Republic from 63 to 80 million, and enlarged its territory from 248,000 to 375,000 sq. km. In terms of its tangible power resources therefore, Germany has increased its capabilities relative to those of other states in the European security complex. Yet as we have seen, material capabilities are 'by no means the whole story'.

German power in Europe – i.e., its capacity 'to affect the behaviour of other nations' – derives from both tangible and intangible resources. This power is manifested in four dimensions: political, economic, military and normative, each of which has two aspects: deliberative and structural. *Deliberative power* refers to the conscious employment of power resources by a political actor to affect the behaviour of others. *Structural power*, by contrast, is largely indirect and unintentional. It is the ability to shape and influence the structures within which other political actors have to operate: 'structural power, in short, confers the power to decide how things shall be done, the power to shape frameworks within which states relate to each other, relate to people, or relate to corporate enterprises' (Strange 1988: 24–6). Turning to Germany, we can see that it has considerable power resources in all four dimensions, but also some liabilities. More significantly, its power is skewed in particular directions.

Political power: during the cold war, Willy Brandt famously described the Federal Republic as an 'economic giant and political dwarf'. In terms of its political power, Germany is widely seen as punching below its weight. When commentators speak of Germany's *Machtvergessenheit* (its 'power-obliviousness' or 'neglect of power'), they are often referring to its attitude towards political power.

Deliberative political power is a function of both a state's economic, military and normative power resources, and its 'national leadership, character and ideology'. A defining feature of the Bonn Republic has been that it has generally eschewed the use of deliberative political power. Commentators frequently spoke of its *Bescheidenheit* (modesty) and *Zurückhaltung* (reserve). The reasons for this *Bescheidenheit* are three-fold. First, cultural and ideational factors: given the legacy of National Socialism, Germany's leaders have traditionally avoided asserting – and sometimes even defining – their 'national interests'. The foreign and security policy behaviour of West Germany has been characterised by a 'culture of restraint'. Second, German is firmly embedded in multilateral structures, which both constrains its ability to exercise deliberative political power, and at the same time provides more fruitful avenues for influencing the behaviour of other nations. Third, Germany's institutional polyphony (see pp. 31–4) weakens its ability to exercise deliberative power (Goldberger 1993: 289–93). As we have seen, the German system of government is characterised by a significant dispersal of authoritative decision-making responsibilities between different institutional actors, each functioning with their own 'organisational routines' and 'standard operating procedures'. This makes the framing and execution of a coherent grand strategy more difficult, and weakens Germany's ability to exercise deliberative political power.

The *Bundesrepublik* has, by and large, a successful track record in post-war diplomacy and statecraft. It possesses a skilled and experienced diplomatic corps, which amplifies German influence on European developments. In contrast to many other states of comparable size and rank, however, these assets are rarely deployed in pursuit of unilateral 'possession' goals. Instead, German statecraft is focused on cooperation with its partners and influence in multilateral organisations. 'German diplomacy has excelled at the patient, discrete pursuit of national goals through multilateral institutions and negotiations, whether in the European Community, NATO or the Helsinki process' (Garton Ash 1996: 85). It is this effective use of multilateral fora and diplomacy that provides the key to understanding German political power in Europe. Germany's political power is primarily *structural,* rather than deliberative. Germany has played an increasingly influential role within both NATO and the EU, but only in cooperation with its strategic partners. In the case of NATO, this is the USA, and to a lesser extent, the UK (Kaiser and Roper 1988). In the case of the EU, France is Germany's close partner, and together they constitute the EU's 'cooperative hegemon' (Pedersen 1998: 34–67).

Germany's considerable *structural political power* also derives from what has been termed its 'indirect institutional power'. This refers to its ability to influence 'the structure, norms, and policy principles of the EU indirectly'. This form of structural political power means that 'it has been possible for the FRG to play an active role in shaping institutional development in such a way as to mobilize a bias in the character of EU governance'. In addition, Germany enjoys 'a kind of empowerment' arising from 'the close congruence between the EU's character and Germany's institutions and identity' which has 'a passive, dispositional power dimension' (Bulmer 1997: 73–6).

Economic power. Germany's economic influence over Europe is considerable, and represents one of the most important sources of German power (Markovits and Reich 1998: 293–4). The Federal Republic is Europe's 'economic giant', and is frequently regarded as the archetypal *Handelsstaat*, or 'trading nation' (Rosecrance 1985). Given the nature of capitalist market economies, this form of power is largely structural, but there are some forms of *deliberative economic power*. These take the form of sanctions, preferential trade agreements, export credits and guarantees, subsidies, tariff and customs regimes, and other forms of economic statecraft. There are, however, two important restraints on Germany's deliberative economic power. First, the European integration process has led to a transfer of a number of important economic and regulatory powers from Bonn/Berlin to Brussels. Second, in late modern Europe's increasingly internationalised economies, economic and commercial activity is less and less contained within the boundaries of the nation-state. As Held and McGrew (1993: 268) note, there is an incontestable 'disjunction between the formal authority of the state and the spatial reach of contemporary systems of production, distribution and exchange'. Thus in a Europe of transnational corporations, cross-national strategic alliances, international mergers and transnational production processes, economic power no longer accrues directly to the nation-state, but is diffused outwards beyond national borders.

Whatever constraints there might be on the deliberative use of German economic power, Germany has substantial *structural economic power*. Indeed, Peter Pulzer has argued that Germany's 'principal institution' for exercising its power is the Bundesbank and its 'principal weapon' the Deutsche Mark. It is with these 'that Germany wields its influence in determining the shape of European institutions and the development of integration' (1996: 315–16). With the end of the East–West divide, the German economy has resumed its earlier role as the hub and powerhouse of the wider European economy. Keynes' observations in 1919 are once again pertinent: 'Round Germany as the central support the rest of the European economic system grouped itself, and on the prosperity and enterprise of Germany the prosperity of the rest of the Continent mainly depended ... The whole of Europe east of the Rhine thus fell into the German industrial orbit, and its economic life was adjusted accordingly' (Keynes 1919: 14–15). Germany's economic preponderance is based not only on the sheer size of its economy, but on 'the quality of its products, the trade surplus, the savings rate, and the reputation of the currency built up over forty years' (Garton Ash 1994: 382).

Yet Germany's economic power should not be exaggerated. Germany is a major economic force in Europe, particularly in Central and Eastern Europe, but it is not an economic superpower. Moreover, there are growing doubts about the future competitiveness of the German economy in a more globalised economy and an enlarged EU. Hence the *Standort Deutschland* question – i.e., 'whether Germany has fundamentally lost its competitiveness as a production location' (Flockton 1996: 229) – is a major worry in the Berlin Republic. The corporatist and consensual nature of decision-making at enterprise level is an undoubted strength of the German economy, but it might also make implementing structural reforms harder. Germany today thus faces a dilemma common to all post-industrial societies: how to combine economic efficiency with social justice and preserve its economic potency (Sen 1999).

Military power. For Treitschke and Meinecke, politics was essentially *Machtpolitik*, and state power was primarily based on military force. From such a perspective, the Federal Republic must seem exceedingly weak indeed. Although Germany has one of the largest armies in Europe, the Bundeswehr is deeply embedded into NATO's integrated command structures, and Germany has voluntarily renounced the right to acquire or possess nuclear weapons. Germany's 'military power in the form of intervention capability and escalation dominance' (Bertele and Mey 1998: 200) is constrained both by institutional factors (its integration into NATO) and normative factors (its identity as a *Zivilmacht*).

By choice and conviction, the Federal Republic's *deliberative military power* has traditionally been limited. In this dimension of power, more than any other, the phenomenon of *Machtvergessenheit* ('neglect of power') has clearly operated. The response of the vast majority of Germans to the experience of a devastating total war has been to reject militarism and disparage military force in general. This has created a strategic culture informed by a *Zivilmacht* identity. Despite this, the Federal

Republic has acquired substantial military assets, giving it significant *structural military power*. Following re-armament in 1955, West Germany built up a powerful conventional capability (especially mechanised units and armoured divisions) designed to stop a first echelon attack by the Warsaw Pact (Seidelmann 1996: 252). It thus constituted the conventional cornerstone of NATO's forward defence strategy, as well as providing basing and infrastructure facilities for Allied forces stationed in Germany. This gave the Federal Republic considerable influence within the councils of NATO that should not be overlooked.

With the end of the cold war, German security has been significantly re-calibrated. As we shall see in chapter 6, the German government in the 1990s has demonstrated a growing willingness to deploy the Bundeswehr in non-article five operations outside the NATO area. The May 1994 ruling by the Constitutional Court was particularly important in removing perceived constitutional restrictions on German participation in military crisis management in Europe and beyond. This recalibration of German security policy was confirmed by Bundeswehr participation in the Kosovo war – the first combat deployment of German forces against a sovereign state since 1945.

The significance of this is that Germany's *deliberative military power* now corresponds more closely to its *structural military power*. The Bundeswehr is the fourth largest contributor to SFOR, and the third largest constributor to KFOR. Its military standing amongst its NATO allies was symbolised by the appointment of a four-star German general, Klaus Reinhardt, to command KFOR forces in Kosovo.[9] The willingness to use military assets for essentially political purposes was also demonstrated by Foreign Minister Fischer's decision to send a (non-combat) Bundeswehr contingent to East Timor in October 1999 as part of a Australian-led UN peace-keeping operation. Changes in German security policy in the 1990s have thus led to an increase in the relative importance of its military power resources (particularly its deliberative military power).

However, developments in German security policy have also revealed a dilemma at the heart of German policy, one central to its identity as a *Zivilmacht*. Germany has demonstrated a new-found willingness to participate in military crisis management within the framework of NATO, the UN and the EU/WEU's 'Petersberg tasks'. Nevertheless, modernising the Bundeswehr and generating the necessary crisis-reaction forces will be expensive. Towards the end of 1999, a number of senior military figures warned that the cuts being made to the defence budget would make it increasingly difficult for the Bundeswehr to fulfil its alliance obligations.[10] Germany thus faces a dilemma: if it is serious about assuming greater responsibility for international peace and security, it must finance the modernisation and restructuring of its armed forces.[11] However, this sits uneasily with its identity as a 'civilian power'. This dilemma will not be easy to resolve, and will place continuing restrictions on the military dimension of German power.

Normative power: this final dimension of power is often under-estimated, but it is a vital dimension of German power in Europe. 'Power', Joseph Nye has argued, 'is becoming less fungible, less coercive and less tangible' (1990: 188). Normative power is the primary example of an intangible power resource and has no coercive capability. Nonetheless, it is a major factor shaping European affairs. 'Rules, norms, values, obligations, decency, dreams and commonality of purpose provide meaningful ends in the light of which political leaders active force and wealth' (Knutsen 1999: 3). Germany's ability to influence the rules, values and dreams of its European neighbours constitutes a major power resource, and provides one of the keys to understanding Germany's role in late modern Europe.

Normative power is 'soft power' par excellence. It reflects the amount of trust and social capital a country enjoys within international society – what Hans-Dietrich Genscher called *Vertrauenskapital* (literally 'trust-capital'). It 'has to do with the overall attractiveness – or magnetism, to recall Schumacher and Adenauer's simile – of a particular society, culture and way of life'. It is related to a country's relative prosperity, but not simply a function of it: 'Other features – individual opportunity, tolerance, culture, security, space, freedom, tradition, beauty – all contribute to the magneticism' (Garton Ash 1994: 383).

The main form of *deliberative normative power* is foreign cultural policy – i.e., official German government support for German language, culture and education abroad. Conceptually, this is seen as contributing to what Ulrich Beck has called 'globalisation with a human face'. It also constitutes an important pillar of German peace policy (*Friedenspolitik*), particularly through cultural programmes designed to strengthen respect for human rights, democracy and tolerance (Leonhard 1999). These examples of deliberative normative power aside, the primarily expression of German normative power is structural, and here Germany excels. Its *structural normative power* emerges almost as an unconscious by-product of German behaviour and practice. It is generated, for example, from Germany's 'policy of the good example' which Genscher spoke of at the time of unification (Hellmann 1999: 838). It is also a by-product of the social market economy, which is 'by far the most influential model for the post-communist regimes' (Gray 1993: 36; see also Markovits and Reich 1991: 16). Germany thus exercises a considerable normative influence over European developments, particularly in the new democracies in Central and Eastern Europe.

The dilemmas of German power

The end of the cold war has left Germany as the 'dominant structural power in Europe' (Hanrieder 1995: 125), with tangible and intangible resources in all four dimensions of power. Nonetheless, its post-war development has skewed its power in certain directions. Germany may no longer be the 'economic giant and political dwarf' it was in the time of Brandt, but its enormous structural economic power is certainly not reflected in its deliberative political power. It has shed its aversion to military crisis management, but its political identity and strategic culture remain marked by the assumptions of a civilian power. Germany will undoubtedly be an influential actor in the new Europe – particularly in Central Europe – but its power to shape its external environment should not be over-estimated.

The essential point to note about Germany is that it is strong enough to be a major factor in the foreign policy considerations of other European states, but not strong enough to dominate European affairs. This was, and is, the central dilemma of German power. Since unification under Bismarck, Germany has figured prominently in the security concerns of its neighbours and other great powers, but has not been able to impose its will on them. Chancellor Kiesinger spoke of this dilemma in 1967, when he warned that 'Germany, a reunited Germany, would be of a critically large size. It is too big not to have an effect on the balance of power, and too small to be able to hold the balance with the powers around it' (quoted in Garton Ash 1996: 81). In contemporary Europe, Germany continues to confront this dilemma of power. United Germany is not strong enough to reshape European affairs on its own, but it will undoubtedly have a decisive impact on the new European order – in ways that other countries might not always like (Nelson 1997: 64).

In framing its grand strategy, therefore, the Berlin Republic faces a difficult balancing act. On the one hand, it is expected to provide an anchor of stability in Central and Eastern Europe, and to assume greater responsibility for international peace and security. On the other, it must avoid stirring up old fears and concerns about its motives and intentions. The history of modern Germany offers different solutions to this dilemma.

Bismarck's response was to construct a complex alliance system and act as Europe's 'honest broker'.[12] He insisted that Germany was a saturated power, and sought to compensate for the relative weakness and strategic disadvantage at the centre of Europe by skilful diplomatic statecraft (Hildebrand 1994). Following the 'dropping of the pilot', Wilhelmine Germany sought to break out of its perceived constraints in the centre of Europe by pursuing an active *Weltpolitik* and seeking a 'place in the sun'. During the First World War, Friedrich Naumann proposed another solution to Germany's geopolitical dilemma: *Mitteleuropa*, a zone of German economic and political domination stretching across much of Central and Eastern Europe (Naumann 1916). Following Germany's defeat in 1918, Stresemann returned to a Bismarckian policy of 'balancing' between East and West, with some limited success. Finally, Hitler's policy of *Lebensraum* and *Vernichtungskrieg* ('war of extermination') offered an extreme response to the dilemmas of German power, thereby providing 'the unforgettable lesson of the perversion of the German presence in Europe' (Magris 1990: 32).

In the light of the national and European tragedy resulting from Hitler's policies, the *Bundesrepublik* strove to define a new identity for itself as both a *Zivilmacht* and a *Handelsstaat*, consciously eschewing power politics and an assertive use of deliberative power. In their place, the Federal Republic sought to manage the dilemmas of power by implementing a grand strategy based around two key foreign policy instruments: multilateral integration and strategic partnerships. As Gottfried Niedhart (1997: 23) argued, from the dilemma of German power followed an imperative: 'German policy must adopt and at the same time credibly practice the principle of self-integration in European and atlantic structures'.

Beyond Machtpolitik: 'milieu goals' and civilian power

Multilateralism and strategic partnerships have been the two defining features of post-war West German foreign policy, and constitute the Bonn Republic's innovative response to Germany's traditional geopolitical dilemmas. In the Adenauer era, these two policies were embodied in *Westbindung* – integration into Western multilateral structures and the cultivation of close bilateral relations with the USA and France. From the Brandt era onwards, *Westbindung* was complemented by an *Ostpolitik* that also combined multilateral diplomacy (in the context of the CSCE) and close bilateral relations (with Moscow and East Berlin). With the end of the cold war, Germany has invested considerable political capital in cultivating a new strategic partnership – this time with Poland, in the context of the dual enlargement process.

The Federal Republic's commitment to multilateralism and strategic partnerships represents a distinctive approach to the problem of order in international society. As we have seen (chapter 4), there are two broad approaches to resolving conflicts of interests between states. The first is the 'power politics approach', the 'unbridled interplay of opposing forces in which the capabilities of the contestants will determine the outcome'. The second is the 'authority approach', which 'can be characterised as the pursuit of decision-making procedures, the legitimacy of which would be recognised by each of the constituent units'. The classic instruments of power politics are diplomacy and bargaining, usually backed up with the threat of military force or other coercive measures – in other words, *deliberative power*. By contrast, the authority approach seeks to establish 'norms, procedures, techniques and institutions that might compensate for the absence of a supreme decision-making body within the international system'. It therefore involves a *negotiated* approach to international relations. As Ian Clark has argued, one of the central points of interest when examining the behaviour of states in international society is 'which tendency is uppermost' or 'how have the two tendencies been combined? (Clark 1989: 14–16).

In the case of post-war West Germany, it is strikingly evident which tendency is uppermost. Bonn's foreign and security policy has consciously avoided the power political approach in favour of an authority approach. German policy has focused overwhelmingly on shaping the processes of international society rather than its substantive outcomes. In Arnold Wolfers's terms (1962: 72–5), it has concentrated on 'milieu goals' rather than 'possession goals', i.e., on shaping the mechanisms, decision-making procedures and norms of behaviour of the multilateral organisations to which it belongs, rather than on possessing things 'to the exclusion of others' (see also Bulmer *et al.* 2000). Although there are plenty of cases of the Federal Republic successfully seeking to shape its regional milieu, there are relatively few cases of Bonn's unilateral pursuit of 'possession goals'. 'German foreign policy over past decades', Christian Hacke has noted (1997: 10), 'has not been pursued through traditional power politics, but much more through the power of diplomacy, economic power, the power of "good example" and of reasonable arguments.'

Given its abstinence from traditional power politics and its concern to strengthen the authority model of international relations, the Bonn Republic has come to embody the characteristics of a *Zivilmacht* ('civilian power'). Hanns Maull and others have employed this concept to describe the character and primary behavioural traits of post-war West Germany. The concept of *Zivilmacht* refers to a strong commitment to multilateral cooperation, institution-building and supranational integration, in preference to national pride, unilateralism and the unbridled defence of sovereignty. Civilian powers seek to 'civilianise' international relations by constraining the use of military force and strengthening the rule of law, the peaceful resolution of disputes and human rights. They are also concerned with building a broad international consensus around a normative commitment to peaceful cooperation, and promoting global justice and sustainable development (see Maull 1990, 1993, 1996, 1997; Senghaas 1997).

The concept of a *Zivilmacht* is an ideal-type, and there has been considerable discussion as to its continuing relevance to united Germany. One problem with the way this concept has been used is the implication that Germany and Japan are somehow unique in being 'civilian powers'. However, 'civilian power' is not a modern German *Sonderweg* ('special path'). A number of countries in Western Europe (particularly in Scandinavia) fit this description even better than Germany. Indeed, most of the mature democracies in the Euro-Atlantic security community share some, if not all, of the traits of a *Zivilmacht*, and are committed to the 'authority model' of international relations. This reflects the fact that the concept of civilian power is closely associated with Kantian and Deutschian theories about 'security commmunities'. For this reason, the concept of 'civilian power' is best regarded as indicating a continuum, with some states acting more or less like civilian powers than others. These caveats aside, the concept of civilian power does help understand the distinctive post-war political identity and strategic culture of the Federal Republic.

The intriguing question to consider is whether united Germany is still a *Zivilmacht*? Does the 'Berlin Republic' remain committed to strengthening the authority model of international relations at the expense of power politics and the unilateral pursuit of possession goals? Or is the balance between the authority model and power politics shifting from the former to the latter? Some have seen in the debates around 'normalisation' and its 'national interests' a gradual but relentless return of Germany to its former great power aspirations. Others have suggested that the very multilateral institutions within which Germany is so firmly ensconced are in crisis, and see in this the underlying cause of a perceived disorientation of post-cold war German foreign policy (Hacke 1997: 10).

On the other hand, the official German government view is that its foreign policy is characterised above all by continuity. At the same time, however, they argue that Germany has been willing to assume greater 'responsibility' (*Verantwortung*) for international peace and security.

In the next section, we shall consider the foreign policy debates in Germany following the demise of the East–West conflict, and explore their implications for German grand strategy in the 1990s and beyond.

National interests and grand strategy

The 'normalisation' of German foreign policy?

The 1990s have witnessed the emergence of a lively debate on Germany's role in Europe and the future of German grand strategy. The debate was slow to begin, primarily because of the overwhelming emphasis placed by the political class on continuity and *Westbindung* in the wake of unification.[13] Indeed, Gunther Hellmann has quipped (1999: 837), 'the most prominent feature of German foreign policy after 1990 has been the continuity in the rhetoric of continuity' used by German policy-makers! Their concern of was, of course, to reassure their allies, neighbours and former adversaries that Germany would remain a reliable member of the Western community and would not revert to recidivist behaviour.

United Germany was shaken out of its foreign policy complacency and domestic preoccupations by two events: the Gulf war and the war in Yugoslavia. Both events exposed a role conflict at the heart of German foreign and security policy. Germany's membership of multilateral organisations gave it obligations which were 'increasingly associated with military commitments' (Schlör 1993: 65). However, these military commitments sat uneasily with its role conception as a *Zivilmacht*. Germany's traditional – and somewhat parochial – security policy was increasingly in contradiction to its commitment to multilateral security structures. Moreover, its 'convenient dependence upon others' for security had ended, and Germany was now expected to assume a new role as a net provider of security for others (Meiers 1995: 85).

This role conflict fuelled a growing debate in Germany on the goals and instruments of its grand strategy, despite the official emphasis on continuity. By 1993–94, therefore, the 'great foreign policy debate in Germany' was finally underway (Garton Ash 1996: 79). As Peter Pulzer has noted (1995: 5), this debate raised some highly charged issues: 'Is there a German national interest? If so, what does it consist of? Has German unification changed its character? Is the new Germany a power?

Should Germans once more feel national pride?' In the context of the legacy of the Third Reich, Germany's past, its national identity and 'the continuities or breaches in institutions or society' are 'sensitive areas, subject to taboos or heavily coded debates'. Yet these debates have often been characterised by 'relentless aggressiveness and gratuitous name-calling ... Germany's leading minds have not been able to engage in a public debate without scratching each other's eyes out'. In part this reflects the fact that '[n]owhere else in Western Europe does academia suffer to such an extent from the open wounds left by 1968, nowhere else are viewpoints asserted with such absolutism and such claims to a monopoly of virtue'.

One of the central themes to emerge in the 'great foreign policy debate' was *normalisation*. This is a very imprecise term, and the debate it generated remained swaythed in double-meanings and conceptual ambiguity. The primary – and ultimately irresolvable – problem was how to define what was 'normal' (McKenzie 1996). For some, it simply meant acting in a more self-confident manner within multilateral structures, and taking greater responsibility for achieving policy objectives shared by the wider international community (Feldman 1996). For others, 'normalcy' was the very antithesis of 'civilian power'. It meant acting more assertively as a traditional great power, and using deliberative military force alongside other instruments of statecraft to achieve Germany's 'national interests' on a global scale.[14] Germany, it was suggested, 'is becoming more self-assured, less military-averse, more global and more assertive than in the past' (Gordon 1994: 230).

The problem with the 'normalisation' debate was not only its conceptual imprecision. It was also that it has never been clear what 'normalcy' is for a country with a past legacy of genocide and *Vernichtungskrieg*. Is it 'abnormal' for a mature democracy anchored in a pluralistic security community to be a *Zivilmacht*? If normalcy is equated with a striving for great power status and the use of deliberative military power, Germany has shown little sign of becoming 'normal'. On the other hand, if it is defined in terms of 'being whole, free, stable, self-reliant, and trusted with power' (Geipel 1994: 363), then contemporary Germany is normal. As Richard von Weizsäcker remarked (1991: 7), the Germans are 'pretty normal people, just like everyone else': 'Germans today can hardly be said to be any more orientated towards comfort, prosperity and generally keeping out of danger than any other nation.'

With the generational change brought about by the 1998 election and the relocation of the seat of government to Berlin, contemporary

Germany has grown out of many of the self-imposed limitations of the
Bonn Republic (Lefebvre and Lombardi 1996: 567). However, as we shall
see in chapter 6, it remains a civilian power – indeed, for the first time in
its history it is evolving into a 'normal *Zivilmacht*'. This aside, one important change is that Germany is increasingly willing to define and articulate its own national interests, in a way that would have been an anathema
to the Bonn Republic.

German national interests

Alongside 'normalisation', the other main issue in the 'great foreign policy debate' in the 1990s was 'national interests'. Defining the national
interest has always been politically contentious and analytically problematic, given the difficulty of distinguishing between sectional and national
interests. In post-war West Germany, however, the very mention of German 'national interests' was avoided, given the perversion of the idea by
Wilhelmine militarism and National Socialism. In its stead, the notion of
Staatsräison (reason of state) was sometimes used, although it was usually defined simply in terms of 'integration into Europe' (Schwarz 1994:
31). 'The nation was demonised, European integration was idealised'
(Hacke 1997: 3). In this context, German political leaders tended to present their own preferences as identical with those of their allies and partners. 'The more European our foreign policy is', Hans-Dietrich Genscher
famously declared, 'the more national it is' (quoted in Garton Ash 1994:
358). German and European interests were often conflated, and Germany
chose to speak and act 'in Europe's name'.

Growing calls in the 1990s for Germany to define its national interests
reflected concern in some quarters about the European integration
process. Following the difficulties involved in ratifying Maastricht, along
with the rising tide of public Euroscepticism across Europe – including
Germany – a number of German commentators began calling for a new
balance between integration and the nation-state. Integration *per se* was
not rejected, but its limitations were stressed. The German state, it was
argued – let alone the French or British – was not going to dissolve in the
EU like a sugar lump in a cup of tea (Schwarz 1994: 28). Germany therefore needed to define its national interests more openly and transparently
than in the past – not in order to pursue unilateral goals in a zero-sum
fashion, but in order to negotiate rationally with other states.

This argument has been developed by Eckhard Lübkemeier (1998:
2–8). Germany, he argues, has always pursued its own interests. To deny
this is to undermine the democratic principle of responsible and

accountable government. Formulating a clear foreign policy involving choices between rival policy objectives is only possible if a state defines its primary interests and concerns. A nation's interests need not be defined in opposition to others – indeed, a sensible foreign policy recognises that cooperation is often the best way to achieve economic and social progress. Thus there is no necessary conflict between interests and morality: '*Ergo und vulgo*: politics without principle are bad politics serving no one's interests, but principles that are not based on a clear definition of interests lead nowhere'.

Formal recognition of the need to define Germany's national interests came in a speech from Federal President Roman Herzog in March 1995. He noted that Germany's partners had no hesitation in defining their national interests, and that German foreign policy had always been based on its national interests. 'It makes no sense to deny this', he argued: 'Our partners would certainly not believe us if we were to claim to act only out of international altruism' (Herzog 1995: 164). He also noted that Germany's partners wanted the German government to define their interests more openly, in order to be able to engage in effective negotiations.

Official definitions of Germany's national interests have sought to underline its continuing commitment to international cooperation, integration, peace and shared prosperity. The 1994 German Defence White Book (*Weißbuch zur Sicherheit*) listed five central interests determining German foreign and security policy. First, the protection of the freedom, security and welfare of German citizens and the inviolability of its territorial integrity. Second, integration with the European democracies in the EU. Third, a durable transatlantic alliance based on shared values and common interests with the US as a world power. Fourth, bringing in, on the basis of equally and partnership, its eastern neighbours into western structures and the shaping of a new comprehensive cooperative security system. Fifth, world-wide respect for international law and human rights and a just global economic order based on market principles (Bundesministerium der Verteidigung 1994: 42). As Dieter Wellershoff has noted (1999: 48), these interests and goals are broadly shared across the political mainstream, and reflect the breadth of the foreign and security policy consensus in contemporary Germany. The only differences lie in how, and with what means, they can best be realised.

In a speech given in November 1999, Chancellor Gerhard Schröder argued that the fundamental determinants of German foreign policy were its 'geographical location in the heart of a Europe growing together'; its experience of 'integration in the Western community of states'; and 'our history and the lessons we have drawn from it'. He went on to specify six key German national interests. First, the deepening of the EU and its widening to the East and the Southeast. Second, to work towards a peace order for all of Europe. Third, to preserve and strengthen transatlantic relations. Fourth, to promote the spread of democracy and respect for human rights in all parts of the world. Fifth, to strengthen the role of the UN so that it can adequately fulfil its role as a mechanism for global order. And sixth, to secure and build up a system of global free trade.

There are three important things to note about the German discussion of their national interests. The first is that these national interests have not been defined in zero-sum ways inimitable with Germany's multilateral and bilateral commitments. Instead, these interests have been defined in terms of international cooperation and integration. This is because 'today, European powers are inescapably caught in the web of interdependence, out of which they cannot escape without heavily damaging their own interests' (Schwarz 1994: 173). In addition, Germany's national interests are primarily concerned with domestic prosperity and security, not great power status. This reflects the fact that German is a mature democracy and that 'in democracies, national interests are generally not plans for greater power or the aggrandisement of a nation'. Rather, they are motivated by a 'concern for the economic well-being of, and the political support by, the national populace' (Bertram 1994: 104)

Second, Germany's national interests have been defined not simply by reference to its *Mittellage* or relative power capabilities, but in terms of Germany's dominant values, principles and identity. These have provided the cognitive prism through which these material factors have been evaluated. Christian Hacke lists seven factors that have shaped Germany's national interests: constitutional values and principles; geopolitical location; Germany's past; the interests of its neighbours and partners in Europe and the world; its membership of multilateral organisations; the political will and capabilities of the government; and the domestic interaction between government, opposition and public (Hacke 1997b: 514–15).

Third, with the coming to power of the Red–Green coalition in late 1998, a new theme has emerged in the discourse of German foreign policy. This is the concept of 'enlightened self-interest' ('*aufgeklärten Eigeninteresses*'), which runs as a *leitmotiv* through the speeches of the new Chancellor, Gerhard Schröder (Schwarz 1999: 5). The significance of this for the practice of German foreign policy is small. The Bonn Republic has always pursued its own interests. *Einbindung* and the emphasis on 'milieu-shaping' were not an expression of selfless, disinterested altruism, but a carefully thought-out form of enlightened self-interest. Nonetheless, this new emphasis on *aufgeklärten Eigeninteresses* constitutes a distinct change of tone, and, as we shall see in chapter 7, does point to a partial recalibration of German *Europapolitik*. It is a reflection more of a change of generation than of governing coalition. Former Chancellor Kohl frequently argued that European integration was a question of war and peace. This reflected his generation's tendency to situate German politics in the context of the Second World War and its immediate aftermath. The 'sixty-eighter' generation of Schröder and Fischer, by contrast, has grown up in a democratic Germany firmly embedded in Western structures, and they therefore have a much more pragmatic, if not instrumental, approach to the EU (Vernet 1999: 12).

One final point to note is that defining, articulating and pursuing the national interest is not an impediment to peaceful international cooperation. The Schröder government's emphasis on 'enlightened self-interest' does not mean that the Berlin Republic is shedding its multilateral and *Zivilmacht* identity. The crucial question is how these national interests are defined. 'Promoting justice in a world of states', David Clinton has argued (1991: 56–8), 'means, in part, working with their evolving national interests'. This involves 'seeking to nudge in desirable ways the shifting definition of a legitimate state interest – furthering restraints and throwing light on areas of common or shared interest as subjects for more positive cooperation'. Clinton therefore also employs the language of 'enlightened self interest', which he equates with de Toqueville's concept of 'interest rightly understood'. De Toqueville did not expect individuals in a society to give up their personal interests for the common good. Rather, he hoped that each would devote some time, energy and resources to preserving the society that allowed them to pursue their own interests, and to moderate their demands in order to compromise with others:

> The principle of interest rightly understood produces no great acts of self-sacrifice, but it suggests daily small acts of self-denial. By itself it cannot suffice to make a man virtuous, but it disciplines a number of citizens in habits of regularity, temperance, moderation, foresight, self-command; and, if it does not lead men straight to virtue by the will, it gradually draws them in that direction by their habits. If the principle of interest rightly understood were to sway the whole moral world, extraordinary virtues would doubtless be more rare; but I think that gross depravity would then also be less common. (De Toqueville, quoted in Clinton 1991: 56)

'A policy grounded in the protection of state interests', Clinton concludes, 'is not a "lofty" doctrine, but if it teaches statesmen temperance, moderation, foresight, and self-command, it will have raised the ethical level of international behaviour' (1991: 56).

Competing grand strategies

In addition to engaging with issues such as normalisation and national interests, the 'great foreign policy debate' in Germany has addressed more substantive questions about the options facing Germany grand strategy. Within the plethora of competing visions and recommendations that have emerged, five main options stand out: these are Carolingian Europe, a wider West, Mitteleuropa, Russia first, and world power.[15]

Carolingian Europe: this option emphasises 'deepening' the EU integration process around a 'core Europe' (*Kerneuropa*). This involves completing Economic and Monetary Union (EMU) and building a political union which would include a common foreign, security and defence policy. The core of this would be the Franco-German 'cooperative hegemon'. The primary objective of this grand strategy would be to strengthening the cohesion of the West European security community, even at the cost of enlargement and the transatlantic relationship.

Wider West: this would focus on enlarging the EU and NATO into East Central Europe, thereby extending the transatlantic security community into the 'intermediate zone' of Europe's regional security complex. It would involve complementing Germany's existing strategic partnerships with France and the USA with a new partnership with Poland, geostrategically the most important of the new democracies of Central Europe. In this scenario, the dual enlargement process would take precedence over a further 'deepening' of EU integration.

Mitteleuropa: this option envisages a more assertive and unilateral pursuit by Germany of its interests in Central Europe. It assumes a perceived lack of support on the part of Western allies for Germany's efforts to strengthen the stability and prosperity of its Eastern neighbourhood. It also assumes a growing conflict of interests between Germany and its major partners, particularly France and Britain (Hellmann 1996: 23). This grand strategy would involve the creation of new multilateral structures in Central Europe and the forging of a new strategic partnership with Poland – even at the expense of existing relationships with Western partners.

Russia first: this is the 'classic eastern option of German foreign policy' (Garton Ash 1996: 90), involving a 'new Rapallo' and a close strategic alliance with Moscow. It would signal a victory for more traditional concepts of great power cartels, and would aim to impose stability on Central and Eastern Europe by reducing the room for manoeuvre of the states in the 'lands between'. In this scenario, Germany would act as the tribune for Russian interests in NATO and the EU, even at the risk of antagonising the USA.

World power: this grand strategy envisages Germany striving to play a more global role as a great power in its own right. This would involve accepting US offers to become its 'partner in leadership', and a greater propensity to deploy deliberative military power around the globe. Institutionally this would entail acquiring a permanent seat on the UN Security Council; positioning itself as the 'captain' of the European Union in its external relations; and perhaps even developing a nuclear capability of its own.

These five options represent ideal-types. In practice they are not mutually exclusive, and most can be combined in various permutations. Indeed, a large country like Germany, situated as it is in the heart of Europe, needs to have many strings to its foreign policy bow. However, Germany's power – although substantial in terms of its structural economic power and political influence – is not unlimited, and Germany needs to set itself clear foreign policy priorities. Timothy Garton Ash notes that throughout its history the Federal Republic has avoided hard choices in preference for what he terms 'the politics of *sowohl-als-auch*: not either-or, but as-well-as'. This he terms 'Genscherism', the 'hard core of which is fudge'. He argues that with 'increased demands on limited resources, the danger is that by trying to do everything Germany will end up achieving nothing'. 'The conclusion', he suggests, 'should be plain: the Federal Republic can and should make clearer choices than in the past. These are not absolute "either-or" choices – to some extent, all major states have to genscher – but choices of priorities ... The obvious starting point for determining such priorities would be a definition of national interest' (1996: 92, 85–6).

Dual institutional enlargement: – the key to the reshaping of Europe
Garton Ash's own preference is for the second option – 'wider West' (which he terms, 'wider Europe'). He argues that Germany should give 'top priority for the next twenty years to building a wider Europe, extending the EU and NATO eastward step by step' (1996: 93). He has thus criticised EMU as a historic error that has detracted from the more important project of bringing stability to the post-communist East through a process of institutional enlargement.

In fact, a broad foreign policy consensus did emerge in Germany in the early 1990s around the objective of enlarging Euro-Atlantic institutions to the east. Gunther Hellmann (1996: 22) notes that the 'wider West' option was 'clearly preferred' by all the five schools of foreign policy thinking he identifies in Germany,[16] 'and, not surprisingly, by government policymakers as well'. This reflected a broad recognition amongst German policymakers that 'East-Central Europe's political elite – and this includes the former communists – have staked their legitimacy on their countries' gradual but steady adherence to the West. Rightly or wrongly, this is understood to have essentially two institutional meanings: the European Union, and NATO' (Allin 1995: 62). Most Germans therefore realised that their own security and prosperity depended on the security and prosperity of their eastern neighbours. The conclusion was clear: enlargement of Euro-Atlantic structures into East Central Europe was a matter of vital national interest to Germany.

However, in the early 1990s this 'wider West' option had to compete with another primary policy objective close to the heart of Chancellor Kohl. This was deepening the European integration process through EMU and Political Union ('Carolingian Europe'). Chancellor Kohl felt very strongly that German unification had to be complemented by deeper European integration. He was also convinced that EU integration must be deepened to provide an 'anchor of stability' for the wider Europe. Kohl was therefore an impassioned advocate of the Maastricht Treaty on European Union, and championed the cause of Economic and Monetary Union despite its domestic unpopularity. Given the experience of his generation, he believed the German 'Ulysses' had to be firmly bound to the mast of European integration in order to avoid the 'sirens of power'.

The German commitment to EU deepening, and the complicated negotiations and preparations that surrounded EMU, meant that there was limited diplomatic time and energy available in the early 1990s to tackle the equally difficult task of enlarging Euro-Atlantic structures. Consequently, the EU was slow to respond to the demands from the new democracies in Central and Eastern Europe. Germany was keen to act as the 'tribune' for its Eastern neighbours, but was not able to translate its vision of a 'wider West' into a concrete programme of action (Mayer 1997: 732). Nevertheless, the East Central Europeans soon came to regard Germany as the leading proponent of enlargement in the EU, and their natural tribune within Western organisations more widely. Only in 1993–94, with the key decisions concerned EMU in place, did German policy-makers begin to devote greater attention to the task of translating their vision of dual enlargement into a concrete set of policy proposals. The key event here was the Copenhagen EU Declaration of June 1993, which for the first time, mentioned an eventual accession of the Central and East Europeans to the EU. During their Presidency of the EU in the first six months of 1994, the Germans became increasingly vocal in promoting Eastern enlargement. At the Essen European Council in December 1994 they succeeding in having approved a 'Strategy to Prepare the Associated Countries of Central Europe for Membership'. This designated the Europe Agreements (EA) as the main mechanism through which CEE countries could achieve EU membership (McManus 1998: 120). However, despite CEE calls for an explicit timetable for accession, none was forthcoming, and it became increasingly clear that EU enlargement was going to be a long, slow and difficult process.

It was in this context that EU and NATO enlargement became 'de-coupled'. Initially it was expected that the enlargement of NATO would follow that of the EU, or at least, that the two would be closely linked. However, as it became evident that the EU would not be in a position to enlarge to the east for some years, the option of an early expansion of NATO became more attractive. This was despite the lack of a clear strategic rationale for enlarging the Atlantic Alliance (Hacke 1997b: 530). As we shall see, a crucial influence behind this decision was Defence Minister Volker Rühe.

The year 1997 – 'Europe's Year of Decision'[17] – was when the crucial decisions on enlarging NATO and the EU were finally taken. At its Madrid summit, NATO formally offered membership to Poland, the Czech Republic and Hungary. Shortly afterwards, at its summit meeting in Amsterdam, EU leaders agreed to begin accession negotiations with five East Central Europeans: Poland, the Czech Republic, Hungary, Estonia and Slovakia. These two historic summits underscored the incontrovertible fact that the reshaping of Europe was going to proceed through a process of institutional enlargement and restructuring. Other options, such as a pan-European system of collective security built around the OSCE, or regional alternatives to the EU and NATO, had been largely discounted.[18] Thus as Alyson Bailes noted at the time, integration was set to become the 'dominant theme' of the next decade in the Euro-Atlantic space. Henceforth, she argued, the most important policy debates would revolve around two questions: 'how best to deepen and how far to widen the two uniquely integrated organizations, the North Atlantic Alliance and the European Union' (Bailes 1997: 28).

The dilemmas of German grand strategy

The decision to enlarge the EU and NATO to the East accords closely with Germany's foreign policy interests in Central and Eastern Europe. However, it also poses a new set of potential dilemmas and role conflicts for German policy-makers. These dilemmas reflect the complexities of enlarging Euro-Atlantic institutions while preserving their cohesion, and at the same time consolidating cooperative security arrangements with states excluded from the enlargement process. Enlargement to the East thus raises questions which strike at the heart of European security. It will inevitably be one of the major foreign policy tasks in the early twenty-first century. 'Depending on how the expansion process is handled it could stabilise a new European security order by consolidating and expanding the integration process, or it could contribute to the unravelling of the whole integration process and the start of a new antagonistic relationship with Russia. Hence it is a complex area where the stakes are high' (Flockhart 1996: 197).

For Germany, the dual enlargement process poses four major foreign policy difficulties. First, balancing *Westbindung* and *Ostpolitik*. Enlarging Euro-Atlantic institutions to the East is essential in order to project stability into Central and Eastern Europe. On the other hand, as Ingo Peters has noted (1997: 374), if enlargement is not accompanied by structural reform of these institutions, then the quality of the integration process could suffer, thereby putting into question Germany's *Einbindung*.

Second, balancing the institutional enlargement of Euro-Atlantic structures to the East with the consolidation of a cooperative security system with Russia. As Heinz Timmermann has argued (1997: 12), the enlargement decisions require Germany and its allies to perform a difficult 'balancing act': integrating the East Central Europeans into Euro-Atlantic institutions, whilst at the same time engaging Russia in European political, economic and security affairs. Finding a balance between integration and institutional enlargement on the one hand, and a cooperative security relationship based on deepening economic interdependencies with Russia on the other, will not be easy. As Timmermann stressed, this balancing act will require '*from both sides* conceptual innovation and a willingness to make material sacrifices'.

The third dilemma facing Germany follows on from the second: it involves managing the competing demands of Berlin's twin-track *Ostpolitik*. For a variety of reasons, the 'Russia first' option holds little attraction for post-unification Germany. Poland and the other Visegrad states in *Mitteleuropa* have become much more important for Germany in the 1990s.

Nevertheless, Germany is keenly interested in good relations with Moscow. Given the legacy of historical animosity and mistrust in Eastern Europe, however, any signs of a 'new Rapallo' are looked on with intense suspicion by the 'lands between'. Germany thus needs to balance relations between Russia and the Visegrad states, the most important of which is Poland. 'At the close of the twentieth century, in a time when states are pursuing their interests cooperatively rather than confrontationally, the task facing German foreign policy is to keep the Russian and East Central European tracks of its *Ostpolitik* in balance, in the same way it has balanced the French and American tracks in its Westpolitik' (Crome 1997:176–7).

The final dilemma facing Germany is finding a balance within its *Westpolitik* (Western policy) between its two strategic partners – namely France and the USA – and between Europe's two most important multilateral organisations – the EU and NATO. This dilemma is not new, but it has been posed anew by the end of the cold war. Germany needs to ensure that the EU and NATO are *interlocking*, not *inter-blocking* organisations in Central and Eastern Europe. It also needs to find ways of harmonising the competing visions of Europe's future held by its most important strategic partners, Paris and Washington.

German grand strategy thus faces a series of new challenges and demands that will sorely test the statecraft of its leaders, diplomats and officials. Gregor Schöllgen has summarised the central task of German foreign and security policy as follows:

> Germany must take up its new role as a European great power without thereby suppressing, forgetting or repeating the incompetence, mistakes and crimes of the first half of this century, the consequences of which can still be felt today. This indeed constitutes the greatest and most pressing challenge facing the Germans on the eve of the twenty-first century. (Schöllgen 1993: 9)

Notes

1 In his memoirs, Konrad Adenauer stressed that gaining the trust of the Western allies was an essential precondition for his policy of partnership with them. 'The most important precondition for parternship is trust. Creating trust – as I repeatedly stressed at the start of this book, was the first commandment for us Germans. The faster and firmer this trust in us grew, the quicker the goal of partnership could be achieved' (Adenauer 1965: 246).

2 This insight provides one of the foundations for security complex theory with its emphasis on regional sub-systems as objects of security analysis (Buzan *et al.* 1998: 9).

3 Geopolitics has been described as 'the applied study of the relationship of geographical space to politics'. It is therefore concerned with 'the reciprocal impact of spatial patterns, features, and structures and political ideas, institutions, and transactions' (Cohen 1994: 17).

4 'Rollensuche, Rollenentfaltung und Rollenerweiterung der Bundesrepublik sind funktional zum Stand bzw. zum Wandel der internationalen Politik – genauer: des Ost-West-Konflikts – zu verstehen' (Niedhart 1997: 16).

5 In the words of its first Secretary-General, Lord Ismay, NATO's purpose was threefold: 'To keep the Americans in, the Russians out, and the Germans down' (quoted in Niedhart 1997: 18). In this context, it is particularly significant that Bonn's acquisition of sovereignty in 1955 was accompanied by its integration into NATO.

6 Egon Bahr has suggested that there were only three 'sovereign gestures or acts' in the history of the Bonn Republic: Adenauer's stepping onto the red carpet in Petersberg; Ostpolitik; and Kohl's agreement with Gorbachev to reduce the size of the Bundeswehr from 600,000 to 370,000 (Bahr 1999: 1,319).

7 In their reconstruction of neorealist theory, Baumann, Rittberger and Wagner focus on economic and military resources as the key determinans of a state's relative power, and explicitly exclude intangible (or 'soft power') resources (1999: 255–6). See also Paul Kennedy (1988).

8 'The most important factor upon which the power of a nation depends', Morgenthau argued, 'is obviously geography … The separation of Great Britain from the European continent by a small body of water, the English Channel, is a factor that Julius Caesar could no more afford to overlook than could William the Conqueror, Philip II, Napoleon or Hitler. However much other factors may have altered its importance throughout the course of history, what was important two thousand years ago is still important today, and all those concerned with the conduct of foreign affairs must take it into account' (Morgenthau 1993: 124–5).

9 Reported in the *Frankfurter Allgemeine Zeitung*, 8 October 1999. The appointment of General Reinhardt to command of KFOR is another historical landmark in European defence and security cooperation. The last time British troops were placed under operational command of a German general in a conflict situation was the Battle of Leipzig, 1813.

10 *Frankfurter Allgemeine Zeitung*, 7 October 1999. The debate on defence expenditure was stoked by the comments of US Secretary of Defence William Cohen who criticized Germany for spending too little on defence arguing that this has a 'profound and lasting impact on the capabilities, not only of [Germany], but of the Alliance as a whole' (quoted in the *New York Times*, 2 December 1999). Germany spends 1.5 per cent of its GDP. The comparative figures for its main allies are: France 2.8 per cent, the UK 2.6 per cent, USA 3.2 per cent.

11 Following the Kosovo war, the government established a new commission on 'Common Security and the Future of the Bundeswehr' chaired by former President Richard von Weizsäcker. Its purpose is to assess what changes are

necessary to the structure and organisation of the Bundeswehr if Germany is to fulfil its new-found obligations for military crisis management and humanitarian operations. All main political parties agreed that at 53,000, Germany's crisis reaction force is too small. Beyond this, there is little consensus on what should be done. Chancellor Schröder has publicly acknowledged that the restructuring and reorientation of the Bundeswehr 'will cost money' (*Bulletin*, no. 83, 6 December 1999, p. 788).

12 As Josef Joffe notes (1994: 80), Bismarck's enduring *Angst* was the 'nightmare of coalitions', the all-European encirclement that threatened to overwhelm Frederick the Great's Prussia. 'Hence in the famous "Kissinger Diktat", Bismarck formulated the following precept for the Second Reich; the basic purpose was to create a "universal political situation in which all the powers except France need us and, by dint of their mutual relations, are kept as much as is possible from forming coalitions against us". Or, as Bismarck told the Russian ambassador Saburov in 1880, his "invariable objective" could be subsumed under a simple formula: "Try to be in a threesome as long as the world is governed by a precarious equilibrium of five great powers. That is the true protection against coalitions".'

13 'In this time of fundamental changes it has been and is especially important to remain true to the guiding principles of our foreign and security policy. They are: cooperation and integration, dialogue and building trust' (Kohl 1998: 9).

14 As Gunther Hellmann notes, a key theme in the normalisation debate was the use of the military instrument in reshaping European order: 'Das vereingte, wieder voll souveräne Deutschland wolle als ebenbürtiges Mitglied in den Kreis der alten Großmächte zurückkehren – jener Großmächte, die sich noch immer anmaßten, über die köpfe der Betroffenen hinweg "Ordnung" schaffen zu müssen und die meinten, diesen Ordnungsauftrag vor allem mit militärischen Mitteln erfüllen zu können' (Hellmann 1997a: 24).

15 These five options are a synthesis of those outlined by Timothy Garton Ash (1996) and Gunther Hellmann (1996).

16 The five schools of thought are Pragmatic Multilateralists, Europeanists, Eurosceptics, Internationalists and Normalisation/Nationalists. Hellmann (1996: 25) presents a very useful table summarising the views of the five schools of thought on the four grand strategic options he identifies (World Power, Wider West, Carolingian Europe and Mitteleuropa).

17 Christoph Bertram, *Die Zeit*, no. 6, 31 January 1997, p. 3.

18 Along with proposals for an OSCE-based system of pan-European collective security, there have been calls for regional security cooperation in Central and Eastern Europe by, inter alia, Polish President Lech Walesa, Belarus President Shushkevich and Ukrainian President Kravchuk. For details, see Cottey (1995: 17–19) and Hyde-Price (1998: 272).

6

NATO
and German security policy

The North Atlantic Alliance remains the backbone for peace and stability in Europe. It will be more than ever the core and motor of a new European peace order. The Alliance is directing itself in spirit and structure towards the new demands of today and tomorrow – crisis prevention and crisis resolution, projecting stability and cooperation with new partners ...

The reorientation of NATO and the reorientation of the Bundeswehr are two sides of the same coin. Both processes must be closely associated. The mission and structure of the Bundeswehr must be brought into harmony with the new peace order in Europe. Our armed forces must be capable of covering, together with our allies, the total spectrum of Alliance missions.

(Defence Minister Rudolf Scharping, Hamburg, 11 November 1998)

The aim of this chapter is to explore one of the twin pillars of post-cold war German grand strategy – the enlargement and restructuring of NATO. Since its foundation, the Federal Republic has based its security policy on the NATO Alliance and the US military security guarantees that it embodies. With unification and the end of the cold war, however, NATO has lost much of its original rationale, and has had to work hard to redefine its role and purpose. At the same time the European security agenda has fundamentally altered. Germany no longer faces any direct military threats, but does have to address a range of non-military security risks and challenges. Above all, German security policy in the 1990s has had to address a question of acute political and historical sensitivity – the role of military force in the reshaping of European order.

The chapter is structured into three sections. The first section reviews Germany's response to the changes brought about to the European security agenda by the end of the cold war. It argues that the Gulf War and the violent break-up of Yugoslavia exposed a tension at the heart of united Germany's foreign and security policy: its commitment to multilateralism and a strategic partnership with the USA on the one hand, and its aversion to military crisis-management on the other. This tension was resolved by evolving a new role for the Bundeswehr in multilateral humanitarian operations.

The second section considers the issues involved in the debate on NATO enlargement. Such strategic decisions, it has been suggested, are 'a function of the political system and the political culture from which they spring' (Heuser 1998: 1). In the case of Germany, the decision to advocate a selective opening up of NATO to new members from East Central Europe was taken following an institutional struggle between the Defence and Foreign Ministries. The decision to enlarge NATO represented a success for a trans-governmental coalition between Defence Minister Rühe and his US counterparts. At the same time, the parameters for this policy shift were set by Germany's *Einbindung* (integration) in multilateral structures and its identity as a *Zivilmacht* (civilian power). German policy towards NATO enlargement thus illustrates the important of including interests, institutions and identities in the analysis of foreign policy decision-making.

The third section of this chapter considers German preferences for NATO's role in Europe. It concentrates on two central issues: *cooperative security governance* and non-Article V military crisis-management operations. For much of the 1990s, controversies over NATO enlargement obscured discussion of an even more important set of questions: the function – if any – of NATO in the post-cold war era, and the role of military force in the reshaping of European order. The Kosovo war came like a bolt of lightening for both these questions, throwing into stark relief the choices and dilemmas facing late modern Europe. NATO's 'Operation Deliberate Force' was a pivotal event in the post-cold war evolution of the European security system. It heralded a further break with the principles and practices of the Westphalian states' system, and pointed to a paradigm shift in the very nature of European order. The consequences of the war for NATO, transatlantic relations, a European Security and Defence Identity (ESDI) and German security policy will be discussed well into the twenty-first century.

Above all, the Kosovo war raises a question that touches deep historical sensitivities in contemporary Germany: the role of military force in reshaping European order. For Germany and Europe as a whole, the *Gretchenfrage* (or key question) of European order in the late modern era is whether or not there is a right to humanitarian intervention. If there is, who has the right to intervene, and on the basis of what legitimate authority? Controversies on these questions are likely to fuel a major debate on the goals and instruments of German security policy for much of the next decade or more.

Germany and the new security agenda

The cold war and West German security policy

Post-war West German security policy was built upon the foundations of the *Bundesrepublik*'s institutional embeddedness in multilateral structures. West Germany's relative rapid integration into the inner sanctums of the Western alliance was made possible by the Berlin Airlift – the 'founding myth of the Federal Republic of Germany'. Germans were transformed from the perpetrators of Nazi aggression to the victims of Stalinist aggression. 'The confused and corrupt "de-Nazification" process was now left more or less in a shambles: the past could be forgotten, as Germans were offered a new and politically virtuous identity based on anti-communism' (Johnstone 1984: 36). In 1955, at the same time as it was rearmed, West Germany was integrated into NATO and the Western European Union (WEU). The Bundeswehr subsequently developed into one of the central conventional military pillars of the NATO Alliance, its military strength lying in its armoured divisions.

German rearmament was not uncontested (Patton 1999: 47–52). There were many domestic critics on the left, who argued that after the experience of the war, Germany's future should be as a neutral and pacifist state. Politically, these concerns were marginalised, given the importance attached by the Adenauer government to the BRD's *Westbindung* (Schwarz 1995b: 475). Nonetheless, throughout post-war German society there were lingering concerns about Germany's authoritarian and militarist traditions, and a strong consensus that democratic Germany needed to break decisively with its militaristic, aggressive and authoritarian past. Consequently, the Bundeswehr was established as a German army of a new type. It was built upon the the notion of 'citizens in uniform', and emphasised individual responsibility for acts carried out under orders. The aim was to create an army imbued with democratic and constitutional principles, anchored into multilateral structures, and designed for strictly defensive purposes.

The emphasis on the strictly defensive character of the *Bundesrepublik*'s army of 'citizens in uniform', along with the fact that from its very inception, the Bundeswehr had been firmly integrated into NATO's multilateral structures, gave rise to a distinctive West German 'strategic culture'.[1]

This strategic culture was characterised by an emphasis on multilateralism, deterrence and conflict prevention. According to this logic, the Bundeswehr would have failed in its mission the moment it fired its first shot in anger (Stratman 1988: 97–8). In part, this reflected the stark logic of Germany's position on the frontline of the East–West conflict, and the realisation that fighting a Third World War on German soil would be as devastating as the Thirty Years War had been in its time.

The Federal Republic's distinctive post-war strategic culture was a manifestation of its post-Holocaust identity as a *Zivilmacht*, or 'civilian power' (Maull 1990, 1993, 1997). As we have seen (pp. 120–1), the concept of *Zivilmacht* is an ideal-type which refers to states that seek to avoid military conflict and resolve international disputes in a peaceful and 'civilised' manner. Civilian powers strive to strengthen the socially textured nature of international society, and encourage wide international acceptance of norms and institutions favouring peaceful cooperation between different political communities. During the cold war, Germany's *Zivilmacht* identity manifested itself in a commitment to *détente* and 'common security' in preference to nuclear deterrence (particularly if this involved nuclear war-fighting scenarios), the balance of power and *Realpolitik*.

This Zivilmacht identity was at times in tension with other key aspects of Germany's strategic culture. During the 'second cold war' of the early 1980s, for example, West Germany found itself facing a tension between *Allianztreuheit* ('Alliance commitment') and the 'special German responsibility for peace'. This tension between deterrence and *détente* arose because the USA, Bonn's key strategic partner within NATO, wanted to deploy Cruise and Pershing II missiles in Germany. Many Germans, however, argued that this was incompatible with the concept of a 'special German responsibility for peace and security'. This tension between deterrence and *détente* was evident throughout much of the late cold war period. When push came to shove, however, West Germany's dominant role conception was as loyal partner for the USA and a reliable NATO ally. *Westbindung* thus remained the decisive feature of its foreign and security policy. This role conception was reaffirmed during the international negotiations on German unification, and was to contribute to the success of Kohl's strategy during late 1989 and early 1990.

Unification and the end of the cold war

The *annus mirabilis* of 1989 fundamentally and irrevocably transformed the parameters of German security policy. To begin with, the decline and fall of state socialism made possible the realisation of a dream, which many Germans had longed for, but few believed attainable – the opening of the Berlin Wall and the unification of their divided country. In the late autumn of 1989, Chancellor Kohl moved swiftly and decisively to 'seize the coat-tails' of history and achieve German unification on the basis of free elections and international agreement.

A decisive issue in the international manoeuvring surrounding the 'two-plus-four' negotiations was Germany's NATO membership (Zelikow and Rice 1995). This had two key aspects. First, Kohl's resolute commitment that a unified Germany should remain firmly integrated into NATO was an important factor in securing American support for unification. US backing for the Kohl government was particularly important given British and French reservations about the pace and implications of Germany's drive for unification (Thatcher 1993: 813). Second, Kohl was able to secure Soviet backing for a united Germany's continued NATO membership by a mixture of diplomatic promises and financial incentives. Gorbachev and other Soviet leaders were repeatedly told by their Western interlocutors that a Germany anchored in NATO would be more constrained, and therefore more predictable, than a neutral and non-aligned Germany. Soviet acceptance for Germany's continued membership of NATO was finally ensured by NATO's July 1990 London Declaration. This announced NATO's transformation into a more political alliance committed to pan-European cooperation. In addition, promises were also given that the incorporation of the former DDR into NATO would be governed by special arrangements. Finally, the Russians believed they had been given informal assurance that incorporating Eastern Germany into NATO would not be the prelude to further rounds of enlargement reaching towards the borders of the USSR (Stent 1999: 213; Eyal 1997: 699).

Whatever the nature of these informal pledges, they were to resurface during the controversies surrounding NATO enlargement, and fuelled Russian suspicions about Western motives (Walter 1996: 742). As regards Germany, the wide public consensus around continued membership of the Alliance underlines the extent to which multilateral *Westbindung* had become part of the *Staatsräison* of the Federal Republic and struck deep roots in German identity and strategic culture (Juricic 1995: 111–12). This deep commitment to multilateral integration in Euro-Atlantic structures was subsequently to colour Germany's response to the new security agenda that emerged in post-cold war Europe.

Germany and the new European security agenda

Not only did the decline and fall of state socialism make possible German unification, it also transformed Germany's external security environment. From being a frontline state in the most militarised region of the international system, Germany became a state 'encircled by friends' (Meiers 1995: 85). Once directly threatened by the first echelon armoured divisions of the Warsaw Pact, and the short-range nuclear warheads of the Soviet Union, united Germany no longer faces any 'clear and present danger'. 'For the first time in history, Germany has – from a military perspective – achieved the status of being absolutely secure!' (Hacke 1997a: 6).

Yet whatever initial hopes and dreams were born in the wave of optimism which followed the *annus mirabilis*, it soon became apparent that post-cold war Europe faced a new set of security concerns. 'We have slain a large dragon', it was suggested, 'but we live in a jungle filled with a bewildering variety of poisonous snakes' (Mueller 1994: 536). The Soviet threat had been vanquished, but a new security agenda quickly emerged, consisting largely of non-military 'risks' and 'challenges' emanating from post-communist Central and Eastern Europe. Some traditional security concerns remained: for example, managing the build-down of conventional and nuclear forces in Central Europe; consolidating the new regime of arms controls and confidence-building measures; addressing the problem of nuclear proliferation; and responding to the problem of international terrorism, particularly state-sponsored terrorism. By and large, however, Europe's post-cold war security agenda has been dominated by non-military risks and challenges.

These security problems primarily derive not from inter-state conflicts, but from the traumas and tensions associated with the 'triple transformation' in the East (the transformation of the economy, political system and external policy). One intractable problem has been the enormous economic and social hardships arising from the dismantling of command economies and the introduction of market capitalism. This has severely complicated the difficult process of state and nation-building which is central to the political agenda in the post-communist East (Vogel 1997: 23). Soon after 1989 it became apparent that transforming and modernising the sclerotic economies which were the legacy of forty years of state socialism was going to be a much more difficult – and painful – undertaking than many had initially imagined. The turmoil and despair that all too often accompanied attempts at macro-economic stabilisation and structural reform threatened to undermine the young shoots of political democratisation, and provide fertile ground for unscrupulous populists, xenophobic nationalists and demogues of all descriptions. At best, this would make international cooperation more difficult. At worst, it could generate new conflicts, up to and including wars.

The dismantling of the iron curtain and the beginnings of the 'triple transformation' thus presented Germany with a new set of security problems. Kurt Biedenkopf, the Prime Minister of Saxony, noted in 1994 that the 'threat to our values has not disappeared', but has taken a very different form. 'The prime military threat from the East has been replaced by a global threat created by disorder. Our sovereignty and security are threatened not by atomic weapons, but by the dangerous proximity of chaos and disorder to our highly developed, albeit sensitive, societies' (Biedenkopf 1994: 17). Most of these new security problems were not a function of the balance of power or geopolitical concerns. Instead, as Federal President Roman Herzog observed in March 1995,

> Social, ecological and cultural destabilisation present additional security risks, which in the long-term are scarcely less dangerous than military threats. Meanwhile the list of these risks has become well-known: population explosion, climate change, economically-motivated migrants, nuclear smuggling, the drugs trade, fundamentalists of different colours, genocide, the collapse of state authority. (Herzog 1995: 161)

This new security agenda is shared by most European countries, but given Germany's central geographical location, it is particularly vulnerable to problems arising from the triple transformation process in Central and Eastern Europe. Germany's response to this new agenda has reflected its identity as a *Zivilmacht* firmly committed to multilateralism. The Federal government has stressed the need for a comprehensive security policy able to tackle the non-military dimension of security. It has also tended to favour multilateral responses to these security concerns, such as strengthening Schengen border controls and the EU's third pillar (Justice and Home Affairs). When such multilateral approaches have not been possible, or have appeared inadequate, Germany negotiated bilateral agreements with neighbours. In general, however, the new security agenda has been met by policy strategies and concepts that reflect Germany's identity as both a civilian power and an advocate of multilateral cooperation.

The emergence of a new security agenda raised two questions for Germany. All European countries were confronted with these questions, but for Germany they proved particularly sensitive given its history, identity and strategic culture. The first question concerned the utility and legitimacy of military force in reshaping post-cold war European order. The end of the cold war has had a paradoxical effect on European security. On the one hand, it has reduced the saliency of military threats and transformed the European security agenda. On the other, it has created a number of situations where the option of military crisis-management is called for. European states, including Germany, have therefore had to think more seriously about 'Military Operations Other Than War' (MOOTW), i.e., humanitarian intervention, peacekeeping and peace-support operations. With the end of the cold war, traditional questions of strategy – the use of military power for political means – is thus firmly back on the security agenda, despite the reduced saliency of military security threats. Consequently, what can be termed 'the agenda of Clausewitz' ('war as the continuation of politics by other means') is firmly back on the European security agenda, after it had been largely displaced by the advent of nuclear deterrence and the East–West military stand-off. This means that Germany, along with other European countries, has increasingly had to confront a series of tough moral and political questions about the legitimacy and utility of military force as an instrument for reshaping European order.

The second question generated by the new security agenda concerned the role of NATO in European order. This question was linked to the first, but not identical, and raised a larger bundle of political and strategic issues. One important consequence of the end of the cold war and the emergence of a radically new security agenda has been the changed importance of NATO for German security. In the context of the East–West conflict, when the BRD was a frontline state in a divided continent, NATO was of existential military and geopolitical importance for the Federal Republic. Today, however, Germany is surrounded by friends, and no longer faces an identifiable military threat to its territorial integrity. Instead, it is seeking to address a new security agenda, one that is dominated by non-military security issues for which NATO is not particularly well-suited (Langguth 1998).

Thus for contemporary Germany, NATO's utility is more political than military. Article V security guarantees are no longer as vital for German security as they were during the cold war. Consequently the relative significance for German security policy of other security institutions such as the EU and the OSCE has grown. In the immediate wake of the fall of the Berlin Wall, the then Foreign Minister, Hans-Dietrich Genscher, even floated the idea that the CSCE (as the OSCE was then known) could provide the core of a new pan-European system of collective security (Rotfeld

1991). This idea received little support from other NATO members and was quietly discarded. Nevertheless, it is clear that the place of NATO in German security policy has changed since unification. For the Berlin Republic, NATO's primary importance will be that it institutionalises the transatlantic partnership with America and provides a multilateral context for German security policy. As we shall see, the debate in Germany on the future role and purpose of NATO has raised sensitive questions touching on core issues of German identity – not least, the balance between its 'European' and 'transatlantic' vocation (Crome 1997: 175), and its future as a *Zivilmacht*.

The Gulf War and the limits of 'cheque-book diplomacy'

Any danger that the end of East–West confrontation would lead to a self-satisfied complacency in German security policy was dispelled by two events in 1990–91: the Gulf War and the violent disintegration of Yugoslavia.

The Iraq invasion of Kuwait in August 1990 provided the first test of united Germany's foreign and security policy. The German government under Helmut Kohl responded by providing substantial financial support for the US-led coalition against Saddam Hussein, and acting as its diplomatic cheerleader in international fora. However, the Kohl government argued that it was constitutionally unable to send Bundeswehr troops to participate in such an 'out-of-area' operation. This position was broadly supported by public opinion, although a small but vociferous anti-war movement campaigned energetically against what was portrayed as an 'oil war'. Whilst popular at home, the German government's policy was criticised by many NATO Allies as being incompatible with the international responsibilities which unification entailed. In particularly, Germany was criticised for its preference for 'cheque-book diplomacy' and its unwillingness to risk Bundeswehr lives in a UN-sanctioned operation.

The Gulf War exposed a tension at the heart of German security policy. On the one hand, Bonn was committed to multilateralism and cooperation with its allies. On the other, it rejected of an out-of-area military crisis-management role for the Bundeswehr. Given that multilateral institutions such as the UN were increasingly associated with military commitments in the 1990s, Germany found itself facing new security policy dilemmas (Schlör 1993: 63). These dilemmas reflected ambiguities within the Bundesrepublik's post-war political identity and strategic culture. On the one hand, West Germany saw itself as a reliable NATO ally enjoying a close strategic partnership with the USA. On the other, many

Germans believed that as a response to the horrors of the Third Reich, democratic Germany had a responsibility to champion non-military solutions to international conflicts (Duffield 1998: 219–20). During the cold war, a time when NATO strategic thinking was dominated by deterrence and war prevention, the potential role conflict inherent in Germany's national identity and strategic culture was less apparent. In the 'New World Order' of the post-cold war period, however, the role conflicts at the heart of German security policy were starkly exposed (Maull and Kirste 1997: 306–7).

The response of the ruling CDU-led coalition under Chancellor Helmut Kohl was to resolve this role conflict in favour of multilateral commitments and its strategic partnership with the USA. This policy choice was a logical consequence of the importance attached to its multilateral *Westbindung* by the Bundesrepublik, and reflected the extent to which Germany's perception of its fundamental national security interests had been transformed by its institutional integration into NATO and the wider transatlantic security community.

Consequently, the years following the Gulf War witnessed a steady recalibration of German security policy. As former Foreign Minister Klaus Kinkel noted, the government used a 'step-by-step' strategy to deploy Bundeswehr troops in UN-sponsored humanitarian missions 'out-of-area'.[2] Initially these did not involve deployments of troops in combat situations. Instead, the Bundeswehr deployed medical and technical support units. Thus for example the Luftwaffe was used in April 1991 to distribute relief supplies to Kurdish refugees, and in July 1992 participated in the humanitarian airlift to Sarajevo. The aim of these and similar missions was to gradually familiarise the German public with the idea of an 'out-of-area' role for the Bundeswehr, and to prepare the ground politically for humanitarian intervention and military crisis-management operations. The first 'blue-helmet' deployment of Bundeswehr troops was in Cambodia (1992–93), where Germany contributed a medical unit to the United Nations Transitional Authority in Cambodia (UNTAC). Bundeswehr units were subsequently committed to Somalia (1992–93), again in non-combat roles.

Yugoslavia and the limits of pacifism

The most important theatre for this gradual re-calibration of German security policy was former Yugoslavia. 'Up until this time, the legitimacy of the German armed forces was mainly based on the fact that alliance and national defence were identical. This context had now been redefined' (Schmidt 1996: 212). The tragic course of developments in the Balkans in the 1990s was the first clear indication that the end of cold war bipolarity was not simply going to be followed by a new age of peace for a Europe 'whole and free'. On the contrary, events in this historically unstable region were to illustrate all too sharply the nature of the new security agenda in Europe. In particular, the violent break-up of Yugoslavia demonstrated how explosive the cocktail of ethno-national differences, historical animosities, economic hardship and unscrupulous political leaders could be. At the same time, developments in this region raised acutely sensitive questions for Germany, given the legacy of Wehrmacht brutality in the Balkans between 1941 and 1945.

United Germany's first engagement with the contorted politics of Yugoslavia was not a happy one (Calic 1996). In late 1990, Slovenia and Croatia responded to Milosevic's attempt to assert Serbian nationalist dominance within Yugoslav federal structures by pushing for independence. In the face of vacillation and uncertainty on the part of the international community, Bonn declared that it would recognise Slovenia and Croatia by Christmas 1991, even if there were no consensus on this matter in the EU (Crawford 1995). This perceived assertiveness on the part of newly unified Germany was widely criticised. Some subsequently accused Germany of seeking to play a great power role in the Balkans, and of precipitating the violent collapse of Yugoslavia.

The explanation for Bonn's approach, however, has less to do with its alleged great power ambitions, and more to do with the normative values underpinning its identity. Bonn had no significant interests in the region, beyond a shared European interest in the political stability and economic accessibility of the Balkans. As Michael Libal has convincingly argued (1997: 105), 'the crucial motives for German behaviour during the first two years of the crisis were rooted in a pervasive pattern of moral and political values'. As a country that had just achieved its national self-determination, Bonn felt compelled to support other states striving for self-determination in the face of communist authoritarianism and military intimidation. 'Equally important was the rejection of violence as a means of politics', which 'basically determined the attitude of both German public opinion as a whole and Germany's political leaders, including Chancellor Kohl and Foreign Minister Genscher'.

Despite this controversial episode, the 'wars of Yugoslav succession' in the 1990s were to provide the context within which a new non-Article V role for the Bundeswehr was legitimised (Maull 1995). As appalling evidence accumulated of atrocities, ethnic cleansing and mass rape in Bosnia mounted, a growing mood developed in public opinion in Germany – as elsewhere in Europe and North America – that 'something must be done'. It was in this context that the German government, led by the Defence Minister Volker Rühe, devised a policy of gradually committing Bundeswehr personnel to multilateral humanitarian and military crisis-management operations. The idea behind these 'salami tactics' was to gradually prepare public opinion for an out-of-area role for the Bundeswehr.

The constitutional position on out-of-area military deployments was finally clarified by a decision of the Federal Constitutional Court (*Bundesverfassungsgericht*) on 12 July 1994. This arose after two earlier rulings by the court. The first concerned the legality of the government's April 1993 decision to authorise the participation of German crews in AWACs (Airborne Warning and Control Systems) deployed to enforce the UN-mandated 'no-fly' zone in Bosnia. The court ruled that the deployment of AWACs was permissible because failure to participate would have jeopardised the confidence of other NATO members. Later, in June 1994, the court ruled on Bundeswehr participation in the Unitend Nations Operation in Somalia (UNOSOM) II deployment in Somalia. This emphasised the importance of involving the Bundestag in decisions concerning missions outside of the NATO area. The constitutional position was finally clarified by the July 1994 ruling, which stated that Bundeswehr forces could participate in military operations outside the NATO area as long as they took place under UN auspices and were approved by the Bundestag. The constitutional basis for this was Article 24(2) of the *Grundgesetz*, which allowed the Bundeswehr to participate in missions associated with membership of a mutual collective security system.

Although the constitutional position was clarified in July 1994, the political conditions governing out-of-area deployments still needed resolving (Dorff 1997: 57). Government leaders began formulating a series of criteria for future deployments shortly after the failure of the UN's Somalia mission. These stressed, inter alia, the need for a clear and legitimate international mandate; multilateral involvement;[3] a clear political concept underlying the military operation; a limited time frame; and German involvement in the decision-making process (Duffield 1998: 211). For the German left, however, the catalyst for a fundamental change of attitude on the issue of military intervention was the massacre in Srebenica in 1995.[4] For many former cold war peace activists, the deepening tragedy in the Balkans raised questions about the moral and political relevance of cold war pacifism in the face of the new security agenda (Hubert 1993).[5]

The pivotal figure in this political reorientation was the prominent Green/Bündnis 90 politician, Joschka Fischer (Sager 1996: 47). In August 1995 he published an open letter to his party colleagues in which he argued that the massacre at Srebenica made necessary a rethink of the hitherto sacrosanct principle of non-violence. He suggested to his colleagues that the German left would lose its soul if it were to fail to intervene in a situation that could only be described as genocide. He made his own position crystal clear: in the event of genocide, it was the political and moral duty of the Greens to support military intervention by multilateral forces, and these forces should include a German contingent (Markovits and Reich 1998: 242; Volmer 1998: 513).

By the mid-nineties, therefore, a significant shift in thinking about German security policy was underway. Prompted the limitations of cheque book diplomacy and driven by public concerns about violence in the Balkans, a new consensus about the role and purpose of the Bundeswehr began to emerge (Dalvi 1998). Volker Rühe was the primary political architecture of the Bundeswehr's new out-of-area role, which was made constitutionally possible by the July 1994 decision of the Constitutional Court. The new cross-party consensus around humanitarian intervention was manifest from the large Bundestag majority (543 in favour, 107 against) for German participation in IFOR, the NATO-led force established to implement the Dayton peace accord (signed in November 1995). Indeed, 'the Yugoslav war and the active involvement of NATO troops in the post-Dayton peacekeeping operation proved to be a catalyst in legitimizing out-of-area deployments of the Bundeswehr' (Calic 1998: 18). The commitment of 4,000 troops to IFOR constituted the largest out-of-area operation in the history of the Bundeswehr, and was thus an important landmark in the evolution of post-unification German security policy (Lantis 1996; Pond 1997).

While the decision to develop a new approach to out-of-area non-article V operations constituted a change in terms of the instruments of German statecraft, in a more fundamental respect it underlined the continuity in normative considerations driving German foreign policy:

> In the context of the new Germany's overall foreign policy orientation, however, the approach to security matters demonstrated not change but continuity. Through its participation in multilateral operations after the end of the cold war, the Federal Republic strengthened its ties with the Western powers amid new circumstances. By 1995 the concerns about unilateralism that had surfaced in the immediate aftermath of reunification had all but disappeared. In the case of security policy, as in the context of efforts to

strengthen and expand NATO and the EU, unity with the Western powers remained a leitmotif of German foreign policy. (Banchoff 1999: 136)

NATO enlargement

The German debate

It was in the context of major debates on humanitarian intervention and an out-of-area role for the Bundeswehr that the issue of NATO enlargement was thrust onto the political agenda. After a brief flirtation with ideas of a pan-European collective security system based on an invigorated and institutionalised CSCE (Conference on Security and Cooperation in Europe), a growing number of Central and East European states began to voice a desire to join NATO. Hungary led the way here, closely followed by Czechoslovakia and Poland. NATO was seen by the new post-communist democracies both as a community of shared values and institutions which they wanted to join, and as the only viable source of credible security guarantees against a recidivist Russia (Pradetto 1997).

Although the security concerns of the East Central Europeans and their evident desire for NATO membership were widely reported in Germany, the debate on the desirability or otherwise of an Eastern enlargement of the Alliance was strikingly low-key. Most public and elite attention at this time was focused on the question of an out-of-area role of the Bundeswehr, and the deepening tragedy in the Balkans. There were certainly few discussions of the issue in the Bundestag, and it did not emerge as a major concern of any of the established political parties.

Instead, the domestic debate in Germany on NATO enlargement was driven by a trio of institutional actors. This institutional triangle consisted of the Defence Ministry under Volker Rühe; the Foreign Ministry under Klaus Kinkel; and the Office of Chancellor Kohl. Once again, Volker Rühe played a central role. It was he who placed the issue of NATO enlargement firmly on the German political agenda. Traditionally, the Defence Ministry has exercised limited political influence in the Bundesrepublik, despite its institutional size and substantial budget. This reflects historical sensitivities about the influence of the military on German politics. However, with the appointment of Volker Rühe as Defence Minister, this began to change. As a relatively young and certainly ambitious CDU politician, he clearly hoped to upstage the FDP Foreign Minister Klaus Kinkel, and stamp his mark on German foreign and security policy.

Although Rühe initially opposed NATO enlargement, by January 1993 there were clear indications that his opinion on the subject was changing. By March 1993, it was evident that he now favoured a selective opening of the Alliance to new members from the east. In a key-note speech to the London-based International Institute for Strategic Studies (IISS) in March 1993, he argued that the Atlantic Alliance 'must not become a "closed shop"', and the future members of the EU should not be denied membership of NATO. More significantly, he called for the de-coupling of the process of NATO and EU enlargement, arguing that '[e]conomic hurdles that present members of the EC can hardly jump across must not become insurmountable obstacles to membership in NATO' (Rühe 1993: 135).

Klaus Kinkel, on the other hand, advocated a slower and more cautious strategy. Although not opposed to enlargement *per se*, he was concerned that 'an over-hasty decision might imperil the security of those countries that were not to be admitted to NATO' (Kamp 1998: 177). He was also aware that NATO was not well-suited to address many of the risks and challenges on the new security agenda. Moreover, there was no direct mil-itary threat to East Central Europe, and the adverse impact of enlarge-ment on cooperative relations with Russia would out-weight any potential benefits. In part, this reflected the ingrained tendency of the Foreign Ministry to attach considerable importance to developing and maintaining good relations with Moscow – coupled with a deep-felt sense of gratitude to the former Soviet leadership for facilitating German uni-fication. As the successor to the long-serving Hans-Dietrich Genscher (whom he replaced in May 1992), Kinkel was concerned to preserve the former's political legacy – which included a close, cooperative relation-ship with Moscow.

'California dreaming': the transatlantic dimension

Within NATO, pressures for eastern enlargement came from a powerful trans-governmental coalition comprising the German Defence Ministry and a group of officials in the Clinton administration around Anthony Lake (Clinton's national security adviser). As the inter-ministerial debate on NATO enlargement intensified in the course of 1993, the Chancellor, Helmut Kohl, mindful of the need to preserve a good working relation-ship with his coalition partner, the FDP, initially supported Kinkel's position. Kohl also shared the Foreign Ministry's concern that early NATO enlargement would place a serious strain on German-Russian relations. In addition, Rühe's advocacy of NATO enlargement had received a lukewarm response from senior Bundeswehr officers. Given the constellation of domestic political and institutional forces arrayed against him, Rühe focused on cementing trans-governmental alliances with the USA and the East Central Europeans.

The key was the USA (Goldgeier 1998). Rühe worked closely with Richard Holbrooke, who was appointed US Assistant Secretary of State for European Affairs in the summer of 1994, with special responsibility for 'enforcing' policy on NATO enlargement within the Clinton administration. Rühe had forged a good relationship with Holbrooke during the latter's stint as US ambassador to Bonn. Rühe also took the novel decision to commission a study on public attitudes towards NATO enlargement by the California-based US think tank, the RAND Corporation. He recognised that in doing so, he would indirectly exert influence on the US Senate, whose support for a future enlargement of NATO would be crucial. In addition, Rühe worked closely with NATO Secretary General Manfred Wörner[6] and US Secretary of State Les Aspen in the autumn of 1993 to draw up proposals for the Partnership for Peace programme. This, they hoped, would be an instrument for preparing the ground for a future Eastern enlargement of NATO. The Partnership for Peace idea was subsequently agreed at a NATO Ministerial Meeting in Travemünde, and later adopted as NATO policy at the Brussels NAC in January 1994 (NATO 1994).

Partnership for Peace was widely regarded as a compromise between those who favoured enlargement and those opposed to it. It provided for the development of new forms of functional military cooperation, aimed at facilitating future multilateral peace-support and non-article V operations involving both NATO and non-NATO members. Along with Russia, CIS states and the East Central Europeans, it included neutral and non-aligned countries such as Austria, Finland and Sweden. PfP members were invited to send permanent liaison officers to NATO headquarters in Brussels, and a separate Partnership Coordination Cell (PCC) was established at Mons in April 1994. In this way, Partnership for Peace was to provide one of the key planks of a new system of post-cold war security governance in Europe.

Whatever PfP's intrinsic merits (and they were manifold), its political function was to provide 'the necessary smoke-screen for an essentially political debate which was conducted within the alliance' on the question of NATO enlargement (Eyal 1997: 703). Between late 1993 and early 1994, the balance of opinion within the Alliance on the question of NATO enlargement shifted perceptibly in favour of enlargement. The change of opinion in the US administration was apparent shortly after the January 1994 Brussels summit, when President Clinton declared that 'the

question was no longer whether NATO will take in new members, but
when and how'. The debate raged throughout 1994 – largely behind
closed doors – and by December 1994, enlargement had become
inevitable. In early 1995 NATO prepared a 'Study on Enlargement', which
was published in September 1995. This spelt out the political criteria governing NATO's 'opening' to the East. Sensing the shift in the middle
ground on the issue – particularly the changed mood in Washington –
Chancellor Kohl revised his stance, and in April 1995 instructed Foreign
Minister Kinkel to formally endorse NATO enlargement. During his visit
to Poland in July 1995, Kohl officially de-coupled the processes of EU and
NATO enlargement, thereby making clear his support for an early
enlargement of NATO (Hampton 1998: 90).

With the clear triumph within NATO of the US–German trans-
governmental coalition in favour of enlargement, two further questions
needed to be resolved. The first was which states to invite to join the
Alliance. In the lead-up to the Madrid NATO Summit in July 1997, two
additional contenders emerged alongside the three front-runners
(Poland, Czech Republic and Hungary): Romania, which enjoyed strong
French backing, and Slovenia. Once again, there were differences within
the German government on this issue. Volker Rühe strongly supported
the US view of limited enlargement. The Chancellor's Office, on the other
hand, leaned more towards the French position. Kinkel and the Foreign
Minister occupied the middle ground, arguing that the German government 'could also support the larger solution, namely four or five members' (quoted in Kamp 1998: 177). In the end, US insistence on a limited
enlargement was accepted by other NATO members, and invitations were
issued to the three Central European aspirants. Nonetheless, the Madrid
communiqué offered indirect encouragement to Romania and Slovenia,
along with the three Baltic states (Lithuania, Latvia and Estonia), by com-
mentating on the 'positive developments' and 'progress' achieved by
these 'aspiring members' (NATO 1997: paragraph 8).

The second key issue was how to minimise Russian opposition
(Ruehl 1994). Here again, Germany played a central role. NATO hoped
that by offering a strategic partnership between the Alliance and Russia,
Moscow's opposition to NATO enlargement would be diluted. Chancellor Kohl was particularly concerned to bring the Russians on board,
and played a leading role in diplomatic initiatives designed to cement a
new partnership between Russia and NATO. The result was the Founding Act of May 1997, which provided for the creation of a Permanent
Joint Council (PJC). The Founding Act was very much a product of

US–German cooperation. Germany and the USA provided the 'greatest stimuli for negotiations and for the agreement's wording', and the Act's 'decisive passages were formulated in Washington's State Department and in the Foreign Office in Bonn in collaboration with NATO headquarters in Brussels' (Kamp 1997: 317). The precise role and powers of the PJC were left deliberately ambiguous, given the different aspirations of the parties involved. NATO believed it would offer Russia a voice in European security issues, without giving them a veto over NATO's policy. The Russians, however, hoped it would provide them with effective leverage over NATO's actions – particularly in terms of future enlargements.

The decision to offer invitations to join NATO to Poland, the Czech Republic and Hungary was finally taken at the NATO summit in Madrid in July 1997. These three countries became full members on 12 March 1999. With the conclusion of this first wave of enlargement, Germany has achieved an important policy goal in terms of 'milieu shaping'. German enthusiasm for further enlargement has subsequently waned, and Berlin is unlikely to play as pivotal a role in future enlargement debates as it did in the first. For Germany and the Alliance as a whole, future enlargement poses some difficult questions. The second and subsequent rounds of enlargement are likely to be much more difficult and controversial than the first round. There is no consensus within NATO on which aspirant countries to invite, although individual members have their preferred candidates. Russia would react strongly if an invitation were offered to Estonia or Latvia. More importantly, further enlargement could weaken the political coherence of the Alliance, and make it more difficult to reach consensus on future NATO policy. Yet not to continue with the enlargement process would generate enormous disappointment in aspirant countries, and raise equally difficult questions about NATO's ultimate purpose.

Chancellor Schröder's government has not yet reached a clear position on the next wave of NATO enlargement. The previous government had been divided on the issue. Volker Rühe insisted that he would support a 'southern round' of enlargement (Romania and Slovenia), but argued that it was essential not to further disrupt cooperation with Russia by offering NATO membership to any of the Baltic three. Klaus Kinkel, on the other hand, saw himself as an 'advocate' of the Baltic states, and was more concerned to address their security concerns. In early 1998, however, both ministries and the Chancellor's Office agreed to a common position: they would oppose an early commitment to a new round of enlargement, and – if the US insisted on a second round – seek to confine it to as few candidates as possible (Kamp 1998: 178).

This view on future NATO enlargement reflects a broader consensus within the German foreign and security policy establishment. It is widely recognised that a public commitment to a continuation of the enlargement process is essential in order to encourage an on-going process of reform in aspirant countries. It is also felt that Germany's standing in NATO would suffer if it were seen to champion membership only for its immediate neighbours. On balance, German opinion seems to favour a process of consolidation and internal restructuring within NATO, and a desire to slow down the NATO enlargement process and re-couple it to the process of EU enlargement. Germany may agree to the membership of Slovenia and Lithuania, and possibly Romania. But it is widely recognised in Berlin that the offer of NATO membership to Estonia and Latvia would precipitate a major crisis in relations with Russia. This would undermine the system of cooperative security governance in Europe that is a primary goal of German grand strategy. Finally, there are tough questions about the future size and membership of the Alliance, given that the larger NATO becomes, the more problematic it is to reach consensus on key issues. Germany is therefore likely to advocate a cautious approach towards subsequent rounds of NATO enlargement, preferring instead to concentrate diplomatic time and energy on EU enlargement.

Cooperative security governance and military crisis management

NATO enlargement dominated German and European security debates for much of the 1990s. In doing so, it largely obscured a more important question: the nature and purpose of NATO, and the role of military force in Europe. These two questions touched sensitive nerves in Gemany, and have led to a partial redefinition of its identity as a *Zivilmacht*.

The first question to consider is the role and function of the Atlantic Alliance in a post-Soviet world. Given the central part NATO has traditionally played in German security policy, this question has far-reaching implications for Germany's approach to the reshaping of European order.

'NATO the elephant'

According to the parable of the blind men and the elephant, there was once a group of blind men who set themselves the task of trying to understand the 'essence' of the elephant. The problem was that as they explored the elephant with their hands, they reached very different conclusions.

Some were most struck by the tusks, and formed an impression of the elephant as a fierce beast. Others were struck by the enormous ears, or the trunk, and formed other impressions of the elephant as a gentle, if not comical, creature. The result was a lively, but inconclusive debate about what constituted the 'essence' of the elephant (Lindfors 1999: 1; see also Puchala 1972).

The metaphor of the elephant is particularly apt when it comes to the contemporary debate on NATO's essential 'role' or 'purpose'. The fact that NATO's Eastern enlargement took place days before the Alliance embarked on its first offensive military campaign raised an awkward question for its members, old and new – what was the essential purpose of NATO? What was the rationale of an Alliance created, in the words of its first Secretary General, Lord Ismay, 'to keep the Russians out, the Americans in, and the Germans down'? This fundamental question had been largely obscured by the controversies surrounding NATO enlargement (Vogel 1997), but was laid bare by the Kosovo campaign.

Like the elephant, NATO has a number of distinct features, each of which is accorded different weight by different observers. First, NATO offers collective territorial defence guarantees, enshrined in Article V of the Washington Treaty. Second, it institutionalises a permanent US security presence in Western Europe, thereby providing the organisational buckle of the transatlantic relationship. Third, it has created a multilateral system of defence cooperation designed to prevent conflict through institutionalised cooperation (historically important given concerns about Germany, and of more contemporary relevance given continued tensions between Turkey and Greece). Fourth, it provides an institutional basis for developing forms of cooperative security governance in postcommunist Central and Eastern Europe. Fifth, it institutionalises a 'community of values' (*Wertegemeinschaft*) based on human rights, democratic government, the rule of law and the peaceful resolution of disputes (Schimmelfennig 1998). It is thus the organisational embodiment of the 'Western Community'. Finally, it facilitates practical military cooperation for non-Article V contingency operations such as the Gulf War, peace support operations such as Bosnia, and offensive campaigns such as the aerial bombardment of Serbia (March–June 1999). This has been dubbed the 'IFOR/SFOR model of NATO' (Schulte 1997).

In the course of the 1990s, the relative importance of these six key roles changed significantly. NATO began to mean different things to different people as the consensus on NATO's post-cold war security rationale began to fragment (Sloan and Forrest 1997). For its original cold war members, the Article V collective defence guarantee lost its over-riding importance. However, for the Central and East Europeans who aspired to NATO membership, Article V security guarantees were what they most coveted. They saw Article V as very *raison d'être* of the Alliance, and were little interested in military crisis management operations in the Balkans or the Gulf. By contrast, the USA increasingly came to see in NATO a potential instrument for global power projection in defence of 'common interests', and as the primary forum for exerting influence over European developments (Dembinski 1999).

For Germany, on the other hand, NATO's primary utility no longer stems from its Article V security guarantees. NATO remains vital to Germany because it provides a multilateral framework for its security and defence policy. The US link also remains important, but its relative significance vis-à-vis Germany's foreign and security policy partnership with France has declined. As regards NATO's future role, Germany's preference is for NATO to function as an instrument for building cooperative security governance in the post-communist East. Germany has also welcomed the development of the 'IFOR/SFOR' model of NATO, above all because it provides a way of reconciling a range of discrete foreign and security policy objectives.[7]

For much of the 1990s, serious discussion of NATO's post-cold war rationale was over-shadowed by the controversies stirred up by the enlargement debate. Stanley Horelik of the RAND Corporation made clear in his evidence to the US Senate that the end of the cold war had left NATO in a torpor. 'In the presence of this conceptual vacuum', he argued, 'virtually the entire burden of reviving NATO has been laid on enlargement. Frankly, this burden is a lot heavier than enlargement can bear' (quoted in Haslam 1998: 123). As is usually the case with NATO, the agenda on NATO's post-cold war purpose was driven by US concerns. Within the Clinton administration, a number of influential figures wanted to use NATO as the key instrument for restructuring European order. They believed this would reinforce US leadership in Europe and stimulate the transformation of NATO into an instrument for US-led military crisis management in defence of 'common interests'.

The testing-ground for this new US conception for NATO was the Balkans. The US-brokered Dayton accords established a clear military role for the Alliance as the organisational core of IFOR. With the perceived success of the IFOR/SFOR mission in Bosnia, American confidence in the ability of NATO to act as an instrument of crisis management grew. At the same time, many Europeans – including Germany – actively sought greater US engagement in the Balkans. In early 1998, for example, at a time of growing conflict between the UCK (the Kosovo Liberation Army) and Serbian security forces, the German Foreign Ministry lobbied Washington to provide 'political leadership'. This reflected their growing frustration at the EU's continued failure to develop a coherent foreign and security policy towards the region (Pradetto 1999: 810). By the end of 1998 it was evident that Washington had decided to use NATO as an instrument for exercising US leadership in reshaping European security. One indication of this new resolve came in early March 1999, when NATO Secretary General Solana argued in *The Economist* magazine that a 'key role for NATO will be to establish long-term stability in the Balkans' (Solana 1999: 29). Shortly afterwards, NATO responded to Serbian brutality in Kosovo by launching 'Operation Deliberate Force', an intensive air campaign against the rump Yugoslav Federation.

Kosovo and the dilemmas of humanitarian intervention
The Kosovo operation has been NATO's most ambitious effort to date to define a new role for itself, and constituted a watershed in the reshaping of post-cold war European security. After four decades of priding itself that it had achieved its goals without ever firing a shot in anger, the 'most successful Alliance in history' embarked on a massive aerial bombardment of a sovereign state. For some, this presaged an ambitious attempt to redefine the basis of European order and the instruments with which it would be forged. The new basis of European order, it seemed, was to be human rights, as understood and practised in the West, not state sovereignty, as it had been since Westphalia (Habermas 1999). The vehicle for enforcing these human rights standards would be NATO, and its instrument would be military force. Consequently, Ulrich Beck suggested, Kosovo represented a defining moment in European history: the end of the Westphalian system and the birth of 'postnational war' based on a 'militaristic humanism'. Rather than war as a continuation of politics by other means, war was now to be a continuation of human rights by other means (Beck 1999).

'Operation Deliberate Force' – the sustained aerial assault on Yugoslav military and special police units, along with the civic infrastructure of the Yugoslav Federation that supported them – constituted a decisive watershed in post-cold war Europe. NATO's intervention took place without a UN Security Council mandate, and with an ambiguous status under international law (Preuß 1999; Bring 1999). It was bitterly condemned by Russia, and precipitated the worse crisis in Russia's relations with the

West since the end of the cold war. The questionable success of the operation, combined with the lack of political will to commit ground troops, places a question mark over the future of such operations. It certainly does not suggest that NATO has succeeded in defining a new role for itself. On the contrary, Kosovo demonstrates that the Alliance continues to face a series of questions about its future rationale and purpose.

Bundeswehr participation in Operation Deliberate Force was certainly a defining moment in the politics of the new Germany. For the first time since 1945, German forces engaged in offensive military operations against a sovereign state. This historic watershed was all the more remarkable because it took place under a 'Red–Green' coalition government, and without a clear UN mandate. Germany's participation in the Kosovo campaign was motivated by three primary considerations. First, a desire to demonstrate its reliability as a loyal NATO ally and partner to the USA. Second, a concern to prevent a wave of refugees heading for Germany and the EU. Third, a normative impulse to respond to ethnic cleansing and widespread violations of human rights. This third factor reflects the continuing impact of Germany's self-perception as a *Zivilmacht* motivated by moral and political concerns to act multilaterally in defence of victims of aggression and persecution. It also reflects the influence of the generation change that has taken place in Germany and a number of other Western countries in recent years. In the case of Germany, this generation change came about following the September 1998 Bundestag elections, and is symbolised by the coming to power of the 'sixty-eighter' generation of Joschka Fischer and Gerhard Schröder. For this generation, human rights concerns are central to their political beliefs, and have been used to give political coherence, direction and legitimacy to their foreign policy objectives (Pradetto 1999: 808).

Given its long-term commitment to fostering a pan-European cooperative security system, the Red–Green coalition pursued a twin-track policy towards the Kosovo crisis. On the one hand, full support for, and participation in, NATO's bombing campaign; on the other, intensive diplomatic efforts to find a solution to the crisis. Given its presidency of the EU, Germany played a pivotal role in negotiations to find a solution to the Kosovo war and to bring peace to the wider region. This involved strenuous diplomatic efforts to involve the UN and Russia in the search for peace.

The emphasis attached to involving Moscow in efforts to reach a negotiated settlement reflects Germany's awareness of the importance of Russia as a partner in a cooperative European security system. Forging such a cooperative security system has been a key aim of post-cold war German foreign policy, and the Red–Green government was concerned to minimise the damage caused by differences over NATO enlargement and the Kosovo war. Throughout the Kosovo war, a steady stream of German diplomats and political leaders travelled to Moscow. The German government also encouraged the Americans to intensify their dialogue with Moscow, and placed considerable emphasis on the G8 as the forum for building a political settlement with Russia. This diplomatic strategy bore fruit at the G8 summit in Bonn, at which a set of 'principles' was agreed for ending the conflict.

The German government's long-established preference for non-military conflict prevention and multilateral cooperation was illustrated by the 'Stability Pact for Southeast Europe'. Germany, as president of the EU, took the initiative in developing this pact, which was designed to stabilise the region through economic investment and support, coupled with the perspective of developing closer relations with the EU, up to and including membership (Ehrhart 1999). The Stability Pact was launched by EU ministers on 10 June 1999 with the former head of the German Federal Chancellory, Bobo Hombach, as its special coordinator (Hombach 1999). Alongside the promotion of economic reform, the pact seeks to develop a new pan-European security system under the auspices of the OSCE based on conflict prevention, and to strengthen the process of democratisation in the region (Rueb 1999: 22–3).

The Kosovo campaign generated a lively debate in Germany that revolved around three key questions. First, the lack of a UN mandate. This was clearly problematic from the start, and violated the Schröder government's previous insistence on 'an unequivocal mandate under international law'.[8] Even if there is a 'right' to humanitarian intervention, self-mandating by NATO sets a dangerous precedent internationally. Joschka Fischer subsequently stressed the 'exceptional' character of Kosovo, and argued that it did not set a precedent for NATO to abrogate to itself the role of 'world policeman'.

Second, the relationship of means to ends. If the end of this military intervention was to prevent genocide and ethnic cleansing, why was there such opposition in the Bundestag to committing ground troops? If *Nie wieder Auschwitz* ('No More Auschwitz') was the moral justification for this intervention, why were so few Germans willing to risk casualties in order to achieve this end (Mayer 1999). How effective was bombing as a means of humanitarian intervention? Did bombing prevent a human catastrophe, or precipitate one?

Third, was a more effective European Common Foreign and Security Policy (CFSP) and a distinctive European Security and Defence Identity (ESDI) more or less necessary after Kosovo? US leadership was clearly crucial to the bombing campaign, but it also raised concerns in some quarters about America's 'arrogance of power'. Such concerns were fuelled by the US Senate's subsequent rejection of the Comprehensive Test Ban Treaty (CTBT) in October 1999, along with indications that the USA was becoming more and more frustrated by the slow and ponderous decision-making processes of multilateral bodies such as the UN, WTO and even NATO. This points to a future source of tension in German foreign policy. On the one hand, the BRD has sought to cultivate a close transatlantic partnership with Washington, and to play the role of 'loyal transatlantic ally'. On the other, Germany regards itself as a *Zivilmacht* committed to multilateral cooperation and the rule of international law. Given its dominant international power position, the USA seems less and less willing to constrain itself by multilateral structures – by the UN, the CTBT or NATO. If in the future the USA chooses to by-pass multilateral institutions and treaties and calls on its allies to support it, Germany may find itself caught in a new role conflict: either to act as a 'loyal ally', or as a *Zivilmacht* committed to multilateralism.

'Cooperative security governance' in Europe

In the context of the debate on NATO's future role, a clear German preference is discernible. As has already been noted, there is a broad consensus across much of the political spectrum that NATO can best contribute to European order by functioning as an integral element of a cooperative European security system, rather than as an instrument of global military crisis management. This reflects Germany's post-war strategic culture, ingrained multilateralism and *Zivilmacht* identity. Karsten Voigt (1997: 39) has argued that such a cooperative security system should be based upon interlocking and functionally diverse institutions, consisting of the OSCE, the EU, the Council of Europe and regional or sub-regional organisations. An important element of such a cooperative security system is the network of arms control agreements and confidence- and security-building measures (CSBMs) agreed in the late 1980s and early 1990s, together with their intrusive verification regimes (Croft 1996: 129–31). Within this cooperative security system, NATO's role is to provide the hub of an emerging network of what can best be called 'security governance'.

The concept of security governance draws from the 'new institutionalism' (see pp. 61–3), regime theory and ideas concerning security communities. Regimes themselves constitute the 'building-blocks of international governance' (Rittberger 1993: 9). 'Security governance' thus refers to the broader corpus of regimes and informal governing arrangements within a regional security complex. These security arrangements generate 'patterned behaviour' based on implicit rules and understandings. They are governed by a distinct set of norms, in the sense of 'collective expectations about proper behaviour for a given identity' (Jepperson *et al.* 1996: 54). The notion of security governance thus refers to patterns of behaviour that are not simply a function of the balance of military forces or the 'hard' security guarantees of military alliances. Cooperative security governance is based on negotiation and policy coordination in a non-hierarchical environment, and consensual decision-making without coercive means of compliance (Rosenau 1997: 146). Such security governance can help reinforce cooperative patterns of behaviour and shared understandings, thereby generating the degree of trust and social capital upon which a stable peace order depends (Adler and Barnett 1998).

NATO contributes to cooperative security governance in Europe through fostering functional military and security cooperation, primarily in the framework of PfP, the EAPC (Euro-Atlantic Partnership Council), the Russia-NATO PJC (Permanent Joint Council) and the NATO-Ukrainian Charter.[9] This functional military and security cooperation derives from, and helps generate and reinforce, shared values and common interests. It also extends beyond the existing nineteen members of NATO to include both EU 'neutrals' and the new democracies of Central and East Europe. This was exemplified by the IFOR deployment in Bosnia, where a Nordic Brigade was created comprising NATO Danish and Norwegian troops, non-NATO Swedish, Finnish and Polish forces, and contingents from the Baltic States. This Nordic Brigade operated along-side Russian troops, 'all under US command and Alliance auspices' (Asmus and Nurick 1996: 136). This form of functional military cooperation reflects an influential German view that the 'most important task facing the transatlantic alliance after the Madrid Summit [is] to ensure that the barriers between NATO membership and non-membership become increasingly blurred' (Francke 1997: 19).

The nature of the new system of security governance emerging in post-cold war Europe can be illustrated by reference to the Baltic Sea region (Scharioth 1997: 34). The restructuring and 'Europeanisation' of NATO around the concept of Combined Joint Task Forces (CJTF) is strengthening the regional dimension of the Alliance (Lepgold 1998: 100–2). This is evident in the Baltic Sea region, where regionally based PfP exercises involving partner countries are being organised by the regional CJTF (Heurlin 1997: 6, 10). One interesting development is the suggestion that Sweden – as a non-NATO member and EU 'neutral' – could play a role in organising regional PfP exercises involving, inter alia, the Baltic states and Russia. This would strengthen NATO's security cooperation with the Baltic states without isolating Russia and fuelling further mistrust in Moscow.

If PfP and the EAPC were to be developed along such lines, NATO could be used to facilitate new forms of security cooperation and dialogue within a broader system of security governance involving other multilateral structures. These include the OSCE, the Council of Europe and the EU, along with regional organisations such as Council of Baltic Sea States (CBSS), the Central European Free Trade Association (CEFTA) or Black Sea Economic Cooperation (BSEC). The OSCE and the Council of Europe provide an important set of political and legal instruments for addressing the problems of democratic transition and minority rights throughout Central and Eastern Europe (Maeder-Metcalf 1997: 5). The EU, for its part, facilitates trade and deepening economic relations and provides a powerful stimulus for a comprehensive reform process. Finally, regional organisations such as the CBSS encourage functional cooperation on issues such as environmental protection, trade, policy harmonisation and transnational crime. Such functional diversity within an interlocking arrangement of multilateral organisations could provide the foundation for a new system of cooperative security governance in Europe.

Germany's preference is certainly for a post-cold war system of European order involving interlocking institutions, security governance and functional diversity. The Federal Republic favours multilateral security cooperation based on shared values and principles, and hopes that such a framework will make it possible to address a range of security issues – from transnational criminal organisations to environmental degradation – on a cooperative and multilateral basis. This perspective underpins the German preference for NATO as an intrinsic element of this cooperative security system.

The development of such a system of cooperative security governance is feasible in the Baltic Sea region given its regional and historical identity (often associated with the concept of a 'new Hansa'); the influence of the Nordic countries; and the success in managing regional ethnonational tensions. Similar forms of cooperative security governance have also emerged in Central and Eastern Europe – embracing the Visegrad countries and Slovenia; and extending into Bulgaria and Romania in the South East, and Ukraine in the East. In some respects, the first round of NATO enlargement has reinforced cooperative security governance in Central and Eastern Europe, in particular, because of Poland's key role as a bridge between the Alliance and its strategic partners, Lithuania and Ukraine (Feldman and Gareis 1998; Tedstrom 1997: 18). Russia's relationship to these nascent forms of security governance is more ambiguous, particularly after Kosovo. Despite a wave of anti-Western sentiment, Russia has not excluded itself from these developing forms of security governance – most notably in the Baltic Sea region, the one point at which Russia is in direct geographical contact with the 'West' (more specifically, the EU).

Despite its obvious preference for security governance, however, tough questions remain which Germany needs to confront more than its European partners. What happens when security governance breaks down? How should Germany and its allies deal with areas (such as the Balkans or the Caucasus) where intractable conflicts make the emergence of security governance highly problematic? How should the West respond to ethnic cleansing, atrocities and widespread violations of human rights? Is there now a right to humanitarian intervention, superseding the Westphalian principle of non-intervention in the internal affairs of sovereign states (Brock 1999)? If so, who has the right to act, and under what authority? Should humanitarian intervention only take place with a UN Security Council mandate, or does NATO have the right to mandate itself to intervene? The fact that these questions are now at the heart of the European security agenda illustrates the extent to which the pillars of the Westphalian system have disintegrated, and suggests that a new 'neo-medieval' system of order based on human rights and ethical concerns is beginning to evolve.

NATO's new security concept

Questions of humanitarian intervention and military crisis management were central to the debates surrounding the historic fiftieth anniversary summit of NATO in Washington in April 1999. This was initially billed as the occasion for a triumphant anniversary celebrations, at which its three new members would be formally welcomed into the fold. In the event, however, the mood in Washington was decidedly sombre. The summit took place at a moment when NATO was engaged in major military operations against a sovereign state, and any anniversary celebrations were overshadowed by unfolding tragedy in Kosovo.

The most important outcome of the Washington summit was the long-awaited 'new strategic concept', which was to provide a clear definition of NATO's post-cold war mission. The debate on the new strategic concept had revolved around three key issues. First, the core functions of the Alliance. There was a broad consensus that collective defence, transatlantic partnership and reinforcing security should remain core tasks. However, Washington favoured giving military crisis management, if not an equal weight with collective defence, then at least a prominent place in the ranking of NATO's core tasks. Indeed, some influential US security analysts advocated giving NATO a key role in tackling threats to global energy sources, proliferation and terrorism (Dembinski 1999: 789). Linked to the question of its core tasks was the second question, the geographical reach of the Alliance. Should NATO be an instrument for world-wide crisis management, or confine itself to crises in and around Europe? Madeline Albright advocated the transformation of NATO into a 'force for peace from the Middle East to Central Africa'. On the other hand, the majority of Europeans – including the Germans – favoured a more limited and regionally focused role for the Alliance (Kamp 1998). Third, the problem of mandating non-Article V operations: could NATO mandate itself, or could the legitimacy of such operations only be provided by a UN Security Council resolution. Whilst the US resisted any restrictions on the Alliance's freedom of action, Germany, France and most European democracies argued that an international mandate was essential for non-Article V operations (Pradetto 1999: 806; Assembly of the WEU 1999: 5).

In the end, the new strategic concept agreed at the Washington summit was a classic compromise document which sought to shroud underlying policy differences in ambiguous diplomatic formulae. The Alliance's 'fundamental security tasks' were defined as follows: first, providing 'one of the indispensable foundations for a stable Euro-Atlantic security environment' based on democratic institutions and the peaceful resolution of disputes. Second: transatlantic 'consultation' on their 'vital interests'. Third: 'deterrence and defence'. In addition, NATO was to 'enhance the security and stability of the Euro-Atlantic area' through 'crisis-management' and 'wide-ranging partnership, cooperation and dialogue with other countries in the Euro-Atlantic area, with the aim of increasing transparency, mutual confidence and the capacity for joint action with the Alliance' (i.e., what has been termed above, *cooperative security governance*). The precise geographical borders of the 'Euro-Atlantic area' were, however, not defined. It was also noted that the security interests of members could be adversely affected by developments in distant regions. The document skirted around the thorny question of the mandate, arguing that crisis response activity must be 'consistent with international law', without explicitly mentioning the need for a UN mandate. In conclusion, whilst the new strategic concept sought to provide some broad definitions of 'NATO's enduring purpose and nature and its fundamental security tasks', in practice the Alliance's future role in European order will be determined by the lessons Alliance members draw from the Kosovo war.

Thus despite the advent of the long-awaited new strategic concept, the debate on NATO's post-cold war role and purpose will remain. The Kosovo operation posed as many questions as it settled, and has therefore not given a precedent for future Alliance policy. The main lesson of 'Operation Deliberate Force' has been the enormous problems and dilemmas associated with humanitarian intervention. Rather than heralding the advent of a new system of European order based on the categorical imperative of human rights, Kosovo indicates that the Europeans have entered uncharted territory. European order is no longer solidly based on Westphalian principles of territorial sovereignty, but neither is it clear who has the authority to respond to gross violations of human rights, and how. As Defence Minister Rudolf Scharping has written (1999: 222–3), a 'new balance between two principles of international law needs to be worked out, namely state sovereignty and the universal validity of human rights. The conflict over Kosovo, the intervention against genocide and major crimes against humanity, is hopefully the start of such an international learning process'. Given the problems NATO faced in trying to achieve its objectives by bombing, and the fact that it now finds itself committed to a long-term presence in the Balkans, Alliance members are likely to be much more cautious before embarking on similar forms of humanitarian intervention. At best, 'coalitions of the willing' involving selected groups of NATO members may be formed to deal with specific security problems.

There are also some indications that one consequence of Kosovo will be intensified efforts to develop a more effective and coherent European Security and Defence Identity (ESDI). The German government has certainly signalled a strong interest in developing an EU capacity to conduct a robust Common Foreign and Security Policy (CFSP), including a military option. This will probably involve using NATO assets under a WEU 'hat' on the basis of the CJTF concept, although what this means in practice is still not clear. German interest in reinvigorating the CFSP was evident at the Cologne EU summit in June 1999, which outlined a strategy for absorbing the WEU into the EU in order to give the latter the capability to conduct 'Petersberg tasks' (i.e., conflict prevention and peace support operations). As we shall see in the following chapter, this opens the way for the EU to play a potentially more active foreign policy role in the reshaping of European order in the twenty-first century.

Conclusion: Germany as a 'normal' Zivilmacht

The preceding discussion suggests three main conclusions about German security policy. First, for a state that has grown through unification with its eastern sibling, and found itself in a radically transformed geostrategic environment, German security policy has demonstrated remarkable continuity. Germany remains broadly committed to a multilateral security policy, and to a security concept that attaches considerable emphasis to the non-military determinants of security and insecurity. The exception that proves the rule is May 1997, when German troops were deployed to help in the evacuation of EU citizens from Albania. More generally, German policy is aimed at consolidating and expanding the transatlantic security community, whilst fostering a pan-European cooperative security order. This reflects Germany's distinctive post-war strategic culture and its continuing self-identity as a *Zivilmacht* – albeit what can be termed a 'normal' *Zivilmacht*. 'German national security culture', it has been argued, 'has placed distinct boundaries on the discourse employed by German political leaders, and it has clearly proscribed some theoretically possible policy responses, such as unilateral military actions (Duffield 1998: 220).

Second, while the strategic direction and underlying policy concepts guiding German security policy have proven remarkably resilient in the 1990s, some new accents have emerged. These are primarily to do with how the strategic aims of German security policy are implemented. The most significant development in this regard is the increasing use of both smaller groupings of states (what is sometimes called 'minilateralism'). Given the problems of making policy in larger multilateral fora such as NATO or the CFSP, Germany has sought to coordinate and define specific policy approaches in smaller groupings.[10] The prime example here is the contact group, which coordinated policy towards former Yugoslavia. Its creation reflected the frustration felt in EU circles over Greece's idiosyncratic Balkan policy, which made consensus in the CFSP impossible. Another example is the G8 (the seven leading economic nations plus Russia). The G8 has become an increasingly important forum for international crisis prevention and management, as its role in ending the Kosovo conflict demonstrated (Dini 1999: 7). Germany is also involved with the 'Group of Five' (Germany, US, Russia, UK and France), which was established through a French initiative. Finally, Germany has encouraged the use of trilateral groupings, such as the Weimar Triangle (Baas 1999), the German–Polish–Danish corps, and the trilateral summits of France, Russia and Germany.

As Vladimir Handl has noted, these minilateral initiatives occupy an 'institutional grey-zone' between multilateralism and unilateralism. The use of informal groupings of states to formulate a common approach to specific policy issues can generate suspicions of a cartel of 'great powers', and may generate worries about Germany's great power ambitions. In general, however, the increasing use of minilateralism is not necessarily an indication that Germany is reverting to great power and *Machtpolitik* inclinations. On the contrary, the Weimar Triangle, for example, represents an interesting attempt to 'multilateralize its Ostpolitik' (Freudenstein 1998: 53). At the same time, the use of the Contact Group represents a pragmatic response to the difficulties of decision-making in larger fora such as the North Atlantic Council (NAC) and the CFSP. The problem of reaching consensus among a large group of states is one that will become increasingly acute as both NATO and the EU enlarge to the East, and will require considerable diplomatic finesse if it is not to undermine collective decision-making in larger multilateral fora.

Third, the most significant shift in German foreign and security policy since unification has been on the question of the use of the Bundeswehr for non-Article V 'out-of-area' missions. Indeed, the debate on the out-of-area question has constituted the most divisive foreign policy issue in the Federal Republic since that over Ostpolitik in the late 1960s to early 1970s (Müller 1994: 131). Constitutional restrictions on non-article V Bundeswehr operations have now been lifted, and Bundeswehr deployments in both Bosnia and Kosovo enjoyed broad public support. However, the influence of a *Zivilmacht* identity continues to be felt, and strong political conditions are likely to surround the use of the Bundeswehr for non-article V missions in the future. While it may be possible to mobilise political support in the Bundestag and wider public for military operations with a strongly 'humanitarian' dimension, reservations will remain about other military deployments – particularly those outside of the Euro-Atlantic area (Kamp 1999: 11).

Future debates on German security policy will thus tend to revolve around two fundamental issues. First, the 'agenda of Clausewitz': namely how best to employ military force in pursuit of political objectives.

Second, the 'agenda of Thomas Aquinas': i.e., upon what principles can a contemporary theory of 'Just War' be constructed? (Mayer 1999)[11] At the point where these two debates converge, German identity as a *Zivilmacht* is being redefined. For some, Germany's participation was the confirmation they have been seeking that the Berlin Republic has finally cast aside its civilian power identity and is now ready and willing to act as a 'normal' great power, deploying deliberative military power for political and strategic objectives.

On closer examination, this version of the 'normalisation' thesis is deeply flawed. The evidence from the 1990s suggests that German security policy remains deeply coloured by the Federal Republic's ingrained identity as a *Zivilmacht*. As Harald Müller has argued (1999: 164), 'the security-political culture of the Federal Republic is as before overwhelmingly civilian'. This is evident from three episodes: the August 1994 Federal Constitutional Court judgment on insults to soldiers; the exhibition on the war crimes of the Wehrmacht; and the legal rehabilitation of Second World War deserters. More recently, the *Zivilmacht* character of German society was demonstrated during the Kosovo campaign. Public manifestations of concern to prevent human suffering; the evident desire to avoid civilian casualties; the emphasis on using Bundeswehr resources to provide humanitarian assistance for refugee camps in Macedonia and Albania; and the strenuous efforts on the part of the Schröder government to reach a negotiated settlement – all these actions offer strong evidence to suggest that the Berlin Republic remains, at heart, a civilian power.

In contrast to the Bonn Republic, however, the Berlin Republic is now a 'normal' civilian power. The political and reservations which the Bonn Republic had towards the use of military force for anything other than territorial defence under Article V of the NATO Treaty gave its 'civilian power' status a decidedly stunted and one-dimensional quality. The Berlin Republic is now willing to use military force for humanitarian purposes within a multilateral framework. It has therefore finally evolved into a 'normal' civilian power, comparable to other mature democracies in the Euro-Atlantic security community. Kosovo has underlined this fact, not changed it.

Notes

1 '*The concept of strategic culture refers* to a nation's traditions, values, attitudes, patterns of behaviour, habits, symbols, achievements and particular ways of adapting to the environment and solving problems with respect to the threat

or use of force ... *The strategic culture of a nation derives from* its history, geography and political culture, and it represents the aggregation of attitudes and patterns of behaviour of the most influential voices; these may be, depending on the nation, the political elite, the military establishment and/or public opinion. *A strategic culture defines a set of patterns* of and for a nation's behaviour on war and peace issues. It helps shape but does not determine how a nation interacts with others in the security field. Other explanations (e.g. technological push) play a greater or lesser role in particular circumstances. Strategic culture helps shape behaviour on such issues as the use of force in international politics, sensitivity to external dangers, civil–military relations, and strategic doctrine. *As a result of continuities* in these matters, it is legitimate to talk about a particular national "style" in the theory and practice of strategy' (Ken Booth in Jacobsen 1990: xvi).

2 See 'Deutsche Aussen- und Sicherheitspolitik bei der Internationale Krisenbewältigung Seit 1990', *Stichworte zur Sicherheitspolitik*, no. 12 (December 1997), 34–8 (p. 35).

3 While the official German 'White Book' on defence policy of 1994 stated that Germany may participate in out-of-area operations, it also insisted that 'it will always be the case that Germany will never act alone, but only with her allies and partners' (*Weißbuch* 1994: 30).

4 Srebenica was the largest mass killing since the Second World War, and provided the most extreme manifestation of Serb aggression. On 8 July 1995, Serb forces led by General Radko Mladic surrounded the UN 'Safe Area' at Srebenica, where over 30,000 Muslims had sought refuge. For the next two days Serb forces shelled the Safe Area. Those Muslims who tried to escape where hunted down and killed. It is estimated that as many 3,000 died in the surrounding countryside to the north and west. The senior UN commander in Bosnia refused to launch air attacks on the Serbs – at one point, because the wrong form was used to request them. Dutch peacekeeping troops deployed in the Safe Area were primarily concerned with their own safety rather than defending the Safe Area. On 11 July they surrendered the Safe Area to the Serbs, and cooperated with them in handing over the Muslim refugees to their care. By 17 July over 4,000 Muslim men and boys abandoned by the UN peacekeepers had been systematically murdered by Serb troops. See Henry Porter, 'Days of Shame', in *The Guardian*, G2, 17 November 1999, 2–3.

5 On his book on the Kosovo war, Defence Minister Scharping quotes a newspaper interview with a gynaecologist, Monika Hauser, who explained her change of mind on the use of military force as follows: 'I was a pacifist feminist when I went to Bosnia in 1995. But I realised that in this situation, pacifism is a luxury-article. I think that when one cannot make any further progress with democratic means, then there is no other way. Milosevic must be sent to the Hague. This regime must go' (Scharping 1999: 137).

6 NATO Secretary-General Wörner, a former German Defence Minister, was also a keen advocate of enlargement. In September 1993, for example, he gave

a speech at the International Institute of Strategic Studies in Brussels in which he stated that: 'NATO is not a closed society. We have always said that the option for membership is open. My view is that the time has come for us to offer a concrete perspective to the countries of Central and Eastern Europe who want to join NATO, and whom we regard as possible candidates for future membership' (Hampton 1998: 88).

7 As Marie-Janine Calic has argued, this IFOR/SFOR model of NATO has a number of advantages from a German perspective. First, participation in the multinational stabilisation force has helped legitimise out-of-area deployments for the Bundeswehr, and thus been an important part of the 'normalisation' of post-unification German foreign policy. Second, 'this model has reconciled divergent, namely pro-American and pro-French, foreign political objectives. Through the deployment of US troops in Bosnia, it has, on the one hand, addressed Germany's strategic interest in a strong and visible American commitment to European security matters. It has, on the other hand, been conducive to strengthening the German–French core through the establishment of the German–French brigade in Bosnia. Generally, French agreement to participate in IFOR under US command has been interpreted as a big step forward for the new European security architecture'. Third, it has provided a practical manifestation of security cooperation with Russia, to which Germany in particular is committed. 'In summary, from the German point of view there are many reasons to believe that the IFOR/SFOR model is, for the time being, more efficient in serving simultaneously military and institutional interests than a pure EU-WEU model' (Calic 1998: 18).

8 At the Wehrkunde conference in Munich on 6 February 1999, Chancellor Schröder made the German position clear: 'But the readiness to assume more responsibility also means that international, out-of-area military missions must be based on an unequivocal mandate under international law. As a rule, this would be a mandate from the UN Security Council or action under the aegis of the OSCE. A community defined by values, such as our transatlantic Alliance, cannot afford to be complacent on this issue. This principle may only be abandoned in exceptional cases: to prevent humanitarian catastrophes and grave violations of human rights, i.e., when immediate action is urgently called for on humanitarian grounds' (quoted in Assembly of the WEU 1999: 9).

9 In his comments to the Hanns Seidel Stiftung in Munich on 4 November 1997, NATO Secretary-General Solana argued that the Alliance 'has assumed the role of catalyst for increased cooperation and integration in Europe. Through the Alliance's cooperative approach, almost all countries in the Euro-Atlantic area are now bound together in a common commitment to a more peaceful, stable future'. In this regard he stressed the importance of the Partnership for Peace programme, which has 'created a pattern of interaction, cooperation and joint activity among the military and defence structures of Allies and 27 Partner countries in Europe (*Atlantic News* 31: 2963, 7 November 1997).

10 'Bonn will follow a double strategy more visibly than in the past. It will try first to launch activity via the EU, but if this leads to no tangible success in a decent timespan, it will cooperate with a smaller group or with partners from outside the Union. France and the USA are the favoured partners in such circumstance. This strategy of "changing partners in the diplomatic dance" is more likely to be forced on Germany from outside than it would be an expression of German national strife' (Rummel 1996: 60).

11 Aquinas argues that there are a number of conditions under which a war may be declared 'just'. First, war must be declared by a proper authority, not by private individuals. In contemporary terms, this suggests that humanitarian intervention requires a legitimate international mandate, and cannot be underaken by individual states or groups of states on their own initiative. Second, even though war is declared by a legitimate authority for a just cause, it may not be just if there is a wicked intention. Aquinas argues that 'it is necessary that the belligerents should have a rightful intention, so that they intend the advancement of good or the avoidance of evil'. Aquinas approvingly quoted Augustine's remark that 'for the true followers of God even wars are peaceful, not being made for greed or out of cruelty, but from desire of peace, to restrain the evil and assist the good' (see Williams 1992: 37–9, and Boucher 1998: 197–9).

7

The European Union
and German *Europapolitik*

The practicability or objective reality of this idea of federation which is to
extend gradually over all states and so lead to perpetual peace can be shewn.
For, if Fortune ordains that a powerful and enlightened people should form
a republic, – which by its very nature is inclined to perpetual peace – this
would serve as a centre of federal union for other states wishing to join, and
thus secure conditions of freedom among the states in accordance with the
idea of the law of nations. Gradually, through different unions of this kind,
the federation would extend further and further.

(Kant 1795 [1992]: 134–5)

'Policy in Europe, from Europe and of Europe – this conviction is and
will remain the guiding principle of German foreign policy.' Chancellor
Gerhard Schröder's words from November 1999 clearly illustrate the
overriding centrality of *Europapolitik* to German foreign policy. 'The first
goal of German foreign policy', Schröder declared, 'is to strengthen
peace, security and a stable environment, upon which in the last instance
our prosperity depends. This involves above all the strengthening and
further development of the structures of European integration'
(Schröder 1999: 786).

The aim of this chapter is to consider the role of the EU in German
grand strategy, focusing on the process of eastern enlargement. The
chapter begins by examining the impact of the European Union on the
constitution of European order. The EU has been central to the process
of post-war West European reconciliation and has made a major contribution to the emergence of a Kantian *foedus pacificum* in the region, with
the *Bundesrepublik* at its core. With the end of the cold war, the European
Union has also come to exert a decisive influence on the new democracies in Central and Eastern Europe, all of which aspire to membership of
the Union. For these reasons, the EU is central to the Federal Republic's

grand strategy and is seen as the key to building a stable peace order in Europe.

This does not mean that Germany's *Europapolitik* is coherent and consistent. As we shall see, since unification and the end of the cold war, the Bonn Republic has pursued conflicting objectives and at times demonstrated a worrying lack of policy coherence. This stems from a role conflict at the heart of German EU policy – between deepening the integration process and enlarging the Union to the East. For most of the 1990s, the German government has denied the existence of this role conflict, insisting that the EU must be deepened in order to provide an 'anchor of stability' for the wider Europe. Further integration is necessary, they argue, in order to make the EU capable of absorbing new members and assuming additional responsibilities for pan-European order. However, this means that the appplicant countries are faced with moving goal posts and are struggling to join a Union that is surging ahead of them towards an 'ever closer union'.

The analysis of Germany and the European Union in the 1990s presented below concludes that the European integration process is on the verge of a fundamental change in its character and direction. Enlargement to the East will make the 'old EU' – what can be termed the 'EEC model' of West European 'deep integration' – ill-suited to a wider Europe growing together. The search is on for a new model of integration, with German academics and policy advisers at the forefront of this 'architectural modelling'. However, the demise of the 'old' EEC/EU, which has played such a crucial part in post-war European order and the *Westbindung* of the Bonn Republic, raises some profound – and disturbing – questions about the future of European order.

German identity and the European integration process

It is hard to over-emphasise the political and psychological importance of the European Union for the Federal Republic of Germany. Post-war West German identity has been decisively shaped by the Federal Republic's integration into the European Union, and this has profoundly coloured Germany's foreign policy role conceptions. The 'Federal Republic and European integration', it has been said, 'are like twins: neither can remember an existence independent of the other. In both economic and political terms the fate of one has a major impact on the other' (Bulmer and Paterson 1987: 15). Not surprisingly therefore, there have been 'scarcely any major differences in opinion over the objective of European integration among the political elite in Germany' (Rometsch 1996: 101).

'All in all', it has been noted, 'a consensus has emerged that the role and influence of Germany should be used to drive European integration forward' (Janning and Algieri 1996: 21).

Germany undoubtedly derives a number of political and economic benefits from the EU. However, the importance attached by German political and economic elites to the European integration process defies a rational cost-benefit analysis, and can only be understood by reference to post-war German identity and political culture. For most Germans, the EU is not simply a free-market zone or latter-day *Zollverein* ('customs union'). Neither is it simply a practical political, legal and administrative solution to economic and social problems. For Germany, the EU is a *Schicksalsgemeinschaft* (a 'community of common destiny'), united by a 'common identity, in a community of values with roots reaching back to the Christian Medieval and to the archaic ages' (Wolfgang Schäuble quoted in Mayer 1997: 726). As Chancellor Schröder declared, the EU 'is more than an alliance of individual nations for the purpose of increasing national prosperity'. It was and is, 'a political vision' shared by both France and Germany (*Frankfurter Allgemeine Zeitung*, 1 December 1999, p. 9).

For the overwhelmingly majority of Germans the EU has come to embody in institutional form a vision of a peaceful, democratic Europe based on institutionalised multilateral cooperation, shared values and common interests. What Tony Judt has called the 'foundation myth of modern Europe – that the European Community was and remains the kernel of a greater, pan-European project' has long been cherished in the *Bundesrepublik*. Support for the EU in Germany has been based on the widely shared belief that it 'was no Zollverein, no mere neo-mercantilist partnership of the rich and famous, no temporary practical solution to daily economic dilemmas. *This* Europe was the Europe of all Europeans – even if there were practical political impediments to their immediate membership of it' (Judt 1996: 41–2). Thus German *Europapolitik* must be understood in terms not of a utilitarian calculation of 'hard' interests, but in terms of a perception of its decisive contribution to peace and cooperation in Europe rooted deep in the identity of post-war West Germany.

The European Union

The EU and European order

Of all the institutions and organisations in contemporary Europe, the European Union is beyond doubt the most important. As we have seen in chapter 4, the European integration process has fundamentally transformed the dynamics of European order. This integration process has eroded defining features of the Westphalian states' system, and created 'an entirely new entity in world affairs; not a federal union, but a remarkable partnership both among states and between them and common institutions' (Hoffmann 1995: 289). The European integration process has provided a means of balancing institutionalised cooperation with the continuing heterogeneity of political communities in Europe. It has, therefore, provided the institutional basis for a *pluralistic* rather an *amalgamated* security community (Deutsch 1957).

The EU is not the only factor responsible for the emergence of this security community, which has been 'over-determined' by a series of related but distinct processes. Nonetheless, it is its most significant institutional expression, and helps ensure its continued stability and cohesion.[1] The role of the EU in facilitating the emergence of a security community in Western Europe has endowed it with the authority to exert a much broader influence on European order more widely. As the then Swedish Prime Minister, Carl Bildt, argued in a speech to the Palais des Académies, Brussels, in September 1993, there have been four main sources of tension and conflict in Europe since the Napoleonic wars. These are French–German relations; Poland's relations with its neighbours; Russia's place in the European states system; and security in the Balkans. The key to the solution of all these conflicts, Bildt argued, was the European Union. It was the 'motor and heart of the new efforts to guarantee security and stability in Europe' (quoted in Agrell 1994: 46).

The EU impacts in all five dimensions of order identified in chapter 3: state behaviour; formal institutional structures; patterns of governance; socio-economic interdependence; and international norms and values. The EU has created an institutional context within which member states are dependent on each other's decisions, thus prompting the development of an EU policy-making process characterised by *Politikverflechtung*, or 'interlocking politics' (Risse-Kappen 1996). The EU is also an important source of law-making for member states. In 1998, for example, over 60 per cent of German legislation originated in form of 'Directives' from Brussels. In addition, the EU exerts a considerable influence over the behaviour of non-member states that either seek to join or to develop closer relations with it.

In terms of formal institutional structures, the EU has a complex and sophisticated network of organisational structures. These structures comprise both inter-governmental fora such as the European Council, and elements of supra-national integration such as the European Commission, the European Court of Justice and the European Parliament. Integration and the pooling of sovereignty is more developed in the 'first pillar' (the EEC, the ECSC and Euratom) than in the second and third (CFSP and JHA). Nevertheless, even in the second and third pillars forms of institutionalised multilateral cooperation are developing which go beyond traditional forms of inter-state cooperation.[2]

These formal institutional structures are impressive, but they are not the key to the success of the integration project. The institutions of the EU are only effective because they rest on a rich sub-structure of governance, involving an elaborate corpus of rules, norms, procedures, codes of behaviour and values. Within the formal institutional structures of the EU, a complex system of multi-level governance has developed in response to the need for 'collective problem-solving' beyond the nation-state (Marks *et al.* 1996). These forms of multi-level governance epitomise the extent to which the boundaries between domestic and international politics have become blurred in late modern Europe (Hurrell and Menon 1996), thereby contributing to the gradual erosion of the key pillars of the traditional Westphalian system (William Wallace 1999).

The development of the EU's formal institutional structures and system of multi-level governance has both been a response to, and stimulated, extensive patterns of socio-economic transactions. As we have seen in chapter 4, the European integration process has involved both 'formal' institution-building and 'informal' integration involving socio-economic flows, transnational exchanges and deepening interdependence. These transnational societal exchanges provide the life-blood of a 'pluralistic security community', helping to foster trust, mutual consideration and a sense of community or 'we-feeling' (Deutsch 1957: 36).

Finally, the EU has come to embody a distinct set of 'European' norms and values. These 'European' norms and values are rooted in the experience of pluralist democracy, the rule of law, market economics and the peaceful resolution of disputes. Rightly or wrongly, the EU is widely seen as embodying these 'European' principles, and consequently exercises an important normative influence in Europe that extends way beyond its existing members.

The EU as a Kantian foedus pacificum

The EU's primary contribution to European order has been to help nurture the development of a more peaceful and stable peace order in post-war Western Europe. This peace order resembles a modern version of Immanuel Kant's vision of a 'pacific union' (*foedus pacificum*), in which states come together in an institutionalised framework of multi-lateral cooperation (Höffe 1995; Dörsam 1995; Bohman and Lutz-Bachmann 1997; Czempiel 1997). In a joint discussion paper by the German and French Foreign Ministries, the EU's impact on inter-state relations is explicitly emphasised:

> European integration, which has broken the earlier tradition of wars, is indisputably *the* political *Novum* of our century. Differences of interest continue to exist between member states, but they have been regulated within a legal framework. No member state thinks of strengthening its influence through power-political means. For the first time in its history, Europe is really constituting itself peacefully and not imperially. (Auswärtiges Amt/Ministere des Affaires Etrangeres 1999: 2)

The EU has contributed to the emergence of a *foedus pacificum* in five main ways. First, it provided an institutional framework for post-war reconciliation – especially, although not exclusively, between France and Germany. The Schuman Plan of 1950 and the subsequent creation of the ECSC (the European Coal and Steel Community) was explicitly conceived as a concrete 'peace project' designed to provide an institutional framework for Franco-German rapprochement (Holland 1994: 24–9). In this way, it has contributed to the solution of the 'German question', the cause of three major wars in Europe.

Second, multilateral integration has helped change EU member states' perception of their interests and preferences. By providing opportunities and mechanisms for exchanges of information, multilateral institutions such as the EU can help states identify common interests and thereby facilitate international cooperation. Institutions also help reduce the 'friction' generated by the interaction of sovereign states in international society. Institutions 'constrain opportunistic behaviour, and they provide focal points for coordination. They make a difference not by imposing order "above the nation-state" but by creating valued networks of ties between states. Among potential adversaries they may alleviate the security dilemma. In short, institutions provide a common reference for leaders trying to struggle with turmoil and uncertainty' (Keohane 1989: 3).

Third, the EU has helped change the process of identity formulation in Western Europe. This is particularly marked in countries located in the cultural and geographical terrain once occupied by the Carolingian Empire, where the EU has helped foster a sense of common purpose and identity. The EU has helped tame nationalism, and has created a situation

in which 'there is nothing especially controversial today about being
"European"':

> In western Europe ... except in the most extreme nationalist circles of
> France, Austria, and among subsections of the British political class, there is
> nothing especially controversial today about being 'European' – it carries no
> suggestion of the lack of properly 'national' sentiment. To be 'European'
> does not entail casting aspersions upon your fellow citizens, nor does it
> imply keeping one's distance from them. This is a real and significant
> achievement for the European Union, and one worth emphasizing. (Judt
> 1996: 76)

Fourth, in the 1980s, the EU helped the process of democratisation in
Southern Europe, thereby helping to lay the foundations for building a
stable peace in Southern Europe (although these foundations remain
somewhat weak in the case of Greece and Turkey).

Finally, the EU exercises a 'presence' (Allen and Smith 1990) in the
international system as a 'civilian power'. It is widely seen as embodying
a community of stable and prosperous democracies, cooperating peacefully together in multilateral institutions. Because of this, the EU began
to act as an important role model and pole of attraction for many in East
Central Europe from the late 1980s onwards. In this way, it helped bring
about the peaceful collapse of communism in Eastern Europe.

The European Union and Central and Eastern Europe
With the end of the cold war, the European Union has acquired 'an
historic new role' as a 'European ordering-power (*Ordnungsmacht*) in
Central and Eastern Europe' (Dauderstädt and Lippert 1998: 10). In
addition to its primary function as a framework for pooling sovereignty
amongst its member states, the EU increasingly exerts a growing political
influence – what has been termed 'soft governance' (Friis and Murphey
1999)[3] – on its neighbours in CEE. It does so in a number of ways.

First, the EU embodies the 'idea' of Europe for many in the new
democracies, and is the focus of their 'return' to Europe. Second, it has
generated a 'new national myth' in CEE, which is altering the process of
identity formation. 'It is the myth of belonging to European culture, the
myth of return to real or imaginary European roots, the myth of normal
development brutally interrupted by the Bolshevik experiment or the
Russian aggression or both' (Zaslavsky 1992: 110). Third, the 'conditionality' of EU aid has helped reinforce the democratisation process and
respect for human rights. It has also encouraged the peaceful resolution

of disputes, notably the Hungarian-Slovak dispute over the Magyar minority in Slovakia and the Danubian dams (Hyde-Price 1996: 93–9). Fourth, the EU has become the major trading partner for the new democracies of East Central Europe. Despite continuing problems with EU restrictions on CEE exports of agricultural products, steel and textiles, market access is an important precondition for security and stability in the region, and will aid the transition process (Mayhew 1998). Finally, the EU-sponsored 'Pact for Stability' (also known as the Balladur Plan) has helped diffuse some of the minority and border disputes which bedevil the post-communist East.[4]

The EU has been able to exert its soft governance in Central and Eastern Europe primarily because all of the new democracies in the region either aspire to join the Union, or are keen to develop close economic links with it (Auswärtiges Amt/Ministere des Affaires Etrangeres 1999: 3). The end of the cold war was accompanied by a marked growth in the attractiveness of the EU and other Euro-Atlantic structures in CEE. This has given the Western democracies a very important foreign policy tool – one that they have been quick to exploit by including a significant measure of conditionality in their dealings with the post-communist East (Flockhart 1996: 211). It is the prospect of eventual membership of the EU that has given the Union such leverage in the post-communist East. Membership was initially seen almost as a *deus ex machina* that would provide democratic government, prosperity and peace. As the enlargement negotiations ground slowly on, however, it became increasingly evident that EU membership would necessitate far-reaching domestic changes in CEE that would take time to implement.

Nonetheless, the aspiration for membership has provided a central drive in the reform process throughout the post-communist East. It has helped both to foster a sense of 'European' identity in Central and Eastern Europe and to consolidate the 'new nationalist myth'. In this way, it can help consolidate democratic government in the region (as it did in southern Europe) and stimulate further economic development. The promise of enlargement also helps the diffusion of 'European' values and norms in the wider Europe, encouraging liberal democracy, respect for human rights and the peaceful settlement of disputes (soft governance). 'Enlargement to the East', as the then EU Commissioner Hans van den Broek noted, is thus 'in the very first place a political issue relating to security and stability on our continent'.[5]

German European policy

Europapolitik *and German grand strategy*

Following the end of the cold war and national unification, the German government has placed European integration at the very heart of its grand strategy. For Chancellor Kohl, further progress in binding ever closer together Europe's *Schicksalsgemeinschaft* was – quite simply – a question of 'war and peace'. With the coming to power of a Red–Green coalition under Gerhard Schröder, the rhetoric has changed, but European integration remains the central thrust of his government's foreign and security policy. On becoming Foreign Minister, for example, Joschka Fischer declared that the 'completion of European integration is the task of my generation' (*Die Zeit*, 9 December 1999, p. 6).

This broad cross-party consensus around European integration is not surprising, given the historic importance of the integration process for the consolidation of democracy in the Federal Republic and formation of a Kantian 'pacific union' in Western Europe. There is also a remarkable institutional congruence between the *Bundesrepublik* and the EU that amplifies the attractiveness of the EU for German politicians. Both the EU and the BRD are characterised by a highly sectorized policy-making process within a cooperative federal system that places a premium on negotiation, consensus-building and compromise. Germany is a 'federal decentralized state, not a unitary one like Britain, and so a supranational Europe looks comfortable: a sort of enlarged Federal Republic' (Treverton 1992: 100). There is therefore 'a good fit between German and EU interests, institutions, and identities' (Bulmer 1997: 50), which must be taken into account when analysing German *Europapolitik*.

The primacy attached to the European integration process constitutes a significant re-calibration of German grand strategy since 1989. During the cold war, German *Westpolitik* had two main axes: transatlantic partnership and European integration. Given the fundamental security imperative of the US nuclear guarantee, Bonn's relations with Washington were seen 'as the most important single element in the Federal Republic's foreign policy' (Morgan 1987; see also Mathiopoulos 1988). With the disappearance of any significant external military threat to Germany, however, US security guarantees have lost their former existential importance. Good transatlantic relations remain politically important for Germany, but the significance of NATO and the US relationship have declined relative to the EU and the European integration process. *Europapolitik* – i.e., policy towards the European Union – is thus now at the heart of German foreign and security policy. 'German foreign policy is in the first instance a policy in and for Europe' (Chancellor Schröder, *Bulletin*, 6 December 1999, p. 790).

The primacy of *Europapolitik* is also evident from Foreign Minister Fischer's speech to the DGAP in November 1999 where he prioritised the three main tasks facing German foreign policy. The first was the 'completion of European integration', which remained 'our calling and our primary interest'. The EU, he maintained, was based on the shared interests of France and Germany, who together constituted the 'motor of European integration', and for whom the 'most important strategic goal today is the enlargement of the EU'. The second foreign policy task was the 'renewal of the transatlantic relationship', whilst the third was strengthening multilateralism and the United Nations (Fischer 1999).

German *Europapolitik* itself has two strategic thrusts: deepening of the integration process, and enlargement of the EU to the East. Deepening has three aspects: stronger coordination of economic and social policy; budgetary reform; and institutional reform (Dauderstädt and Lippert 1998: 13). The importance attached by the German government to deepening was a direct consequence of unification. Chancellor Kohl and his advisors were convinced that a united Germany needed to be anchored in a more integrated Europe. 'Binding Leviathan', they believed, would reassure Germany's neighbours and prevent any recidivist behaviour by future German governments (Dyson 1999). This political concern was one of the main driving forces behind the Maastricht Treaty on European Union, and provided an important political rationale for what constitutes the most ambitious 'deepening' project in the history of the integration process – Economic and Monetary Union. EMU was regarded by Chancellor Kohl as essential in order to give the EU the capacity to act as Europe's 'anchor of stability', and has been accompanied by efforts to build a 'political union'. This involves a greater use of 'qualified majority voting' (QMV) in the European Council and Council of Ministers, along with the strengthening of the CFSP and the development of cooperation in the area of JHA. In both the second and third pillars (CFSP and JHA), Germany has consistently championed the principle of more extensive forms of multilateral cooperation (Janning and Algieri 1996).

While acting as a motor of EU 'deepening' (in cooperation with France, its fellow 'cooperative hegemon'), Germany has also been the leading proponent of EU enlargement to the East. Germany is particularly interested in the accession of Poland, the Czech Republic and Hungary. In a speech to the Bundestag on 29 October 1993, for example,

Chancellor Kohl stressed that it would be unacceptable to Germany if, in the long term, the western frontier of Poland or the Czech Republic were to remain the eastern frontier of the European Union.

From 1996 to 1997, Germany's commitment to enlargement appeared to wane, as Kohl's visionary approach gave way to more nitty-gritty negotiations by individual ministries, each of which sought to protect their vested interests. In part, this was inevitable, as the 'age of "big leaps", historic gestures and symbols' was replaced by 'hard work on details, interrupted by the "ups and downs" of political normality' (Pflüger 1995: 228). However, the central thrust of German grand strategy has remained constant: to enlarge the Union to the east – in the first instance, into East Central Europe. Chancellor Schröder has stressed that EU enlargement is both necessary given the West's historic responsibilities to Central and Eastern Europe, and economically and politically advantageous (*Frankfurter Allegemeine Zeitung*, 1 December 1999, p. 9). Germany remains the primary political advocate of EU eastern enlargement, even if it continues to grapple with the contradiction between integrating East Central Europe into the West and protecting EU markets from low-cost products from the east (Zaborowski 1998: 77–8). Berlin's continuing commitment to EU enlargement reflects Germany's role conception as a 'bridge' between East and West, and the German government's decision to respond to the dilemmas of the *Mittellage* by enlarging Euro-Atlantic structures eastwards.

German commitment to EU enlargement derives from four key factors. First, a desire to stabilise the security environment along its eastern borders by projecting the benefits of institutionalised multilateral cooperation into East Central Europe. Günther Verheugen, Germany's EU Commissioner for Enlargement, has stressed that the primary argument for eastern enlargement is the need to 'create a peace order for the whole of Europe' based on 'democracy, the rule of law and human rights' (*Die Zeit*, 9 December 1999, p. 6). EU enlargement will help Germany and its neighbours find cooperative solutions to many of the non-military issues on the post-cold war security agenda, particularly those associated with economic transformation and the state- and nation-building process.

Second, enlargement promises to bring substantial economic benefits to Germany by facilitating trade and investment, and creating a single market area in CEE. Indeed, 'central Europe is turning out to be a more and more profitable site for investment; with comparatively cheap and comparatively highly skilled labour, it will provide an excellent opportunity to intensify the division of labour in industrial production that is required by economic globalisation' (Freudenstein 1998: 45). On the other hand, some in Germany harbour fears about the free movement of labour, and worry that this will be destabilising for the domestic labour market (Holtbrügge 1996: 545). Yet as Günther Verheugen has warned, the economic alternative to eastern enlargement is 'a poverty border, a *Limes* running through the middle of Europe', which is in nobody's interest – least of all the Germans (*Die Zeit*, 9 December 1999).

Third, enlargement will provide a multilateral context for German relations with its smaller neighbours in East Central Europe. This will help address some of the concerns about German domination of *Mitteleuropa* which remain widespread throughout the region. It will also help spread some of the costs of stabilising Central and Eastern Europe amongst EU members, thereby relieving the burden on Germany.

Fourth, the broad support of German political and economic elites for EU enlargement reflects the extent to which multilateralism has become ingrained in Germany's 'genetic code' (Goetz 1996: 24). Multilateral integration played an important role in consolidating German democracy and facilitating its rapprochement with its Western neighbours. The Germans along with 'some of the smaller European states have embraced Europe as a means of strengthening and projecting existing state identities', and this has resulted in a significant 'Europeanization of state identity' in the Federal Republic (Katzenstein 1997: 31–2). Germans overwhelmingly believe that the new CEE democracies would benefit from multilateral integration and cooperation, and are thus firm advocates of opening the integration process up to the East.

This faith in the virtues of multilateral integration has coalesced with a strong sense of historical debt and moral responsibility towards Central and Eastern Europe (see for example Dauderstädt and Lippert 1998: 20). This reflects the Federal Republic's continuing sensitivity to its past, and its self-identity as a state with a particular responsibility for peace in Europe. The memory of the war has generated a sense of moral responsibility that has been an important factor in German support for East Central European aspirations to 'return to Europe'. Many Germans also feel indebted to the Poles, Czechs and Hungarians for their part in ending the cold war and making possible the peaceful unification of Germany (Freudenstein 1998: 46). Consequently, there is a strong normative impulse driving Germany's commitment to EU enlargement, which colours German perceptions of their national interests in *Mitteleuropa*.

Institutional polyphony and German Europapolitik

Whilst the broad direction of German *Europapolitik* is shaped by its iden-tity and its dominant role conceptions, day-to-day policy decisions reflect the specific interests of individual ministries. This has always been a feature of German policy-making, which by its very nature is highly decentralised and sectorised (Bulmer and Paterson 1987: 25–31). Powers of decision-making are dispersed horizontally, between different Federal ministries, and vertically, between the Federal authorities and the Länder (Jeffery 1996). Other actors – notably the Bundesbank, the Federal Constitutional Court, political parties, the Bundestag and the Bundesrat – also have a significant input into policy formulation.

One important consequence of this institutional polyphony is that specific policy decisions by individual institutional actors do not always accord with the long-term goals mapped out by German grand strategy. Individual federal ministries sometimes have particular concerns or styles of policy-making that are not congruent with the government's long-term objectives. The Finance Ministry, for example, tends to oper-ate with an accountant's cost–benefit analysis that sits uncomfortably with the Foreign Ministry's emphasis on the political importance of mul-tilateral cooperation. The classic example of an individual ministry pursing an institutional interest at variance with the broader goals of Ger-man *Europapolitik* is the Federal Ministry of Agriculture (BML). This ministry has frequently sought to protect the interests of German farm-ers in ways that are not easily compatible with the need to prepare the EU for eastern enlargement (Webber 1999). By blocking implementation of Agenda 2000, the agricultural ministry has consistently defended narrow sectional interests at the expense of Germany's strategic commitment to EU enlargement.

In seeking to understand Germany's role in the reshaping of European order, therefore, it is essential to consider not only the broad policy objec-tives set by its grand strategy (which are shaped by its identity and national role conceptions), but also the influence of institutional actors. German policy towards the EU – and Europe more widely – is made and implemented by a cocktail of actors. This raises problems for the coher-ence of German *Europapolitik*, especially in coordinating day-to-day tactical decision-making. The danger is that decisions on Europe may reflect negotiated compromises or package deals between different domestic actors (and their transnational allies), rather than a strategic assessment of national interests. Given the difficulties of coordination inherent in a highly sectorised policy-making area, it is sometimes hard for the *Bundesregierung* to formulate and implement a coherent grand strategy for Europe.

The problems of sectorisation and policy coordination have certainly made it harder to resolve a number of contradictions at the heart of German *Europapolitik*. Both the Kohl and Schröder governments identified three policy objectives: 'leaving the CAP basically untouched; reducing the German share in the EU budget; and speedy eastward enlargement of the EU' (Freudenstein 1998: 48). Unfortunately, it is impossible to achieve all three goals. Germany's emphasis on budgetary reform, for example, openly conflicts with the goal of eastern enlargement (Anderson 1999: 54). Similarly, EU enlargement is impossible without substantial reform of the CAP. The problems generated by policy sectorisation are likely to increase as the integration process encompasses new policy areas, such as Justice and Home Affairs along with foreign and defence policy. Without strong central direction from the Chancellor's Office, therefore, the contradiction between different elements of *Europapolitik* will be impossible to resolve. German European policy may therefore remain prone to preoccupations with short- and medium-term considerations at the expense of the longer-term objectives of grand strategy.

The dilemmas of EU enlargement

Official German statements on *Europapolitik* emphasise the Federal Republic's continuing commitment to European integration, and the complementary nature of deepening and widening. German officials and policy-analysts nearly always present deepening and widening as two sides of the same coin. In the words of a joint Franco-German paper, 'Enlargement and deepening always go hand in hand' (Auswärtiges Amt/Ministere des Affaires Etrangeres 1999: 1).

However, such a *sowohl-als-auch* ('as well as') approach cannot hide a central dilemma at the heart of German *Europapolitik*. This is the unavoidable tension between deepening and widening. In part, this tension is about how political leaders prioritise scarce diplomatic time and energy between competing policy goals. 'Whatever one says', Timothy Garton Ash has argued, 'there is a day-to-day tension between concentrating on deepening or on widening the EU' (1996: 88). The crucial dilemma facing German *Europapolitik* is that eastern enlargement will necessitate fundamental changes in the key policies and decision-making procedures of the EU. This poses a major difficulty: how to enlarge to the east, whilst preserving the benefits of existing forms of multilateral cooperation and integration. If enlargement significantly weakens the cohesion and effectiveness of the EU's institutionalised multilateralism, this will weaken the foundations of European order and make the construction of a durable peace more difficult.

This tension between enlargement and deepening has existed throughout the history of the European integration project. Indeed, it has been argued that the 'original "project" – a gradual pooling of sovereignties – has in fact been sacrificed to the politics of enlargement: enlargement and what Maurice Schumann used to call "deepening" have turned out incompatible' (Hoffmann 1995: 221). Whilst it is too simplistic to see enlargement and deepening simply in terms of a zero-sum game, there is certainly a tension between the two. The increasing heterogeneity of the EU has made it more difficult – although not impossible – to build unanimity around policies designed to deepen the integration process. The EU currently faces the most ambitious and complex wave of enlargement in its history. The Helsinki summit of December 1999 identified thirteen candidates for membership, the majority of whom had socio-economic structures very different from those of existing members.

Consequently there can be little doubt that the eastern enlargement of the EU will fundamentally transform the multilateral structures within which Germany is embedded, and alter the dynamics of the integration process. As Chancellor Schröder has noted, the forthcoming round of enlargement will 'mark a deep-seated watershed in the history of the European Union'. Eastern enlargement will 'propel the European Union into a new dimension', raising fundamental questions about the goal and future form of the integration process (*Frankfurter Allgemeine Zeitung*, 1 December 1999, p. 9).

To begin with, enlargement will force fundamental changes in the two key policies of the EU – the Common Agricultural Policy (Comes 1995) and the structural funds (Axt 1997). Changes to both these policies would still have been required even if enlargement was not on the agenda (Freudenstein 1998: 44). Enlargement, however, means that these long over-due reforms can no longer be postponed, despite the objections of the influential German agricultural lobby and its transnational allies.

Second, it will precipitate changes in EU decision-making procedures and structures. The EU was originally designed for six members: over the years its membership has grown to nine, then twelve, and currently stands at fifteen. Existing structures are already beginning to creak at the seams: with twenty or more members, they are likely to grind to a halt. Enlargement will make necessary a re-balancing of authority within the triangle formed by the Commission, the Council and the Parliament. Enlargement also poses questions concerning the number of Commissioners in an enlarged Union; the size of the European Parliament; and the weighting of votes in the European Council (Deubner and Janning 1996).

Third, enlargement threatens to unravel the complex pattern of package deals and compromises within the EU. Decision-making within the EU involves a series of reciprocal agreements between different states and groups of states – between, for example, the richer states in the north and the less well off southern states (Wallace 1985; Hayes-Renshaw and Wallace 1996). The importance of issue-linkage for the negotiation of compromise package deals amongst EU members was clearly demonstrated by Chancellor Schröder at the EU summit in Berlin in March 1999.[6] However, with far-reaching changes to key policies such as CAP and the Structural funds, such package deals will be much harder to negotiate.[7]

Fourth, reform of EU decision-making structures may increase tensions between larger and small states within the EU, particularly over issues such as qualified majority voting (QMV) and the allocation of Commissioners. Enlargement will mean that the EU becomes an organisation comprised primarily of small states, who might come to begrudge the leading role played by larger states (particularly France and Germany).

Finally, in an enlarged EU, new coalitions of states will emerge. This may weaken the authority of the Franco–German motor of integration within the EU – particularly if new members from East Central Europe look to Germany to defend their interests (Kolboom 1996: 123–4). A subtle re-balancing of the Franco-German relationship has been underway since 1989, which has generated some strains within this crucial partnership. As Hans Stark has noted (1999: 21), 'the years from 1995 to 1998 were characterised by the accumulation of misunderstandings and divergences that could only be covered up by the two governments' repeated declarations of friendship'. With enlargement of the Union to twenty or more members, it is unlikely that Paris and Berlin alone can continue to function as the motor of the integration process. Consequently, a new 'cooperative hegemon' (Pedersen 1998: 3) must be forged – perhaps by building on the experience of the 'Weimar Triangle' and including Poland in Franco–German deliberations.

The central dilemma at the heart of German *Europapolitik* is that enlargement increases the 'logic of diversity' within the EU (Hoffmann 1995: 84). This sets limits on the operation of spill-over, reinforces the importance attached to national interests and constrains further integration. Enlargement will not just exacerbate the logic of diversity between established West European member states and the new East Central

European members, it will also bring into the Union states with very different national identities and role conceptions. In the case of Poland and the Czech Republic, for example:

> Czechs see Poles as nobles and peasants lost in the modern world, too disorganised to manage anything but folly; Czechs see themselves as rational, modern citizens, the only true democrats in eastern Europe. (The Polish word for 'the state', means 'courtly ladies and gentlemen' in Czech, and appears mainly in fairy tales). Poles see Czechs as burghers who want peace to enjoy their beer and dumplings; Poles see themselves as the only nation willing to sacrifice for freedom in eastern Europe. These attitudes reflect real differences between Polish and Czech society; they will surface as European integration proceeds, and will perhaps influence the character of European life in years to come. (Snyder 1999: 55)

Enlargement and the future of Europe

EU enlargement and the reshaping of European order

Towards the end of 1999, the process of EU enlargement received some important new impulses. In part these represented a post-Kosovo awareness that enlargement was vital as an instrument for stabilising Central and Eastern Europe as a whole, including South-eastern Europe. Consequently the Tampere EU informal summit in October 1999 proposed bringing a further six applicants into a flexible and multi-speed accession process, alongside the six already engaged in membership negotiations. It also recognised Turkey as an applicant country. What has been called the 'regatta' principle was subsequently adopted at the Helsinki summit in December 1999, bringing the number of countries involved in enlargement negotiations to thirteen. These countries will all negotiate the thirty-one 'chapters' of the *acquis communautaire* (which currently runs to about 80,000 pages, but which continues to grow apace), with the expectation that the front-runners might be ready for accession in 2001–2. Meanwhile the EU itself will have to embark on the equally complex task of internal restructuring in order to be fit to accept new members. Chancellor Schröder has suggested that the EU should aim to complete this process 2003, with key reforms being implemented during the French Presidency in the second half of 2000.

Whatever the precise institutional and political consequences of enlargement, one thing is clear: enlargement means the end of the postwar West European form of multilateral cooperation (the 'EEC model'), and the birth of a new form of European integration. Post-war Western

Europe has been transformed by a process of 'deep integration', involving both formal and informal integration. It has resulted in a significant pooling of sovereignty and the proliferation of expanding networks of multi-level governance which have fanned out across the EU. This deep integration process was possible because it took place within a geographically compact region and between a relatively cohesive group of states. However, it is unlikely that existing forms of 'deep integration' will be appropriate for a larger and more diverse group of states.

Enlargement will therefore change the EU and the nature of the integration process itself. As Joachim Fest has argued, we must recognise that 'the first stage in the creation of Europe definitely lies behind us and that it is time for the second to begin' (1994: 64). The integration process that began in the early 1950s was designed to address the specific West European needs and concerns of that time (namely agriculture, coal and steel). It took placed in the context of a divided Europe protected by the US nuclear umbrella; its geographical scope was set by the iron curtain and the Berlin Wall; and at its core was the old Carolingian Empire – Latin, Catholic, Rhineland Europe. 'Public protestations to the contrary notwithstanding', Tony Judt has written (1996: 43), 'the European Community of the 1970s and 1980s not only presumed the permanence of Europe's division but depended upon it'.[8] This West European model of integration reached its zenith at Maastricht, but is no longer viable in a Europe of twenty-six or more – particularly one stretching from Lapland to the Mediterranean, and from the Atlantic to the Black Sea (Weidenfeld and Janning 1997: 82). A new model of integration is thus required, one more appropriate to the changed political, economic and geopolitical circumstances of post-cold war Europe.

This new model of EU integration will probably involve some form of 'flexibility', 'variable geometry' or 'differentiated integration' (Cziomer 1997: 31). The public debate on differentiated integration emerged following the generally hostile reception accorded to a CDU/CSU position paper on European policy (Schäuble and Lamers 1994).[9] This paper, modestly entitled *Reflections on European Policy*, was written by Wolfgang Schäuble and Karl Lamers and published in September 1994. It represented a response to the 'unavoidable dilemma between widening and deepening' (Janning and Algieri 1996: 17). Schäuble and Lamers suggested that in the absence of broad consensus for further deepening amongst the existing membership, integration should proceed amongst a smaller core willing to pool sovereignty in a number of crucial areas. This core would consist of the original EEC founders, who were willing to continue with the sort of 'deep' integration that was only possible amongst a small and homogenous group of states sharing common interests and aspirations. The EU could then take in new members from CEE who would not have to adopt the full *acquis communautaire* immediately upon accession.

Their ideas were given a more thorough conceptual elaboration in 1995 by Christian Deubner. In his book on *Kerneuropa* ('core Europe'), he outlined a model of a single core built on the structures of the Benelux Union and the cooperation provisions of the Franco-German Treaty. This would combine EMU, political union, a robust CFSP (including defence) and extensive cooperation in JHA. The problem with this idea, however, is that some states might want to join in certain areas of cooperation but not others. Austria, for example, is a natural candidate of 'Euroland', but is unwilling to join a defence union. On the other hand, European defence and security identity without the UK would lack credibility.

Consequently, the debate has shifted from ideas of a single core to the notion of 'differentiated integration' (Janning 1994) and 'enhanced cooperation' (Dauderstädt and Lippert 1998: 40). The concept of differentiated integration involves the effective creation of several cores, each with different members and different functional concerns. This would allow different states to 'opt in' to some areas of integration but not others, whilst remaining within a broad institutional framework. The essence of German thinking on this issue is that if some EU members wish to deepen integration between them, other members should not prevent them. This idea (which has been developed in cooperation with the French),[10] has received a sympathetic but not enthusiastic hearing within the EU. Indeed, the notion of 'flexibility' was formerly incorporated in the Treaty of Amsterdam (Section V), and already operates *de facto* within the EU (i.e., in the areas of EMU and the Social Chapter).

Differentiated integration seems to offer a solution to the growing heterogeneity of an enlarged union. Its advocates claim it has three main strengths. First, it could provide a way of involving the CEE states in some areas of the EU but not others. Thus, for example, although many of the post-communist democracies might not yet meet the economic criteria necessary to compete in the single market, they could participate in the second and third pillars. Second, it may help maintain a balance of unity and diversity within a wider Europe, allowing those states which want to deepen their integration to do so. Third, it may facilitate the emergence of more flexible forms of cooperation and multi-level governance across a wide spectrum of policy-areas, despite its heterogeneous membership.

On the other hand, some fear that differentiated integration may pose problems for existing forms of multilateral cooperation in Europe. It will make 'package deals' across a range of policies and issue areas more difficult, particularly given a cut in the structural funds. This might in turn weaken the EU's internal cohesion, as different states head off in diverse directions, opting in and out at will. The issue here is whether 'differentiated integration' involves 'multi-speed' structures or 'variable geometry'. Multi-speed means that whilst all members share common policy goals, some embark on deepening integration before others are ready to join them. Variable geometry, by contrast, means that some states opt out of a policy because they do not agree with its objective. Maastricht contained elements of both: Britain, Denmark and Sweden opted out of EMU because they did not agree with the idea of a single currency, whilst Greece did not meet the convergence criteria.

In addition, it is not clear how much control the wider membership should exert over the core group (or groups), and whether all members should contribute financially to activities undertake by some members only. 'Differentiated integration' has also been described a concept for the avant-garde, not the rear-guard. It may leave the CEE states feeling that they have been relegated to a second division within the EU. Similarly, it may lead smaller states to feel they are being sidelined by the major powers.

Whatever their pros and cons, it is already clear that concepts of 'differentiated integration' and 'flexibility' in their various permutations are now central to the German debate on the future of European integration. This is inevitable because they are the only way to manage the tension between deepening and widening which lies at the heart of German *Europapolitik*. Whether they will do so or not is impossible to judge in advance. As the former Minister of State for Defence Lothar Rühl has argued, 'no mathematical formula' exists to determine what the outcome of the enlargement process will be. 'It is an open one and everything depends on how enlargement is managed, in what spirit, with what common purpose and approach, and, above all, according to what concepts and means' (Assembly of the WEU 1997: 52).

EU enlargement and Central and Eastern Europe

Enlargement will not only transform the internal workings of the Union, it will also have important implications for domestic and international developments in Central and Eastern Europe. On the positive side, the tangible prospect of membership provides incentives for structural reforms in the new democracies and reinforces the 'new nationalist myth'. This will contribute towards greater multilateral cooperation and the peaceful resolution of disputes, and strengthen the rule of law and respect for human rights.

On the other hand, enlargement might have negative implications for emerging patterns of cooperation and conflict in the region (Amato and Batt 1999). The enlargement process is already creating new divisions within CEE between those involved in accession negotiations (the 'pre-ins') and those with no prospect of membership (the 'outs'). With the opening up of the 'iron curtain', the EU has become increasingly concerned about the problems of transnational crime, migration and illegal economic activity. This was highlighted by the decision to incorporate the Schengen *acquis* into the Treaty of Amsterdam. However, the EU's insistence that applicant states prepare for accession by applying Schengen border controls and EU trading regulations has already begun to adversely affect the relationship of the 'pre-ins' to the 'outs'. Poland has expressed concerned about the implications of this for its strategic partnerships with Ukraine and Lithuania; the Czech Republic is concerned about the implications of Schengen for its special relationship with Slovakia; and Hungary is concerned about how EU membership will affect its links with Magyar communities in neighbouring states. The frustration of the Ukrainian ambassador to Poland was clear from his comment that 'the Berlin Wall was dismantled. Are we going to build a new one in the east from the pieces of the pulled down Berlin Wall'? The essence of the problem is that the EU wants two contradictory things. It wants the 'pre-ins' to develop good relations with their eastern neighbours, but it also wants them to enforce a strict border regime in order to prevent crime and illegal cross-border activities.

In the light of the danger that enlargement will create new lines of division and exclusion in Central and Eastern Europe, the EU needs to develop a dual-track strategy: eastern enlargement and new forms of pan-European cooperation. On the one hand, member states need to overcome the resistance of narrow sectional interests and short-term national thinking in order to push forward with the enlargement process. Only in this way can the EU fulfil its historic post-cold war mission of extending the Kantian *foedus pacificum* into Central Europe. On the other hand, the EU must forge new forms of multilateral cooperation with countries in pan-Europe excluded from the integration process – particularly Russia and the Ukraine, but also Belarus, Moldova and some of the successor states of former Yugoslavia. These need to build on the modest achievements of existing Partnership and Cooperation Agreements with Russia and Ukraine.[11] One positive example of this is the Northern Dimension initiative which Finland has championed (Jopp and Arnswald 1998; Jopp and Warjovaara 1998). This was a major concern of the Finnish Presidency in the second half of 1999, although it was somewhat overshadowed by the Kosovo war. The aims of the Northern Dimension were two-fold: to emphasise the positive interdependence between Russia, the Baltic Sea region and the EU; and to help integrate Russia into European and global structures through increased cooperation.

Alongside initiatives like the Northern Dimension, the EU needs to develop strategies for positive engagement with the excluded states of Eastern Europe and the Balkans. A significant role in this respect can be played by the 'pre-ins', who can function as a 'bridge' between the EU and Eastern Europe. Of particular importance in this regard is Poland, a country which is emerging as a central player in the new international relations of CEE. Poland is well situated to play a pivotal role as the linchpin between the European integration process and the development of pan-European forms of cooperation and 'soft governance'. At the same time, the EU itself needs to consider more creative forms of multilateral cooperation with the 'outs' of Eastern Europe and the Balkans. This could take the form of 'new flexible arrangements which represent more than association but less than membership' (Friis and Murphy 1999: 227). An example of such flexible new arrangements is the development of different kinds of membership and participation in pillars two and three (CFSP and JHA).

Towards 'European overload'?

The EU is now attempting the most complex agenda in its history: EMU; enlargement (the largest, most complex and most difficult round of enlargement in its history); political union (as outlined in the Treaties of Maastricht and Amsterdam); strengthening the CFSP and forging a common defence and security policy; and creating new forms of cooperation and integration in JHA. All these policy areas involve questions of money, power and sovereignty, and are therefore bound to be controversial. Individually, each of these steps is an enormous undertaking in its own right. EMU is without doubt the most ambitious step in the history of the European integration process, and will have far reaching implications for the political identity and economic interests of 'Euroland'. Enlargement, as we have seen, will necessitate fundamental changes in the key policies and decision-making structures of the Union. Taken together, the EU currently faces an agenda of enormous complexity and far-reaching implications. The enormity of what is being attempted raises concerns that the EU agenda is becoming so 'overloaded' that the integration process as a whole could suffer.

The problem for the EU is that it is struggling with this extensive agenda at a time when scepticism about the benefits of the integration process is growing in nearly all member states – including Germany (Rattinger 1994). The problems involved in ratifying the Maastricht treaty (particularly in Denmark and France) demonstrated that the 'permissive consensus' that underpinned integration in the post-war period has ended. The EU is now the central political cleavage in the domestic politics of nearly all member states. In 1990, over 70 per cent of those asked described their country's membership of the EU as a 'good thing'. By 1997, his had fallen to 46 per cent. In Germany, the change of mood was even more dramatic, the comparable figures being 70 per cent in 1990 and 36 per cent in 1997 (Dauderstädt and Lippert 1998: 16).

In addition, the issue of the EU budget is also on the agenda. This threatens to generate renewed financial disputes between member states precisely at the moment when enlargement will create new budgetary demands. Most importantly, Germany has made clear its unwillingness to go on being the '*Milchkuh*' (milk-cow) of Europe. This shift in policy began during Kohl's last years as Chancellor, but has become more apparent with the change of government in 1998. The Schröder government has been particularly keen to argue that EU enlargement cannot take place before a reform of EU finances.

A further complication is that the EU faces the problems of EMU, enlargement, budgetary negotiations and political union at a time when bilateral relations in Europe are more fluid than at any period since the early 1950s. Since its inception, the EEC/EU has faced complex problems. But it has always been driven forward by the Franco-German 'cooperative hegemon', galvanising the energies of a relatively coherent group of Rhineland states. Today, however, the Franco-German axis is not so solid, and differences between the EU's fifteen members are wider than previously. The danger here is that without clear direction from a core group acting as a 'motor' of integration, the EU may lose its sense of direction and urgency.

A final problem is that increasingly the EU is expected not only to regulate affairs between its member states, but also to provide the foundation for security and order in the wider Europe. This poses an acute danger of overloading the EU's capabilities. The problem is that there is a tension between the provision of 'hard governance' inside the EU and the exercise of 'soft governance' in the wider Europe (Smith 1996). As Lykke Friis and Anna Murphy have argued (1999: 229), the export of EU 'soft governance' to CEE countries weakens the '"carrying capacity" of the EU's internal governance system'. Resolving this dilemma will not be easy. The EU has certainly not been adept at tackling the more intractable problems on the new security agenda, as its failure in Yugoslavia demonstrates. The ill-fated words of Jacques Poos of Luxembourg, who as President of the Council of Ministers announced in the early months of the Yugoslav crisis, 'this is the hour of Europe', will haunt EU policy-makers for years to come (Kintis 1997: 148). The underlying problem is that the EU punches below its diplomatic and economic weight, as the Kosovo war has demonstrated recently. Consequently, at the end of the 1990s, the spotlight has come to rest on the EU's Common Foreign and Security Policy – an area that experienced a remarkable flurry of activity in the course of late 1998 and 1999.

Germany and the CFSP

One of the most important developments in European integration in the late 1990s was the strengthening of the CFSP. In the course of 1999, Europe has made more progress in forging a robust European defence capability than at any time since the failure of the European Defence Community (EDC) in 1954. The catalyst for this change was the Kosovo war, which marks a defining moment in the brief history of post-cold war European security.

The political conditions for a qualitative leap forward in forging a credible European Security and Defence Identity (ESDI) were a convergence in the security policies of France and the UK around that of Germany. Germany has long argued that there is no inherent contradiction between NATO and an autonomous European defence capability. Both France and the UK, however, argued that there was – from opposite positions. However, from the mid-1990s onwards France began inching closer to NATO and now accepts that an ESDI can be constructed *within* the Atlantic Alliance. In the case of the UK, the Blair government now recognises that a credible CFSP with a defence component will not undermine NATO. The symbolic landmark here was the Franco-British St Malo summit of 3–4 December 1998 (Mathiopoulos and Gyarmati 1999). With positive signals emanating from Washington, Germany used the opportunity of its combined Presidency of the EU and the WEU in the first half of 1999 to drive forward the process of closer European defence and security cooperation.

The EU Cologne summit (3–4 June 1999) was the occasion for some landmark decisions on CFSP. First, former NATO Secretary-General Javier Solana was appointed as the EU's High Representative for Foreign Policy ('Herr GASP'). A German proposal that he also be appointed as the new Secretary-General of WEU was approved at the same time. Unfortunately, the division of responsibilities between him and the EU Commissioner for External Affairs, Chris Patton, was not completely clarified.[12] The Cologne Summit also approved a German Presidency 'Report on the Strengthening of Common Defence and Security Policy', which proposed giving the EU credible means for taking autonomous action in response to international crises. Cologne built on earlier decisions taken at the Bremen WEU summit in May 1999, when it was agreed that WEU would be incorporated into the EU Treaty structure, probably by the end of 2000.

The Helsinki EU summit (10–11 December 1999) witnessed further important decisions on CFSP. Most importantly, EU leaders agreed to create a European rapid reaction corps of fifteen brigades (50–60,000), with attached naval and air assets, capable of being deployed within sixty days. The aim was to give the EU an 'autonomous capacity to take decisions where NATO as a whole is not engaged', in order to conduct 'EU-led military operations' within the framework of the Petersberg Declaration (Van Ham 2000). In addition, discussions are underway about possible EU 'convergence criteria' for defence spending and interoperability. These political and institutional developments have been underpinned by a series of mergers in the European defence industry, which are laying the industrial and technological foundations for a European Security and Defence Identity.[13]

The convergence of French and British security policy around that of Germany seems to vindicate the latter's policy of *sowohl als auch* – i.e., their refusal to choose between the transatlantic alliance and the aspiration for a robust ESDI. More importantly, it seems to presage the emergence of a 'New EU'. The 'old' EU (the 'EEC model'), was a civilian power which exercised 'soft governance' in CEE and a 'presence' in the wider international system. The 'New EU', it appears, will not only have substantial economic, financial and political power resources at its disposal (strengthened by a single currency), it will also have an autonomous capability to project deliberative military power. We are, it seems, on the verge of a 'brave new world'.

However, Germany and its allies have a long way to go before they translate the Cologne and Helsinki decisions into practical military and security cooperation. In the words of T.S. Eliot, 'Between the idea / And the reality / Between the motion / And the act / Falls the Shadow.' The practical difficulties involved in creating an effective rapid reaction corps are enormous, and will demand a tremendous expenditure of time, resources and political will. There is also a host of institutional and architectural questions that will need to be addressed, and which have been exacerbated by the de-coupling of NATO and EU enlargement. The 1995 NATO *Study on Enlargement* maintained that the 'enlargement of NATO is a parallel process with and will complement that of the European Union'. It also stressed that an 'eventual broad congruence of European membership in NATO, EU and WEU would have positive effects on European security'. Yet it also recognised that EU and NATO enlargement 'will proceed autonomously according to their respective internal dynamics and processes' which means that 'they are unlikely to proceed at precisely the same pace'.

The 1995 enlargement of the EU to include Austria, Sweden and Finland brought into the Union three more non-NATO 'neutral' countries (in addition to Ireland). On the other hand, the first round of NATO enlargement to the east has given the Alliance three more non-EU European countries (in addition to Norway and Turkey). The problem of divergent memberships between the EU and NATO will be further exacerbated if the dual enlargement process remains de-coupled. This will complicate the development of a coherent CFSP. 'Policy-making in the EU', it has been pointed out, 'cannot proceed smoothly if there is a parallel process in NATO in which several EU members are not taking part … It remains difficult to see how the European Union's Common Foreign and Security Policy (CFSP) and that of NATO can be reconciled if their membership becomes increasingly different.' Thus, a 'growing gap in European membership of NATO and EU/WEU would have a corrosive effect on the effectiveness of all the institutions' (Rühle and Williams 1995: 85). This problem is particularly acute in the Baltic region, where the creation of an 'extended non-aligned zone' would curtail ambitions to create a common EU foreign, security and defence policy. Indeed,

> The latter would require reducing the gap between allied and non-allied EU member states instead of widening it. Even if the development of a full-fledged common defence policy is, anyway, one of the most difficult undertakings of integration, it is questionable whether a true CFSP can

materialise with a growing number of member states with a security status
different from the rest of the Union. (Jopp and Lippert 1998: 16–17)

The issue of divergent membership touches upon another question
which remains unresolved within German grand strategy – the place of
the USA in Europe. Although Germany is no longer dependent on American nuclear guarantees, the German government has explicitly defined a
strong and healthy transatlantic partnership as one of its vital national
interests. The Clinton administration has been broadly supportive of
European aspirations to develop a defence capability, but remains somewhat schizophrenic on the issue.[14] The USA is concerned about an 'EU
caucus' within NATO and about what is termed 'sequencing', i.e., the
sequence in which NATO and the EU address security issues: does the EU
have first say, or NATO? Beyond a shared desire to avoid a damaging
transatlantic row, little is clear in the debate on the practical implications
of an autonomous European defence and security identity for transatlantic relations. Discussions around the strengthening of the CFSP do,
however, suggest a growing need to find a new balance between an
enlarged EU with a single currency and an emerging defence capability,
and the world's last remaining superpower. Given its political and economic influence within both the EU and NATO, Germany will be a
leading player in defining a transatlantic partnership appropriate to the
changing realities of the twenty-first century.

Continuity and change in German Europapolitik

In the late 1990s, there were some indications of a partial shift in German
Europapolitik. This reflected three factors. First, the increasing sectorisation of German Europapolitik, as new institutional actors were drawn into
a widening EU policy-making process. Second, the end of the 'permissive
consensus' in Germany on EU integration. Third, the lack of a clear policy concept for reconciling the twin imperatives of EU enlargement and
structural reform. In addition, the September 1998 election resulted in
a change of government and – more importantly – a change in generation. This new generation has a more pragmatic approach towards EU
integration and a greater willingnes to articulate Germany's national
interests. Thus for example in his inauguration address in November
1998, Chancellor Schröder spoke of the 'self-confidence of a grown-up
nation that doesn't have to feel superior or inferior to anyone, that
accepts its history and responsibility – but is looking forward'.

Some commentators have thus suggested that the Berlin Republic will be more 'British'[15] – i.e., that it will define and assert its national interests more directly and forcefully than in the past. Such views were given greater credence by Schröder's initial insistence that he intended to be resolute in pressing for German interests within the EU, especially in terms of its budgetary contribution. The Berlin government's insistence that the German language be accorded equal status with French and English in all EU business was also seen by some as an indication of Germany's new-found assertiveness and self-confidence.

There may be some truth to this, but the jury is still out. Despite their previously combative rhetoric, at the EU Berlin summit in March 1999, Schröder and his colleagues demonstrated a willingness to reach compromises and make concessions with their EU partners (*Frankfurter Allgemeine Zeitung*, 27 March 1999). More significantly, the growing pragmatism of German *Europapolitik* has not meant a more Eurosceptic policy. When push comes to shove, Germany will not risk multilateral cooperation in the EU by forcefully pressing its own national interests. After the Berlin summit, Joschka Fischer explained that when 'faced with the alternative, either "represent our national point of view" or "reach a decision for Europe"', his choice was clear. 'We have held the EU together', he proudly announced (*Süddeutsche Zeitung*, 27 March 1999).

There is, therefore, little evidence that the German political and economic elite (with the possible exception of some elements in the Bavarian-based CSU) have seriously questioned the benefits of European integration and multilateral cooperation. If there is a new accent in German *Europapolitik*, it is a stronger focus on the pragmatic advantages integration offers for Germany. Rather than seeing integration as a question of 'war and peace', it is seen as a practical response to problems of globalisation.

A significant shift has taken place in the discourse within which German *Europapolitik* is embedded. The visionary elements have not been completely discarded, and remain more in evidence in Germany than in many other EU countries (notably Britain). However, the overall tone has become much more pragmatic. At the same time, German financial constraints mean that the BRD is no longer willing to be the *Milchkuh* for the EU and finance major integration projects and undertakings. In 1984, by contrast, Kohl was so concerned to prevent a British veto of EU business that he was willing to fund much of the British rebate demanded by Thatcher from German coffers. This age of 'cheque-book diplomacy' has clearly ended (Sperling 1994). Indeed, Schröder has subsequently blamed Germany's 'excessive' EU budgetary contributions on Kohl's penchant for 'cheque-book diplomacy' (*Frankfurter Allgemeine Zeitung*, 27 March 1999, p. 2).

One way of conceptualising the shift in Berlin's *Europapolitik* is in terms of a switch from what Kjell Goldmann has termed a 'radical internationalism' to a more pronounced 'nationalist internationalism' (Goldmann 1997: 269–70, 81). This signifies a shift from an idealistic commitment to international integration to a more pragmatic calculation that multilateral cooperation serves a nation's interests better than a more assertive unilateralism. In the early 1990s, the German position was 'close to the internationalist programme'. It advocated the 'spread of multilateralism and the strengthening of international institutions' in order to 'counter nationalist tendencies in Germany and elsewhere and to strengthen the commitment to democracy, which was seen as a pillar of a new European order'. German policy thus comprised 'a substantial measure of self-entanglement – a remarkably anti-nationalist stance for being a great power'. However, even in the case of Germany, 'the institution of national independence and related concerns remain a constraint on far reaching change in the direction advocated by internationalists'. As a consequence, the late 1990s have witnessed a shift in rhetoric towards a 'nationalist internationalism'. This recognises that, in the words of Chancellor Schröder (1999: 786), 'in the context of our history and geography there is no alternative to the firm integration of Germany in the European Union'.

Conclusion: 'here be dragons'

The European Union is clearly central to German grand strategy, even more so in the 1990s than during the cold war. The EU not only provides a multilateral framework for German influence in *Mitteleuropa* and beyond, it is seen as providing the crucial 'anchor of stability' for Europe as a whole. In this context, EMU is of vital importance because 'all current German concepts of European order with its various layers will stand or fall with either the success or failure of EMU as its central anchor' (Mayer 1997: 736).

There is, however, an unresolved tension at the heart of German *Europapolitik* between deepening the integration process (through EMU and political union), and enlarging it by up to ten new members from CEE. The German government has no clear solution to this problem, despite the existence of a veritable cottage industry of academics and think tanks busily drafting elaborate schemes for 'flexible integration', 'differentiation' and the like. There is also a broader tension at the heart of the dual enlargement process, which reflects the failure of Germany and its partners to develop a coherent *Gesamtkonzept* ('comprehensive concept') for NATO and EU enlargement. This concerns the future of the transatlantic relationship and the role of the USA in European affairs. Finally, insufficient thought has been given to the impact of EU enlargement on relations within CEE. Enlargement will inevitably create new lines of inclusion and exclusion in the region, to the detriment of existing patterns of cooperation. Enlargement also raises difficult questions involving the future of relations between the EU and East European states like Russia and Ukraine.

Above all, it is increasingly clear that the dual enlargement process will not simply mean the 'Westernisation' of CEE, but will be the catalyst for profound changes in the institutions and identity of Western Europe. This is particularly evident in the case of the EU – an organisation which has had a significant impact on the political and economic contours of Europe, and which provides one of main pillars of contemporary European order. The old 'EEC model' of European integration has had its day, and the search is on for a new model of integration appropriate to a more heterogeneous EU of twenty-six or more members. Germany and its partners have thus entered uncharted territory, *terra incognito* – the place where on ancient maps it was sometimes written, 'Here be dragons!'

Notes

1 As Michael Smith has noted, 'it is evident that there is an intimate linkage between the internal development of the EU and its institutions and the broader European order, which is not solely attributable to the interests, power or policies of major European states. Whilst some analysts have noted this connection, it is doubtful whether it can be accounted for simply within an interstate or intergovernmental framework' (Smith 1996: 8–9).

2 The EU integration process has an impact on member state's attitudes and behaviour which goes beyond the formal pooling of sovereignty in pillar one. In terms of the Second pillar (CFSP), for example, '[t]wo decades of European Political Cooperation have transformed the working practices of West European foreign ministers and ministries … The COREU telex network, EPC working groups, joint declarations, joint reporting, even the beginnings of staff exchanges among foreign ministries and shared embassies: all these have moved the conduct of national foreign policy away from the old nation-state national sovereignty model towards a collective endeavour, a form of high-level networking with transformationalist effects and even more potential' (Hill and Wallace 1996: 6). Thus they argue, 'Intergovernmentalism in theory

does not erode sovereignty; in practice, over time, it too has ties that bind ... habits of cooperation, accepted advantages of shared information, responses to common threats, cost saving through increased collaboration, have all significantly altered patterns of national policy-making. This is an intensive system of external relations, in which the cooperating actors which constitute the system intertwine' (Hill and Wallace 1996: 11–12).

3 'Soft governance', Friis and Murphy argue, 'reflects the fact that EU governance is not limited to formal interaction but to the development of norms and values which condition the actions of its members. These concern a commitment to democracy, respect for the rule of law and negotiation which give the EU the character of a security community and civilian power in the international system' (1999: 214).

4 Reinhardt Rummel notes that Bonn was initially unhappy with French proposals for a stability pact, fearing that it might delay EU enlargement. However, he notes that German officials now grudgingly admit that 'French diplomacy has (again) shown how to handle diplomatic grand designs' (Rummel 1996: 56).

5 'Six Must Wait for EU Date', *The Guardian*, 5 November 1994.

6 Schröder's issue-linkage strategy was praised by *Die Welt* (26 March 1999): 'He throws everything together in one pot: agricultural reform, the new seven year plan for regional aid and the redistribution of budgetary contributions'.

7 Many southern Europeans (i.e., France, Greece, Spain and Portugal) fear that 'a united Europe, in short, has become a zero-sum game in which the extension of its benefits to newcomers from the east will be achieved only at some real cost to the current members' (Judt 1996: 91). The potential for eastern enlargement to exacerbate north–south/rich–poor divisions was evident in November 1998 when British, German, Dutch, Swedish and Austrian finance ministers called for a seven-year freeze on EU spending. This was opposed by Spain, Portugal and Greece (who receive 25 per cent, 12 per cent and 9 per cent of cash transfers from the structural funds respectively), along with the Commission. British sources were reported as saying that stringent control of community expenditure was 'the way to ensure that we can pay for EU enlargement when the time comes' ('North–South Clash Looms Over EU Budget Freeze', *The Guardian*, 21 November 1998).

8 Tony Judt has argued that the post-war West European integration process was a singular success in modern European history, but that 'What made possible the Western Europe we now have was almost certainly unique – and unrepeatable. To suppose that it can be projected indefinitely into the future is an illusion, however worthy and well intentioned'. 'Public protestations to the contrary notwithstanding, the European Community of the 1970s and 1980s not only presumed the permanence of Europe's division but depended upon it. The more secure the division, the easier it was to imagine a closer and more prosperous union of nations to the west of the line – while at the same time holding out the illusory prospect of that union's hypothetical expansion

to the east "one day".' His conclusion is that 'in its *strong* form the idea of "Europe" has had its day ... the likelihood that the European Union will fulfill its own promises of ever-closer union, while remaining open to new members on the same terms, is slim indeed' (1996: 24, 43, 128–9).

9 'The recently touted German idea of a small inner core of European states moving at full speed toward integration and setting demanding macro-economic criteria for membership in their club', Judt argues (in characteristically provocative terms), 'is merely the latest evidence that the future of Europe will be on German terms or not at all' (1996: 123)

10 The Germans and French issued a joint paper on 'enhanced cooperation' on 17 October 1996.

11 Alan Mayhew (1998: 35) has argued that EU policy towards Russia is 'of great importance for the successful future enlargement of the Union to Central Europe. Successful reform and democratisation in Russia (and indeed in the Ukraine) is an important criterion for economic development and political stability in the CEE countries. Bilateral agreements between Member States and Russia and the Partnership and Cooperation Agreement (PCA) with Russia at the Union level together with Community assistance programmes and attempts to draw Russia closer to many aspects of Community affairs are all important for creating an environment in which the Union can enlarge eastwards'.

12 See Friedbert Pflüger, 'Es Bleiben Zwei Nummern', *Frankfurter Allgemeine Zeitung*, 18 October 1999, and 'Nur Ein Missverständnis', *Der Spiegel*, no. 39, 27 September 1999, p. 220.

13 The prime example is the merger of Germany's Daimler-Chrysler Aerospace AG (DASA) and France's Aerospatiale Matra SA to create a new defence industrial giant 'European Aeronautic, Defense and Space Company' (EADS). See *Frankfurter Allgemeine Zeitung*, 15 October 1999, p. 1. On the implications of procurement policy and the defence industries for EU policy-making see Ulrika Mörth (1998).

14 NATO's new Secretary-General Lord Robertson has commented that there 'has always been a bit of schizophrenia about America, on the one hand saying "You Europeans have got to carry more of the burden" and then when the Europeans say "OK, we'll carry more of the burden", they say "Well wait a minute, are you trying to tell us to go home?"'. *Financial Times*, 15 September 1999.

15 'Die Deutsche Europa-Politik wird "Britischer"', *Frankfurter Allgemeine Zeitung*, 30 October 1997.

8

Conclusion:
Germany and Europe
in the twenty-first century

I saw a big autumn leaf which the wind
Was driving along the road, and I thought: tricky
To reckon that leaf's course.
                    (Bertolt Brecht, *Poems* 1913–1956: 383)

TESMAN: But, good heavens, we know nothing of the future.
LOVBORG: No, but there is a thing or two to be said about it all the same.
                    (Ibsen, *Hedda Gabler*)

'International relations', the US Ambassador to the United Nations Richard Holbrooke is fond of remarking, 'is like jazz: continual improvisation around a theme.'[1] This is a very apt metaphor, pertinent to both German grand strategy and European order. It reminds us that the reshaping of European order in the twenty-first century Europe will not proceed on the basis of grand designs and the discipline of a conductor's baton. Rather, it will involve continuous improvisation around a theme.

Successful statecraft requires an ability to respond flexibly to the chaotic play of contingency and the unexpected. Nonetheless, if states are not to find themselves adrift on a sea of fate, they need a broad set of policy objectives – defined in terms of their vital national interests – that provides them with a sense of orientation and strategic direction. All states, in other words, need a 'grand strategy' that defines their international role and how best to fulfil or defend that role. In this conclusion, we will summarise the primary aims and objectives of post-cold war German grand strategy, and consider the central dilemmas and difficulties facing its implementation. We will also consider the political character of the 'Berlin Republic', and its likely impact on the future of European order in the early twenty-first century.

Reordering Europe

Germany and the dilemmas of a 'multilateral Mittellage'

Germany's grand strategy, and the set of national role conceptions it embodies, is the product of its distinctive 'national situation' (see pp. 29–30). Its grand strategy has been shaped, in other words, both by its domestic characteristics (primarily its democratic institutions and its post-Holocaust identity) and its position in international society. As a 'situated actor', Germany's position in international society is defined by two decisive factors: its institutional embeddedness in the multilateral structures of the Euro-Atlantic security community, and its proximity to post-communist Central and Eastern Europe. Germany thus faces the dilemmas of its *Mittellage* (its 'central geographical location'). However, these are not the same dilemmas which confronted Bismarck, Strese-mann or Hitler. Rather, in the context of Germany's *Westbindung* and the dual enlargement process, they are the dilemmas of an increasingly *mul-tilateral Mittellage* (see pp. 107–8).

German grand strategy has three main elements. These reflect its national situation as a 'normal' *Zivilmacht* firmly ensconced in the West European zone of peace, but adjacent to a post-communist east that is grappling with a difficult process of 'triple transformation' (Rühl 1996: 118–19). The three elements of German grand strategy are, first, consol-idation of the Euro-Atlantic security community. Second, enlargement of this security community to the east by the integration of Central Euro-pean democracies into Euro-Atlantic structures. Third, nurturing a pan-European system of cooperative security embracing Russia and other democratising countries in Eastern Europe and the Balkans. These three broad policy goals provide German policy-makers with a sense of strategic direction and purpose. They also represent a considered and carefully calibrated response to the complexities of Germany's geopoliti-cal situation, and the fact that 'as usual Germany has to juggle more balls than most' (Joffe 1994: 86). However, they are not without their contra-dictions, inconsistencies and dilemmas.

Consolidating the Euro-Atlantic Security Community: for Germany, this is an over-riding priority. The 'German question' in its traditional form was resolved by the institutional *Einbindung* of a democratic Germany in the multilateral structures of the Euro-Atlantic community. Any weaken-ing of the cohesion and integrity of these multilateral structures would raise disturbing questions for both Germany and its partners and neigh-bours. In addition, German policy-makers see a robust and effective

Euro-Atlantic community as an essential anchor of stability for Central and Eastern Europe. Consequently, consolidating the Euro-Atlantic community has been a primary objective of German grand strategy.

This has two dimensions: deepening EU integration and restructuring NATO. Deepening EU integration has proceeded primarily through EMU – the most ambitious project in the history of European integration. This has served to add an additional layer of 'deep integration' to the Franco-German relationship, and has underlined Bonn's preference for *Kerneuropa* rather than *Mitteleuropa* (Axt 1996). German policy-makers hope EMU will be complemented by building an 'ever closer *political* union', and have thus championed the strengthening of the CFSP and the development of closer cooperation in JHA. Whilst most emphasis has been placed on the pivotal role of the EU in reordering post-cold war Europe, NATO remains an important element of German foreign and security policy. For the Federal Republic, its importance stems from its role as the institutional buckle of the transatlantic partnership; its contribution to *cooperative security governance* in CEE; and its utility as an instrument of multilateral military crisis-management.

There are, however, some unresolved problems inherent in German *Westpolitik*, many of which have lain dominant for some time, but which have been exacerbated by the process of institutional adaptation and enlargement (Sperling 1999: 187). To begin with, EMU and steps towards political union raise controversial questions about the future direction and shape of the European Union. Having to address these questions could undermine consensus within the Union and paralyse the integration process. Second, building a European Security and Defence Identity (ESDI) and strengthening the CFSP brings to the fore unresolved questions about the US role in Europe and the future of the transatlantic alliance. Linked to this are the profound differences in political and strategic goals between Germany's two closest partners – France and the USA. Third, the process of restructuring NATO and redefining its purpose in the post-cold war world has exposed deep fissures within the Alliance. New and aspirant members want the focus to remain on Article V security guarantees and territorial defence; the USA would like NATO to become an instrument for global power projection in defence of 'common interests'; Germany and many other European alliance members, on the other hand, want the emphasis to be placed on pan-European cooperative security governance. These preferences will not be easy to reconcile, and reflect the uncertainty that surrounds NATO's future mission in an era without a 'clear and present danger'.

Enlarging the Euro-Atlantic Security Community into Central Europe:
German policy-makers are keenly aware that the prosperity and security
the Federal Republic enjoys within the Euro-Atlantic community would
be threatened by instability and turmoil around its eastern borders. More
positively, they also believe that Germany would benefit from growing
prosperity and security in *Mitteleuropa*. A broad consensus has thus
emerged in Germany around the goal of opening up Euro-Atlantic structures to new members from East Central Europe. Germany has been a
driving force behind EU and NATO enlargement, and prides itself on
being the 'tribune' of the CEE states within Euro-Atlantic organisations.
Since Europe's historic 'Year of Decisions' in 1997, the dual enlargement
process has been the central motor driving the reordering of Europe, and
will continue to figure prominently on the European policy agenda for
much of the early twenty-first century.

Once again, however, there are tensions and ambiguities at the heart of
German policy. First, the de-coupling of NATO enlargement from that of
the EU. This has exacerbated the problem of divergent memberships
between the two organisations, and will complicate the building of a
coherent CFSP and an autonomous ESDI. Second, the decision to push
ahead with EU enlargement has been taken at the level of 'high politics'.
Its implementation, however, has been resisted by vested interests in
some sections of German society. There is thus a pressing need for more
effective policy coordination within the Federal government itself, as well
as between EU member states more generally. Third, whatever the spin,
there are problems inherent in trying to enlarge the EU at the same time
as the integration process is being deepened. At the very least, it means
that applicant countries are faced with a moving target, and find themselves struggling to catch up with a Union which is surging ahead with
new forms of integration. Finally, there is the impact of the enlargement
process on existing patterns of cooperation in CEE, particularly given the
requirement that applicant countries enforce Schengen regulations at
their borders. This raises the broader question of how to minimise the
sense of exclusion felt by countries left out of the enlargement process,
and takes us to the third plank of German grand strategy.

Nurturing a pan-European cooperative security system: 'cooperation'
not 'integration' is the operative word here. Central to this plank of
German grand strategy is Russia – Eastern Europe's great power and an
important contributor to European civilisation over the last millennium
(Kumar 1992: 458). Germany has not been tempted by the 'Russia First'
option, but it has sought to develop a cooperative partnership with

Russia (Stent 1999). This was evident from Chancellor's Kohl leading role in negotiating the NATO-Russia Founding Act, and the unstinting efforts of Foreign Minister Fischer to bring the Russians 'back on board' during the Kosovo war. This German–Russian relationship has been an important element in the new 'Concert of Europe' between Europe's great powers which emerged after the end of the cold war (Zelikow 1992; Kupchan and Kupchan 1991; Treverton 1993). The primary institutional expression of this new 'concert' has been the Contact Group, along with the G8 and the Permanent Joint Council (PJC).

In the 'outer zone' of Europe's fractured 'regional security complex' more broadly, Germany and its allies have sought to develop new patterns of cooperation and governance. The aim has been to embed the democratising states of Eastern Europe and the Balkans in networks of institutionalised cooperation based on deepening socio-economic interdependence and shared normative values (Hanson 1993). The primary institutions involved in this are the OSCE and the Council of Europe (Erhart 1996), along with regional organisations such as the CBSS, CEFTA and BSEC (Bremmer and Bailes 1998). The main mechanism for reshaping order in this outer zone has been *governance*, both in the form of the EU's 'soft governance' and NATO's 'cooperative security governance'. By enmeshing the Eastern Europeans in webs of institutional cooperation and governance, Germany and its allies hope, traditional patterns of *Machtpolitik* and balance of power thinking will be eroded and the 'authority model' of international relations strengthened.

The problems with this aspect of German grand strategy are threefold. First, despite the NATO-Russia Founding Act and the EU–Russia Partnership and Cooperation Agreement (PCA), the Euro-Atlantic community still lacks a clear vision of how Russia is to be included in pan-European networks. 'Russia's proper place is a critical issue that the governments of the West, led by Germany and the United States, but including Britain, have failed to address' (Haslam 1998: 129). Second, there is an intractable tension between enlarging Euro-Atlantic structures eastwards and nurturing pan-European security cooperation. Russian policy analysts are increasingly seeing a common strategy underpinning the dual enlargement process, involving NATO and the EU 'opening their doors' to the Central Europeans whilst 'putting off Russia's admission for the future'. 'When such a course in economic affairs is combined with a similar one in the military sphere, suspicions about isolating Russia and splitting up Europe are evoked still higher' (Pichugin 1996: 95). Third, a pan-European cooperative security system requires that the

many multilateral organisations that constitute Europe's security architecture are 'interlocking' not 'inter-blocking'. There is pressing need to
ensure that the primary organisations involved in European security –
the UN, OSCE, EU, NATO and Council of Europe – synchronise their
efforts and work together harmoniously. To return to the jazz metaphor
employed above, in a large band of many ambitious musicians there is a
great danger of a discordant cacophony unless there is firm agreement on
rhythm and chord structures, on who plays solos and when.

Twenty-first-century Europe

In addition to the antinomies of German grand strategy summarised
above, this study has identified four factors that will have important
implications for Berlin's foreign and security policy in the twenty-first
century. These four factors have to do with the deep-seated processes of
change that are transforming the nature of European order in the late
modern age.

First, the crucial dynamics of change in the continent of Europe are not
those associated with EU deepening. Rather, they are those associated
with the altered relationship between the West European security community and the countries of Central and Eastern Europe. Despite the
importance of EMU for the future of European integration, the most far-
reaching changes to the nature of European order are those taking place
between Western Europe and the post-communist East. New patterns of
cooperation and conflict are emerging across the old East–West divide
that are transforming the economic, political and strategic contours of
Europe. This will have important – and unknown – implications for
order in twenty-first century Europe.

Second, the 'return to Europe' of the Central European democracies will not simply involve their 'Westernisation', but will alter the
institutional pillars of the Euro-Atlantic community. Enlargement will
significantly change patterns of institutional governance in Europe,
transforming the networks of multilateralism that have been so important for 'embedding' Germany in wider Euro-Atlantic structures.
As Heinz Timmermann has argued, the notion of 'eastern enlargement' is therefore somewhat of a misnomer (Timmermann 1997: 10).
Enlargement will not simply 'Westernise' Central and Eastern Europe,
but will act as the catalyst for the birth of a new Europe. This is most
obviously the case with the EU, where eastern enlargement spells the end
of the 'EEC model' of deep integration. As we have also seen, however,
NATO too is trying to re-define its mission in the post-cold war world.

In addition, not only will the key institutions of the Euro-Atlantic community change through enlargement, but established patterns of bilateral relations will differ. This is most evident in the case of the Franco-German partnership, which will have to adjust to a new environment where Poland is an increasingly important interlocutor for Berlin.

Third, the Kosovo war has thrown into stark relief the extent to which the ordering principles of the Westphalian system have been undermined, and in doing so, has raised some intractable moral and political questions for Germany. The Westphalian system was built on the principle of the territorial inviolability of sovereign states. This ordering principle has been gradually undermined in the post-war years, initially by the Nuremberg trials, and later by the ambivalent provisions of the 1975 Helsinki Final Act. After Kosovo, however, it is not clear what is left of sovereignty in its traditional, Westphalian form. It is certainly not apparent what new ordering principle will replace it, and what the implications of a post-Westphalian system will be for existing concepts of statehood, citizenship and democratic accountability. The crucial question is whether there is now a right to humanitarian intervention in the internal affairs of sovereign states in the case of gross violations of human rights. If so: under what conditions, by whom and how? This raises complex political and ethical considerations that expose sharply the agonies of a *Zivilmacht* faced with large-scale organised violence and appalling abuses of human rights.

Finally, one of the inescapable facts about contemporary Europe is the existence of a major fault-line running through continent. It broadly corresponds with the old East–West divide, and overlays older historical fractures and fault-lines in Europe. This fault-line is no longer military or ideological, but social and economic. It runs through *Mitteleuropa*, between the relatively wealthy social market economies of Germany and Austria, and the new democracies of East Central Europe. Despite the dismantling of the iron curtain and the Berlin Wall, huge socio-economic disparities and power asymmetries still mark the relationship between West and East. 'Germany, which is the world's highest cost production area, is immediately adjacent to the very low cost areas of Hungary and the Czech Republic. This gradient between Germany and eastern Europe is steeper than that between Mexico and California, and far steeper than the gradient between Japan and other parts of southeast Asia' (Kaletsky 1997: 36). This will place enormous strains on German and the EU's social partnership model, given the competitive pressures of low cost labour and industrial restructuring than will accompany the eastward expansion of the European economy.

More importantly, perhaps, it raises questions about the prospects for extending the Euro-Atlantic security community into Central Europe. Karl Deutsch argued that a security community did not simply involve shared institutions and economic exchanges, but a sense of community or 'we-feeling' based on trust and social capital. However, as Dieter Senghaas has suggested (1997: 15), this sense of community is difficult to achieve in the absence of a degree of economic fairness and social justice. The existence of substantial socio-economic inequalities impedes the accumulation of trust and social capital that is vital to the emergence of a durable peace order. It also complicates the process of constructive conflict resolution. Economic asymmetries may impede the emergence of a security community in two ways. First, perceived economic disparities will make the process of defining common interests harder to achieve. This is already evident given the fear of some in Germany that they will not be able to compete with relatively cheap Polish labour. Second, it will make the emergence of shared identities and a sense of 'we-ness' more difficult, particularly as socio-economic asymmetries may serve to reinforce existing cultural differences and historical animosities between 'slavs' and 'teutons'. The existence of a major socio-economic cleavage between Germany and its East Central European neighbours will thus make it harder to build a Europe 'whole and free'.

'Negotiated' or 'imposed' order in Central Europe?

The existence of sharp asymmetries between the West Europeans and their Central European neighbours raises questions about the way in which European order is being reshaped through the dual enlargement process. In particular, it poses the question: is Germany and the Euro-Atlantic community of which it is an influential member *imposing* order on the post-communist East, or *negotiating* it (see pp. 65–6).

The dual enlargement process certainly seems at times to CEE countries to smack of *imposed order*, in the sense of an order 'deliberately fostered by dominant powers or consortia of dominant powers' using 'some combination of coercion, cooptation, and the manipulation of incentives' (Young 1989: 88). Both the EU and NATO have insisted on strict requirements for accession, and attached conditionality clauses to their cooperation with CEE countries. The position of the applicant countries appears especially weak given that they are seeking to join

Euro-Atlantic structures – they are the supplicants, which the West can either accept or reject.

In reality, however, the situation is much more complicated than this. The dual enlargement process does involve the 'explicit consent on the part of subordinate actors', and thus does not fit the archetype of *imposed order*. Rather, the situation involves a form of leadership (what we shall term below '*benign hegemony*') 'in which an actor (or small group of actors) that is markedly superior to others in natural and human resources or other bases of power plays a critical role in designing institutional arrangements and inducing others to agree to their terms'. The Euro-Atlantic community (the collective actor in this case) has not simply dictated terms to applicant countries, but has engaged in a process of negotiation involving considerable give-and-take. 'In such cases', Oran Young argues (1989: 88), 'the distinction between imposed regimes and negotiated regimes begins to blur, and it is not helpful to insist on a hard-and-fast separation between the two.'

One important consideration is that the relationship between the Euro-Atlantic community and the Central European democracies tends to involve what Alexander George has called a 'strategy of reciprocity', rather than a 'bargaining strategy'. A bargaining strategy is 'an effort to achieve through negotiation an *explicit, specific* exchange that is usually carried out by the two parties *simultaneously*'. Reciprocity, on the other hand, refers to a 'unilateral initiative taken by one side in the hope that it will encourage the other side to take a conciliatory action in return. The terms of the exchange are not negotiated and are left somewhat *diffuse*, and the action that constitutes the reciprocation comes later, *not simultaneously*' (George 1988: 693).

The element of *negotiated order* inherent within the dual enlargement process has been greatly strengthened by the normative component of German *Ostpolitik*. Both the German public and German policy-makers have a powerful sense of historical indebtedness to CEE countries for their contribution to the fall of the Berlin Wall. In addition, they are aware of the painful legacy of *Vernichtungskrieg* in the East, and of the open wounds it has left on the body politic of CEE. This has altered the dynamics of power relations in *Mitteleuropa*, and effectively strengthened the negotiating hand of Poland and other East Central Europeans vis-à-vis their powerful Western neighbour (Hampton 1998: 85; Pond 1996: 32–3; Freudenstein 1998: 46). This was already evident in the negotiations Germany conducted with its eastern neighbours in the early 1990s. Despite the clear power asymmetries between CEE states and Germany,

Ann Phillips has argued, the 'new constellation of international, regional and domestic factors has enhanced their ability to exercise more authority over their own futures than they had enjoyed in recent memory. Germany's policy of reconciliation, continued from West Germany's *Ostpolitik*, in particular, has augmented CEE leverage in the process of rewriting the terms of German-CEE relations' (1998: 74).

Germany's role within the Euro-Atlantic community as an advocate of eastern enlargement and a tribune for the interests of the East Central Europeans is thus important in strengthening the element of *negotiated order* in the dual enlargement process. German politicians continually stress the importance of eastern enlargement and the sense of mission that surrounds it. Chancellor Schröder, for example, has declared enlargement to be an 'imperative arising from our historic responsibility towards [our friends and partners in Central and Southeast Europe], as well as political and economic good sense' (*Frankfurter Allgemeine Zeitung*, 1 December 1999, p. 9). Similarly Günther Verheugen, the EU Commissioner for Enlargement, has described his job as 'contributing to overcoming the division of Europe'. The exclusion of Poland or Czechoslovakia from the EEC over forty years ago, he argues, was a result of the outcome of the Second World War, 'and therefore a consequence of German guilt'. EU enlargement thus has an important 'moral and historical dimension which must be emphasised'. Moreover, enlargement is 'the political task of my life, of my generation' (*Die Zeit*, 9 December 1999, p. 6). Germany's active engagement in the dual enlargement process has thus been an important factor in facilitating the East Central Europeans 'return to Europe' on the basis of *negotiated* rather than *imposed* order.

Hegemony in Central Europe

The relationship between the Euro-Atlantic security community and the Central European democracies is not just characterised by sharp power asymmetries and socio-economic disparities, but also by a desire on the part of the Central Europeans to 'rejoin Europe'. The primary factor driving the 'triple transformation' in Central Europe is the influence of the West. This is not simply a function of relative power capabilities, but reflects the ability of the Euro-Atlantic community to articulate values, norms and codes of behaviour that the Central Europeans wish to emulate. This suggests that a distinctive mechanism is at work in this relationship – not domination or coercion, but rather a form of '*benign hegemony*'.

'Hegemony', as Knutsen has argued (1999: 11–12), is a much-used word, but many who use it 'have overlooked the consensual connotation which informs the term'. There is an important distinction to be made between 'great power based on force and great power rooted in consent. And only the latter qualifies as "hegemony"'. Hegemony thus has a 'moral dimension', and a hegemon owes its influence to its effective articulation of 'a code of values, norms and rules for social conduct that other countries embrace'. If a hegemon looses its normative influence, 'it will also forfeit its commanding position'. Hegemony is therefore not synonymous with great power, and

> a hegemon is more than a great power. To be hegemonic means to possess the authority of command. It includes a notion of primacy based on a component of just and legitimate leadership. Pre-eminence in wealth and force is a necessary but not a sufficient precondition of hegemony. Hegemony involves pre-eminence which is sustained by a shared understanding among social actors of the values, norms, rules and laws of political interaction; of patterns of authority and the allocation of status and prestige, responsibilities and privileges.

This concept of hegemony was shared by no less a historical personage than Otto von Bismarck. He described hegemony as 'an unequal relationship established between a great power and one or more smaller powers which is nevertheless based on judicial or formal equality of all the states concerned. It is not an empire. It is not based on "ruler" or "ruled" but on "leadership" and "followers"'.[2] Bismarck's definition underlines that there is an important distinction in the way large powers exert influence over smaller powers. The distinction is between 'domination' (or 'empire') and 'hegemony'. Domination is a function of a unilateralist foreign and security policy,[3] and involves the pursuit of what Arnold Wolfers called 'possession goals'. Imperial powers seek to 'impose' order through the deployment of deliberative power, particularly the threat or use of the instruments of coercive power. Dominance is thus based on *Machtpolitik* and reinforces the 'power politics' model of international relations (see pp. 66–7).

Hegemony, on the other hand, involves an asymmetrical power relationship in which the larger state (or group of states) exercises power with a view to strengthening the 'authority model' of international relations. Hegemons are primarily concerned with 'milieu shaping' and 'negotiated order', and rely on non-coercive forms of structural power. A hegemon will tend to focus on establishing 'an institutional environment which is favourable to its own interests', even if this means shouldering the burden of 'being the mainstay of the system (providing financial services, a source of capital, and a pattern of military support)'. A hegemon is thus 'the main beneficiary of the system but also the main provider of externalities to the other members: it receives disproportionate benefits but accepts disproportionate burdens' (Clark 1989: 106–7). Finally, the successful exercise of hegemony will depend on what Joseph Grieco, drawing on Albert Hirschman's concept of 'exit, voice and loyalty' (Hirschman 1970), terms 'effective voice opportunities':

> 'Effective voice opportunities' may be defined as institutional characteristics whereby the views of partners (including relatively weaker partners) are not just expressed but reliably have a material impact on the operations of the collaborative arrangements … states (and particularly weaker states) may view effective voice as a 'good' that they enjoy as part of being in a collaborative arrangement, and enjoyment of a satisfactory level of this 'good' may itself be a basis for assessment by states of their satisfaction or dissatisfaction with the arrangement. (Grieco 1996: 280)

In Central Europe, hegemony is exercised in the first instance not by Germany alone, but collectively, by the Euro-Atlantic community organised in NATO and the EU. The Euro-Atlantic community thus functions as a *benign collective hegemon*. When exercised collectively through multilateral institutions, hegemonic leadership can 'soften' perceptions of power asymmetries, thereby providing an incentive for other states to cooperate. Charles Kindelberger himself suggested that two or more participants can 'take on the task of providing leadership together, thus adding to legitimacy, sharing the burdens, and reducing the danger that leadership is regarded cynically as a cloak for domination and exploitation' (1981: 252). The Euro-Atlantic community thus serves as a 'collective hegemon' in Central Europe, seeking to lay the foundations for a durable peace order by utilising the tools of cooperative governance and multilateral cooperation. Its hegemonic influence on Central Europe rests on its capacity for institutionalised consultation, negotiation, compromises, agenda-setting and shared normative principles.

Germany's relationship with its neighbours in East Central Europe is also best understood in terms of hegemony. However, Germany does not exercise its hegemonic power unilaterally. As we have seen, German foreign and security policy is characterised by a deep-seated commitment to multilateralism and a series of close strategic partnerships. This is not an altruistic abnegation of its national interests, but an example of what de Toqueville called 'interest rightly understood' (i.e., 'enlightened self-interest'). 'Germany has become a team player by conviction; its population has internalized multilateralism, not for reasons of altruism but for the sake of efficient foreign and security policy in an interdependent world' (Rummel 1995: 193).

For this reason, therefore, Germany's role in Central Europe is that of a '*benign multilateral hegemon*'. This definition underlines the fact not only that Germany's power in the region is overwhelmingly benign, but more importantly, that it is embedded in a broader set of multilateral structures and relationships.[4] From a structural realist perspective, it is impossible to explain why Germany, 'considered to be the strongest state in Europe', supports institutional arrangements that accord weaker states in Central Europe such power over key decision-making processes (Spirtas 1996: 403). Indeed, this can only be understood in terms of Germany's foreign policy identity and role conception as a multilateralist *Zivilmacht* with a special responsibility for peace and cooperation in Europe.

Germany's *benign multilateral hegemony* is primarily based on its accumulated stockpiles of trust and social capital – what Hans-Dietrich Genscher called *Vertrauenskapital* (literally 'trust-capital'). Genscher argued that Germany had successfully accumulated reserves of *Vertrauenskapital* over the years through its policy of *Westbindung* and rapprochement with the East through *Ostpolitik* (Genscher 1991: 7). 'These reserves of trust', as Garton Ash notes, 'as much as the reserves of DM – and the capital of trust was also partly trust in German capital – were heavily and successfully drawn upon to achieve German unification' (1994: 358). This *Vertrauenskapital* is a primary instrument of German structural power, and is a vital resource for Germany's grand strategy for reshaping late modern European order. As Gunther Hellmann has stressed, the foreign policy *Vertrauenskapital* collected over the last forty years, together with the instinctive multilateralism of German diplomacy 'are priceless – and frequently undervalued – intangible power resources' (Hellmann 1998: 282). At the same time, he warns, they are also 'more diffuse and precarious', given their intrinsic character and the legacy of Germany's past.

Germany and Poland

One final aspect of German grand strategy that emerges from this study is the importance of Germany's relationship with Poland. As we have seen (pp. 119–20), the *Bundesrepublik*'s response to the dilemmas of German power in Europe involved two policy instruments: integration in multilateral organisations and the cultivation of a series of close strategic partnerships – primarily with the USA and France. With the end of the cold war, Germany has responded to the dilemmas of its '*multilateral*

Mittellage' by forging a new strategic partnership with Poland, the largest and geopolitically most important of the new democracies in Central Europe. This new bilateral relationship, which has been from the start embedded in a broader multilateral context, is of pivotal importance for the reordering of Europe. Whilst it would be an exaggeration to claim that Europe's future hinges upon Polish–German relations, 'it is certainly the case that, first, the way things work out between these two states is highly relevant to everything else that happens in Europe in the decades to come; and second, this relationship encompasses many of the east-west problems that Europe as a whole faces' (Freudenstein 1998: 41).

For Poland, Germany's importance stems from the inescapable fact that 'our road into the West European house leads through Germany and can perhaps be made easier with German help' (Lipski 1996: 262). For Germany, Poland is important because it is the pivotal country in Central and Eastern Europe, and because a stable, prosperous and secure Poland is vital for a stable, prosperous and secure Germany. These shared concerns have given rise to the emergence of what the then Polish Foreign Minister, Krzysztof Skubiszewski, termed a Polish-German 'community of interests' (Pfluger and Lipscher 1993). At the heart of this 'community of interests' is the dual enlargement of NATO and the EU – a goal which has been championed by both countries. The dual enlargement process is also important because it provides a multilateral context for German–Polish relations – as does the 'Weimar Triangle' with France (Baas 1999).

Poland's importance to German grand strategy, however, goes beyond a simple desire to see its largest eastern neighbour incorporated in Euro-Atlantic structures. This is of course very important to Germany. At the same time, however, many in Berlin are aware that Poland is emerging as a pivotal actor in Central and Eastern Europe. By virtue of its size, location and national role conception, Poland is coming to act as a crucial hinge between the core and outer zones – between the transatlantic community and Eastern Europe (Feldmann and Gareis 1998). In the 1990s, Warsaw has cultivated a series of strategic partnerships with Lithuania and – more importantly – Ukraine. It has also striven hard to foster and consolidate good working relations with Moscow, despite historical animosities and conflicts over the question of NATO enlargement. As a new member of NATO, Poland is active in the Partnership for Peace programme and is keen to promote wider patterns of cooperative security governance in the CEE area. Poland also aspires to carve out the EU's 'Eastern Dimension' of its external relations as its own special domain (Handl and Zaborowski 1999: 31). Poland thus aspires to play a pivotal role in the new international relations of Central and Eastern Europe, and to act as a conduit and multiplier for cooperative security governance throughout its neighbourhood in CEE – including the Baltic Sea region. By developing a strategic partnership with Poland, therefore, Germany is also serving the broader goals of its grand strategy – developing a pan-European system of cooperative security.

'As long as the world exists', conventional wisdom in Poland has it, 'a German would never be a brother to a Pole' (Rachwald 1993: 232). The decade since unification and the end of the cold war has confounded such views, and demonstrated that it is possible for Germans and Poles to live together in Central Europe as cooperative neighbours. Problems at a social and individual level persist, of course, and the economic asymmetries between the two countries set limits to the prospects of building a sense of common identity or 'we-feeling', but in general, remarkable progress has been achieved. The emergence of a Polish–German 'community of interests' is one of the most important developments in post-cold war Europe, and augurs well for building a stable peace order. As former Polish Foreign Minister Wladyslaw Bartoszewski – himself a survivor of Auschwitz – said in 1995, the 'change wrought in Polish–German relations is one of the most positive transformations in European history' (Pritzel 1998: 124).

Germany and the reordering of Europe

Since unification with its illegitimate Eastern sibling in 1990, the coordinates which have defined post-war West German foreign and security policy have fundamentally altered. The ground has shifted under the feet of Europe's 'gentle giant'.[5] At the same time, Germany itself has changed through unification, and is now the only country in Europe having to grapple simultaneously with the problems of post-industrialism and the legacy of state socialism. United Germany thus faces complicated domestic challenges at a time when it is also having to rethink its role and identity in a Europe growing together.

Given its central location, size and influence, and the demands placed upon it by its neighbours and allies, Germany faces a barrage of competing demands. Its central task is to preserve its *Westbindung* and ensure the continuing cohesion of the Euro-Atlantic security community, at the same time as fostering new patterns of integration and cooperation with Central and Eastern Europe. In the twenty-first century, the historic task facing the Berlin Republic is to preserve and expand the Kantian *foedus pacificum* that developed in post-war Western Europe, and thereby to lay the foundations for a durable *Friedensordnung* throughout the continent. If Germany lacks the vision, the commitment or the energy to work towards this end, the losers will not only be the Germans themselves, but also the wider international community.

The Berlin Republic and the future of Europe

The Berlin Republic

The Bonn Republic, Hans Magnus Enzensberger once observed (1989: 100), represented 'the very paradigm of a government lacking in aura'. This, he added, was no bad thing, for there was much to be said for the 'mediocre sort of government' embodied by Rhineland, provincial Bonn. The transfer of the capital and seat of government to Berlin corresponds to the new geopolitical realities of a larger 'Europe', and perhaps makes unification seem less like *Anschluss* to East Germans. Perhaps, too, as Gunther Hellmann has mused, in ten, twenty or fifty years we may, when we look back on the period since unification, use the metaphor of the 'Berlin Republic' to describe a novel foreign policy mix of 'civilian great power, national self-assuredness and multilateral normality' (Hellmann 1999: 842).

Yet there are concerns that with the relocation of political power to Berlin, the virtues that Bonn symbolised – modesty, quiet self-confidence and above all, *Westbindung* – might be lost among the Wilhelmine grandeur of Unter den Linden and the Reichstag. The debate on normalisation and national interests in the mid-1990s was seen by some as heralding the advent of a Germany less committed to multilateralism and more concerned to pursue its own self-interest. Bundeswehr participation in military crisis management was also seen by some as marking the death of *Zivilmacht Deutschland*. Unification and the move to Berlin have therefore fuelled concerns that the Berlin Republic will be a very different creature from the accommodating and reticent Bonn Republic.

Chancellor Schröder addressed these concerns in his speech to the French National Assembly on 30 November 1999 (*Bulletin*, 6 December 1999, p. 781). He recognised that some harboured fears that a 'Germany governed from Berlin' would 'displace the coordinates of German foreign policy', thereby weakening the Franco-German relationship. He argued, however, that even if German politics were conducted in a more 'dynamic, exciting city much closer to reality', German foreign policy would continue to be characterised by continuity. Like France, he declared, Germany would continue to pursue its 'enlightened self-interest whilst being embedded in the European Union and the North Atlantic Alliance'. Together, he concluded, France and Germany would pursue goals shared by all Europeans: above all 'peace, freedom, prosperity and our own national as well as European identity'.

Schröder's words are instructive about the subtle re-calibration of foreign policy discourse underway in Germany. Gone is the *Bescheidenheit* and *Zurückhaltung* (modesty and reserve) of the Bonn Republic. Gone too is the unwillingness to talk about 'national interests' and preference for a 'European' rather than a 'national' identity. In its place is the self-confidence of the 'sixty-eighter' generation, and a recognition of Germany's responsibilities as a 'large power' (the current euphemism for 'great power'). This does not signify a new spirit of assertiveness and a yearning for unilateral power projection. The crucial question is not *whether* Germany defines its 'national interests', but *how*. To date, there is no indication that the Berlin government is defining its interests in ways incompatible with those of its partners and neighbours. At the same time, there are no indications that Germany's post-Holocaust identity is weakening, whatever the concerns stirred up by the 'normalisation-nationalists' (see pp. 39–40). Indeed, the continuing vitality of its post-Holocaust identity is evident from the debates surrounding the Goldhagen book, the Bubis–Walser dispute and the Holocaust Memorial in Berlin.

One additional point is the continuing importance of the normative dimension of German foreign policy. This runs as a red thread through the post-war history of German foreign policy, from Willy Brandt's sublime *Kniefall* to the Kosovo war. This means that much of the official discourse surrounding German foreign policy is phrased in terms of its morality and ethics, rather than in the traditional diplomatic language of *Realpolitik* and international law. Of course, this striving for an 'ethical' foreign policy generates its own dilemmas, as the British government has recently discovered. Thus Germany, for example, has faced a set of role conflicts over the question of arms sales to Turkey (a NATO ally, but one with a dubious human rights record), and the dilemma of how best to respond to Putin's war against Chechnya. At the same time, this normative concern with human rights, rapprochement with former adversaries and international justice has a very real impact on the conduct of German foreign policy – as we have seen in the case of its policy towards the Central European democracies.

Germany and the 'arrogance of power'

Given the Berlin Republic's political weight, economic strength and accumulated reserves of *Vertrauenskapital*, the new Europe will have a strong German influence. Yet, German power and influence in the new Europe will not be exercised unilaterally, but multilaterally. It will therefore tend to be mediated through multilateral organisations, informal 'minilateral' groupings of states (see pp. 166–7) and strategic partnerships. Despite this, Europe's new age may well be 'a German age, perhaps to the degree that the age of Louis XIV was French, that the age of Victoria was British and the that the twentieth century has been American' (Rees-Mogg 1989).

Germany's considerable influence on the reshaping of Europe will not necessarily be malign. The Germans today are different from those who acted 'as Hitler's willing executioners'. They are concerned, not with *Lebensraum* in the East or military glory, but with environmental protection and human rights, with 'quality of life' and gender issues, with participation and *Bürgerinitiativen* – all of which will be concerns of growing saliency in late modern Europe. With its social market economy, vibrant civil society, liberal-democratic political system and increasingly 'multi-kulti' culture, Germany has in many respects come to embody the 'European dream', particularly for those in Central and Eastern Europe. 'When in 1989 people east of the Iron Curtain spoke of returning to Europe and normality, West Germany was a central part of the liberal, democratic, civil and bourgeois "normality" they had in mind' (Garton Ash 1996: 83).

There is of course a danger that the Berlin Republic may use its considerable tangible and intangible power resources for selfish and short-sighted ends. The most serious concern regarding Germany is not of a recidivist 'Fourth Reich', but that Germany may yield – like so many major states in history – to the 'arrogance of power'. 'Under these circumstances', Stanley Hoffmann has warned (1990: 295–96), 'Germany might behave less like a wise "hegemon", understanding the need to take account of the interests of lesser powers, than like a selfish player concerned above all with relative gains and insensitive to the claims and fears of others'.

In the end, there can be no foolproof safeguard against this eventuality, but two points are relevant here. First, as Joseph Rovan said four months after his liberation from Dachau concentration camp, we get *l'Allemagne de nos merites* ('the Germany we deserve'). He coined this phrase in order to indicate the need at that time for mutual reconciliation and a shared responsibility for the democratic development of Germany. Today, this means treating the Germans as our allies and partners in a new Europe, working with them, not against them – and not treating them as if they were suffering from 'angst, aggressiveness, assertiveness, bullying, egotism, inferiority complex, sentimentality' (as an infamous Whitehall memorandum in the late Thatcher years suggested).

Second, the best way to ensure that the tremendous dynamism and creativity of the Germans benefits Europe as a whole is through nurturing multilateral forms of cooperation and integration in Europe – not only, the EU, NATO and the OSCE, but also the Council of Europe and sub-regional organisations such as the CBSS. This is the most realistic way to realise the dream of Thomas Mann in 1952 – a 'European Germany' rather than a 'German Europe'. As Peter Katzenstein has argued (1997: 304), the 'legitimate exercise of German power can occur only through Europe's complex institutional arrangements'. Moreover, he suggests, because 'institutional integration describes a process in which the character of states also changes, German domination over contemporary Europe is a mirage – both close at hand and receding'. Thus 'the "Germanization of Europe" and the "Europeanization of Germany"', he concludes, 'are part of the same political process'.

Germany will clearly be an influential actor in the reshaping of Europe, but there are good grounds for believing that this German influence will help reinforce trends towards cooperation and integration in the continent. A Germany embedded into a expanding Euro-Atlantic security community, and enjoying good relations with its neighbours, strategic partners and former adversaries, is well situated to become a positive motor for pan-European cooperation. In this way, the Berlin Republic will be able to fulfil both aspects of its constitutional duty laid down in the preamble to the *Grundgesetz*: preserving 'its national and political unity', whilst at the same time serving 'the peace of the world as an equal partner in a united Europe'.

Conclusion

Politicians, Harold Macmillan once remarked, have only one thing to fear: 'events, old boy, events'. Academics reflecting on future developments should bear Macmillan's admonitions in mind when tempted to prognosticate about the future. In the case of Germany and Germany's role in the reshaping European order, much is in flux. It is therefore particularly difficult to make any predictions about future trends and developments with any confidence.

However, one thing can be said with some confidence that has a crucial bearing on the future of Europe. This is that Germany has changed. Contemporary Germany is not the Germany of Bismarck, Stresemann, Hitler or even of Adenauer. The dominant values, norms and principles of late modern Germany are those of a mature liberal-democracy, firmly embedded within the multilateral structures of a pluralistic security community. Germany's national identity and its dominant foreign policy role conceptions are those of a 'normal' *Zivilmacht*, committed to the shaping of pan-European cooperative security order buttressed by enlarged Euro-Atlantic structures. As recent public debates have demonstrated, most Germans remain sensitive to the need to find new and authentic ways to remember the lessons of the past, and do not seek to repress, deny or relativise memories of the Holocaust. This does not mean that Germans can be complacent, but it does mean that others have little reason 'to fear the Germans' (see Markovits and Reich 1991; Goldberger 1993).

In this context, the words of the *Selige Knaben* ('Blessed boys') in the closing scene of Goethe's *Faust: Part Two* are appropriate to contemporary Germany. Of Faust, the errant hero whose ceaseless strivings for development and self-fulfilment had inflicted such great tragedy and suffering on others, they declare;

> *Doch dieser hat gelernt,*
> *Er wird uns lehren.*
> ('This one, however, learned,
> And he will teach us'.)

Germans, at the end of the twentieth century, have learnt. They have, as Chancellor Kohl said in his speech on German unification to the Reichstag on 4 October 1990, faced up to the 'darkest chapters' of German history, and not tried to 'forget, push aside or belittle what crimes were carried out by the Germans this century, and what pain has been inflicted on individuals and peoples'. Germany today is stable, democratic, prosperous and secure. It is also a 'normal' civilian power, with a well-functioning federal system, and welfare and educational services that are the envy of many. Perhaps, therefore, Germany also has something to teach us about building a more peaceful, cooperative and socially just Europe.

Notes

1 Quoted in *Die Zeit*, no. 50, 9 December 1999, p. 2
2 Quoted in *The Economist*, 23 October 1999, p. 8.

3 'Unilateralism' involves 'the pursuit of one's own interests with no consideration or only a minimal consideration for the interests of others. Such insistence on pursuing one's own agenda often goes hand in hand with domination
over others, even if done with good intentions. It rests on a "fait accompli"
backed by superior power' (Bertele and Mey 1998: 198).

4 In this respect, it is interesting to note that Michael Dauderstädt and Barbara
Lippert have argued that 'Germany's increasing importance for the internal
development of the EU and for its capacity to act externally' requires from
Germany a 'willing to exercise a political leadership characterised by self-
binding (*Selbstbindung*)'. 'What Germany is seeking from the EU', they argue,
'is the chance to embed itself in structures that can Europeanise its national
interests and bring them into harmony with the national interests of its neighbours' (1998: 10, 20).

5 As Simon Bulmer notes, the notion of a 'gentle giant' expresses two important
facets of Germany's role in Europe. First, German diplomacy is 'gentle' in the
sense that it is not characterised by 'unilateral, deliberative power'. Second,
that 'Germany is a giant, particularly in the economic sphere' and thus exercises 'the dispositional form of unintentional power' (Bulmer 1997: 79).

Bibliography

Adenauer, K. (1965) *Erinnerungen, 1945–1953*, Stuttgart, Deutsche Verlags-Anstalt

Adler, E. (1997) 'Seizing the Middle Ground: Constructivism in World Politics', *European Journal of International Relations*, 3: 3 (September), 319–64

Adler, E. and Barnett, M. (1998) *Security Communities*, Cambridge, Cambridge University Press

Aggestam, K. (1999) *Reframing and Resolving Conflict: Israeli–Palestinian Negotiations 1988–1998*, Lund Political Studies 108, Lund University Press

Aggestam, L. (1997) 'The European Union at the Crossroads: Sovereignty and Integration', in Landau and Whitman, 75–92

Aggestam, L. (1999) *Role Conceptions and the Politics of Identity in Foreign Policy*, ARENA Working Paper no. 8 (February), Oslo, University of Oslo

Agrell, W. (1994) *Alliansfri – Tils Vidare*, Stockholm Natur och Kultur

Albright, M. (1997) 'Review of Foreign Policy Agenda' (confirmation hearing before the Senate Foreign Relations Committee), *Official Text*, United States Information Service (USIS), London, US Embassy, 9 January 1997

Allen, D. and Smith, M. (1990) 'Western Europe's Presence in the Contemporary International Arena', *Review of International Studies*, 16: 1 (January), 19–38

Allin, D. (1995) 'Can Containment Work Again?', *Survival*, 37: 1, 53–65

Allison, R. (1993) *Military Forces in the Soviet Successor States*, Adelphi Paper 280 (October), London, Brassey's for the IISS

Alten, J. von (1994) *Die Ganz Normale Anarchie: Jetzt erst Beginnt die Nachkriegszeit*, Berlin, Siedler Verlag

Amato, G. and Batt, J. (1999) *The Long-term Implications of EU Enlargement: The Nature of the New Border*, Final Report of the Reflection Group, Badia Fiesolana, Robert Schuman Centre for Advanced Studies and European Commission Forward Studies Unit

Anderson, J. and Goodman, J. (1993) 'Mars or Minerva? A United Germany in a Post-Cold War Europe', in Keohane, Nye and Hoffman, 23–62

Andreae, L. and Kaiser, K. (1998) 'Die "Aussenpolitik" der Fachministerien', in Eberwein and Kaiser, 29–46

Armstrong, D. (1999) 'Law, Justice and the Idea of a World Society', *International Affairs*, 7: 3 (July), 547–61

Anderson, J. (1997) 'Hard Interests, Soft Power, and Germany's Changing Role in Europe', in Katzenstein, 80–107

Anderson, J. (1999) *German Unification and the Union of Europe*, Cambridge, Cambridge University Press

Archer, C. (1996) 'The Nordic Zone as "Zone of Peace"', *Journal of Peace Research*, 33: 4, 451–67

Ashe, F., Finlayson, A., Lloyd, M., Mackenzie, I. Martin, J. and O'Neill, S. (1999) *Contemporary Social and Political Theory: An Introduction*, Buckingham, Open University Press

Asmus, R. and Nurick, R. (1996) 'NATO Enlargement and the Baltic States', *Survival*, 38: 2 (spring), 121–42

Assembly of the WEU (1997) 'Enlarged Security: The Security Problems Posed by the Enlargement of NATO and the European Institutions', Colloquy, Athens, 11–12 March 1997, Paris, Assembly of the WEU

Assembly of the WEU (1999) *The NATO Summit and Its Implications for Europe*, Report submitted on behalf of the Defence Committee by Mr Cox, Rapporteur, Document 1637, Paris, Assembly of the WEU, 15 March 1999

Auffermann, B. and Visuri, P., eds (1995) *Nordeuropa und die deutsche Herausforderung*, Baden-Baden, Nomos Verlagsgesellschaft

Auswärtiges Amt/Ministere des Affaires Etrangeres (1999) *'Ein Europa mit dreißig und mehr Mitgliedern': Ausgangspunkte der deutsche-französischen Überlegungen*, Bonn/Paris, Auswärtiges Amt, Planungsstab/Ministere des Affaires Etrangeres, Centre d'analyse et de prévision

Axt, H.-J. (1996) 'Mittellage oder Kerneuropa: Perspektiven deutsch-französözischer Beziehungen', *Europäische Rundschau*, 24: 1 (winter), 109–24

Axt, H.-J. (1997) 'Strukturpolitik und Köhesion in der Europäischen Union: Reform in der Perspektiven der Osterweiterung', *Zeitschrift für Politikwissenschaften*, 17: 3, 885–927

Baas, R. (1999) 'Das Weimarer Dreieck: Von Regionaler Kooperation zu Europäischer Integration', *Internationale Politik*, 54: 11 (November), 41–6

Bahr, E. (1999) 'Ein Deutschland, Das Nein Sagen Kann', *Blätter für Deutsche und Internationale Politik*, 44: 11 (November), 311–23

Bailes, A. (1997) 'Sub-Regional Organizations: The Cinderellas of European Security', *NATO Review*, 45: 2 (March), 27–31

Baldwin, D., ed. (1993) *Neorealism and Neoliberalism: The Contemporary Debate*, New York, Columbia University Press

Banchoff, T. (1998) 'German Identity and European Identity', *European Journal of International Relations*, 5: 3 (September), 259–90

Banchoff, T. (1999) *The German Problem Transformed: Institutions, Politics, and Foreign Policy, 1945–1995*, Michigan, University of Michigan Press

Baring, A., ed. (1994) *Germany's New Position in Europe: Problems and Perspectives*, Oxford, Berg

Barnett, M. (1996) 'Identity and Alliances in the Middle East', in Katzenstein, 400–47

Bartsch, S. (1998a) 'Aussenpolitischer Einfluss und Aussenbeziehungen der Parteien', in Eberwein and Kaiser, 167–84

Bartsch, S. (1998b) 'Politische Stiftungen: Grenzgänger Zwischen Gesellschafts- und Staatenwelt', in Eberwein and Kaiser (1998), 185–98

Baumann, R., Rittberger, V. and Wagner, W. (1999) 'Macht und Machtpolitik: Neorealistische Aussenpolitiktheorie und Prognosen über die deutsche Aussenpolitik nach der Vereinigung', *Zeitschrift für Internationale Beziehungen*, 6: 2 (December), 245–86

Beck, U. (1999) 'Über den Postnationalen Krieg', *Blätter für deutsche und internationale Politik*, 8 (August), 984–90.

Bender, P. (1996) *Die "Neue Ostpolitik" und ihre Folgen: Vom Mauerbau bis zur Vereinigung*, 4th edition, Munich, Deutscher Taschenbuch Verlag

Bertele, M. and Mey, H. (1998) 'Unilateralism in Theory and Practice', *Contemporary Strategy*, 17: 2, 197–207

Bertram, C. (1988) 'Change in Moscow: Continuity in Europe?', *The World Today*, 44: 8–9 (August–September), 137–9

Bertram, C. (1994) 'The Power and the Past: Germany's New International Loneliness', in Baring, 91–106

Biedenkopf, K. (1994) 'Facing the Challenge of Upheaval in Europe', *NATO Review*, 42: 3 (June), 15–17

Blackbourn, D. and Eley, G. (1984) *The Peculiarities of German History: Bourgeois Society and Politics in Nineteenth Century Germany*, Oxford, Oxford University Press

Bloom, W. (1990) *Personal Identity, National Identity and International Relations*, Cambridge, Cambridge University Press

Bohman, J. and Lutz-Bachmann, M., eds (1997) *Perpetual Peace: Essays on Kant's Cosmopolitan Ideal*, Cambridge, Mass., MIT Press

Booth, K. (1995) 'Dare Not to Know: International Relations Theory versus the Future', in Booth and Smith, 328–50

Booth, K. and Smith, S., eds (1995) *International Relations Theory Today*, Cambridge, Polity Press

Boucher, D. (1998) *Political Theories of International Relations*, Oxford, Oxford University Press

Boulding, K. (1978) *Stable Peace*, Austin, University of Texas Press

Bowker, M. and Brown, M. (1993) *From Cold War to Collapse: Theory and World Politics in the 1980s*, Cambridge, Cambridge University Press

Braudel, F. (1975) *The Mediterranean and the Mediterranean World In the Age of Philip II*, two volumes, London, Fontana

Bremmer, I. and Bailes, A. (1998) 'Sub-regionalism in the Newly Independent States', *International Affairs*, 74: 1, 131–48

Brettschneider, F. (1998) 'Massenmedien, Öffentliche Meinung und Aussenpolitik', in Eberwein and Kaiser, 215–26

Breuilly, J., ed. (1992) *The State of Germany: The National Idea in the Making, Unmaking and Remaking of a Modern Nation-State*, London, Longman

Bring, O. (1999) 'Should NATO Take the Lead in Formulating a Doctrine on Humanitarian Intervention?', *NATO Review*, 47: 3 (autumn), 24–7

Brock, L. (1999) 'Normative Integration und Kollektive Handlungskompetenz auf internatinoaler Ebene', *Zeitschrift für Internationale Beziehungen*, 6: 2 (December), 323–48

Brown, C. (1992) *International Relations Theory: New Normative Approaches*, London, Harvester Wheatsheaf

Brown, C. (1995) 'International Theory and International Society: The Viability of the Middle Way', *Review of International Studies*, 21: 2 (April), 183–96

Brown, C. (1997) *Understanding International Relations*, London, Macmillan

Brown, S. (1995) *New Forces, Old Forces and the Future of World Politics*, New York, HarperCollins

Brzezinski, Z. (1989) 'The Future of Yalta', *Foreign Affairs*, 63: 2 (winter), 279–302

Bühl, W. (1994) 'Gesellschaftliche Grundlagen der Deutschen Aussenpolitik', in Kaiser and Maull, 175–202

Bull, H. (1977) *The Anarchical Society: A Study of Order in World Politics*, London, Macmillan

Bull, H. and Watson, A., eds (1984) *The Expansion of International Society*, Oxford, Oxford University Press

Bulmer, S. (1993) 'The Governance of the European Union: A New Institutionalist Approach', *Journal of Public Policy*, 13: 4, 351–80

Bulmer, S. (1997) 'Shaping the Rules? The Constitutive Politics of the European Union and German Power', in Katzenstein, 49–79.

Bulmer, S. and Paterson, W. (1987) *The Federal Republic of Germany and the European Community*, London, Allen and Unwin

Bulmer, S. and Paterson, W. (1989) 'West Germany's Role in Europe: "Man-Mountain" or "Semi-Gulliver"?', *Journal of Common Market Studies*, 28: 2 (December), 95–117

Bulmer, S. and Paterson, W. (1996) 'Germany in the European Union: Gentle Giant or Emergent Leader?', *International Affairs*, 72: 1: 9–32

Bulmer, S., Jeffery, C. and Paterson, W. (2000) *Germany's European Diplomacy: Shaping the Regional Milieu*, Manchester, Manchester University Press

Bundesministerium der Verteidigung (1994) *Weißbuch zur Sicherheit der Bundesrepublik Deutschland*, Bonn Presse- und Informationsamt

Burley, A.-M. (1990) 'The Once and Future Question', *Foreign Affairs*, 68: 5 (winter), 65–83

Burton, J. (1993) 'Conflict Resolution as a Political Philosophy', in *Conflict Resolution Theory and Practice: Integration and Application*, edited by Dennis Sandole and Hugo van der Merwe, Manchester, Manchester University Press

Buruma, I. (1994) *The Wages of Guilt*, London, Cape

Buzan, B. (1991) *People, States and Fear: An Agenda for International Security Studies in the Post-Cold War World*, 2nd edition, London, Harvester Wheatsheaf

Buzan, B., Jones, C. and Little, R. (1993) *The Logic of Anarchy*, New York, Columbia University Press

Buzan, B., Waever, O. and de Wilde, J. (1998) *Security: A New Framework for Analysis*, London, Lynne Rienner Publishers

Byers, M. (1999) *Custom, Power and the Power of Rules: International Relations and Customary International Law*, Cambridge, Cambridge University Press

Calic, M.-J. (1996) 'German Perspectives', in *International Perspectives on the Yugoslav Conflict*, edited by Alex Danchev and Thomas Halverson, London, Macmillan, 52–75

Calic, M.-J. (1998) 'Post-SFOR: Towards Europeanization of the Bosnia Peace Operation?', in *The Issues Raised by Bosnia, and the Transatlantic Debate*, Chaillot Paper 32, edited by Sophia Clement, Paris, WEU Institute for Security Studies, 10–22

Calleo, D. (1978) *The German Problem Reconsidered: Germany and the World Order: 1870 to the Present*, Cambridge, Cambridge University Press

Caporaso, J. (1996) 'The European Union and Forms of State: Westphalian, Regulatory or Post-modern?', *Journal of Common Market Studies*, 34: 1, 29–51

Carlsnaes, W. (1992) 'The Agency-Structure Problem in Foreign Policy Analysis', *International Studies Quarterly*, 36, 245–70

Carlsnaes, W. (1994) 'In Lieu of a Conclusion: Compatiblity and the Agency–Structure Issue in Foreign Policy Analysis', in Carlsnaes and Smith, 274–87

Carlsnaes, W. and Smith, S., eds (1994) *European Foreign Policy: The EC and Changing Perspectives in Europe*, London, Sage

Cassels, A. (1996) *Ideology and International Relations in the Modern World*, London, Routledge

Cerny, P. (1993) 'Plurilateralism: Structural Differentiation and Functional Conflict in Post-Cold War World Order', *Millennium*, 22: 1, 27–51

Cerny, P. (1997) 'Paradoxes of the Competition State: The Dynamics of Political Globalization', *Government and Opposition*, 32: 2 (spring), 251–74

Checkel, J. (1993) 'Ideas, Institutions, and the Gorbachev Foreign Policy Revolution', *World Politics*, 45 (January), 271–300

Checkel, J. (1997) 'International Norms and Domestic Politics: Bridging the Rationalist–Constructivist Divide', *European Journal of International Relations*, 3: 4, 473–95

Checkel, J. (1998) 'The Constructivist Turn in International Relations Theory', *World Politics*, 50: 2, 324–48

Clark, I. (1989) *The Hierarchy of States: Reform and Resistance in the International Order*, Cambridge, Cambridge University Press

Clark, I. (1997) *Globalization and Fragmentation: International Relations in the Twentieth Century*, Oxford, Oxford University Press

Clinton, D. (1991) 'The National Interest: Normative Foundations', in Little and Smith, 47–58

Cohen, S. (1994) 'Geopolitics in the New World Era: A New Perspective on an Old Discipline', in Demko and Wood, 15–48

Coker, C. (1992) 'Post-Modernity and the End of the Cold War: Has War Been Disinvented', *Review of International Studies*, 18: 3 (July), 189–98

Comes, S. (1995) *Die Agrarpolitik der EU und die Osterweiterung: Aktuelle Kurzanalyse*, no. 13, Bonn, DGAP

Cooper, R. (1996) *The Post-Modern State and the World Order*, London, Demos

Corterier, P. (1990) 'Quo Vadis NATO?', *Survival*, 32: 2, 141–56

Cottey, A. (1995) *East-Central Europe after the Cold War: Poland, the Czech Republic, Slovakia and Hungary in Search of Security*, London, Macmillan

Cox, R. (1986) 'Social Forces, States and World Orders: Beyond International Relations Theory', in Keohane (1986), 204–54

Craig, G. and Gilbert, F. (1986) 'Reflections on Strategy in the Present and Future', in Paret, 863–72

Crawford, B. (1995) 'German Foreign Policy and European Political Cooperation: The Diplomatic Recognition of Croatia in 1991', *German Politics and Society*, 13: 1, 1–34

Croft, S. (1996) *Strategies of Arms Control: A History and Typology*, Manchester, Manchester University Press

Crome, E. (1997) 'Noch Einmal über die NATO-Osterweiterung, die europäische Sicherheit und das Perzeptionsproblem', *WeltTrends*, no. 15 (summer), 162–77

Czempiel, E.-O. (1996) 'Kant's Theorem. Oder: Warum Sind die Demokratien (Noch Immer) Nicht Friedlich?', *Zeitschrift für Internationale Beziehungen*, 3: 1 (June), 79–101

Czempiel, E.-O. (1997) 'Die Neuordnung Europas: Was leisten NATO und OSZE für die Kooperation mit Osteuropa und Russland?', *Aus Politik und Zeitgeschichte*, B1-2/97 (3 January), 34–45

Czempiel, E.-O. (1998) 'Foreword' to *The Promise and Reality of European Security Cooperation: States, Interests, and Institutions*, edited by Mary McKenzie and Peter Loedel, Westport, Praeger, ix–xii

Cziomer, E. (1997) 'Polen auf dem Wege zur EU-Mitgliedschaft', *Zeitschrift für Politikwissenschaft*, 7: 1, 21–32

Dalvi, S. (1998) 'The Post-Cold War Role of the Bundeswehr: A Product of Normative Influences', *European Security*, 7: 1 (spring), 25–44

Dauderstädt, M. and Lippert, B. (1998) *Die Deutsche Ratspräsidentschaft: Doppelstrategie zur Vertiefung und Erweiterung der EU*, Bonn, Friedrich Ebert Stiftung

Davies, N. (1996) *Europe: A History*, Oxford, Oxford University Press

Davies, P. and Dombrowski, P. (1997) 'Appetite of the Wolf: German Foreign Assistance for Central and Eastern Europe', *German Politics*, 6: 1 (April), 1–22

Dembinski, M. (1999) 'Verteidigungsbündnis ohne Feind', *Blätter für Deutsche und Internationale Politik*, 44: 7 (July), 787–90

Demko, G. and Wood, W., eds (1994) *Reordering the World: Geopolitical Perspectives on the 21st Century*, Boulder, Westview

Deporte, A. (1979) *Europe Between the Superpowers*, London, Yale University Press

Deubner, C. (1995) *Deutsche Europapolitik: Von Maastricht nach Kerneuropa?*, Baden-Baden, Nomos Verlag

Deubner, C. and Janning, J. (1996) *Zur Reform des Abstimmungsverfahrens im Rat der Europäischen Union: Überlegungen und Modellrechnungen, Ausgehend von einer Veränderung der Stimmgewichtung*, SWP–IP2971 (September), Ebenhausen, Stiftung Wissenschaft und Politik

Deutsch, K. (1957) *Political Community in the North Atlantic Area*, Princeton, Princeton University Press

Dini, L. (1999) 'Taking Responsibility for Balkan Security', *NATO Review*, 47: 3 (autumn), 4–7

Diez, T. (1996) 'Postmoderne und europäische Integration: Die Dominanz des Staatsmodells, die Verantwortung gegenüber dem Anderen und die Konstruktion eines Alternativen Horizonts', *Zeitschrift für Internationale Politik*, 3: 2 (December), 255–81

Diez, T. (1998) 'Perspektivenwechsel: Warum ein "Postmoderner" Ansatz für die Integrationsforschung doch relevant ist', *Zeitschrift für Internationale Politik*, 5: 1 (June), 139–48

Donnelly, J. (1998) 'Realism: Roots and Renewal', *Review of International Studies*, 24: 3 (July), 399–405

Dorff, R. (1997) 'Normal Actor or Reluctant Power? The Future of German Security Policy', *European Security*, 6: 2 (summer), 56–69

Dörsam, P. (1995) *Zum Ewigen Frieden 1795–1995: 200 Jahre Nach Kant's "Zum Ewigen Frieden" Was Nun?*, Heidenau, PD-Verlag

Doyle, M. (1983) 'Kant, Liberal Legacies, and Foreign Affairs', *Philosophy and Public Affairs* (summer), 205–35 and (autumn), 3–29

Duffield, J. (1994) 'German Security Policy after Unification: Sources of Continuity and Restraint', *Contemporary Security Policy*, 15: 3, 170–98

Duffield, J. (1998) *Political Culture, International Institutions, and German Security Policy after Unification*, Stanford, Stanford University Press

Dunne, T. (1995) 'The Social Construction of International Society', *European Journal of International Relations*, 1: 3 (September), 367–90

Dunne, T. (1998) *Inventing International Society: A History of the English School*, Basingstoke, Macmillan

Dyer, H. and Mangasarian, L., eds (1989) *The Study of International Relations: the State of the Art*, London, Macmillan

Dyson, K. (1980) *The State Tradition in Western Europe: A Study of an Idea and Institution*, Oxford, Martin Robertson

Dyson, K. (1999) 'The Franco-German Relationship and Economic and Monetary Union: Using Europe to "Bind Leviathan"', *West European Politics*, 22: 1 (January), 25–44

Eberwein, W.-D. and Kaiser, K., eds (1998) *Deutschlands neue Außenpolitik. Band 4: Institutionen und Ressourcen*, Munich, R. Oldenbourg Verlag

Ehrhart, H.-G. (1996) 'EU, OSZE und der Stabilitätspakt für Europa: Präventive Diplomatie als gemeinsame Aufgabe', *Integration*, 1, 37–48

Ehrhart, H.-G. (1999) 'Stabilitätspakt für Südosteuropa', *Blätter für deutsche und internationale Politik*, 8 (August), 916–18

Enzensberger, H. (1989) Interview in *New Left Review*, 178 (November–December), 87–104

Evans, P., Rueschemeyer, D. and Skocpol, T., eds (1985) *Bringing the State Back In*, Cambridge, Cambridge University Press

Evans, T. and Wilson, P. (1992) 'Regime Theory and the English School of International Relations: A Comparison', *Millennium*, 21: 3, 329–52

Eyal, J. (1997) 'NATO's Enlargement: Anatomy of a Decision', *International Affairs*, 73: 4, 695–719

Fawn, R. and Larkens, J., eds (1996) *International Society after the Cold War: Anarchy and Order Reconsidered*, London, Macmillan

Feldman, L. (1996) 'The Impact of German Unification on German–American Relations: Alliance, Estrangement or Partnership?', in Heurlin, 179–209

Feldmann, E. and Gareis, S. (1998) 'Polens Rolle in der NATO: Zur Bedeutung externer Hilfen bei der Stabilisierung Osteuropas', *Zeitschrift für Politikwisssenschaft*, 8: 3, 983–1003

Finnemore, M. (1996) *National Interests in International Society*, Ithaca and London, Cornell University Press

Fischer, J. (1994) *Risiko Deutschland: Krise und Zukunft der deutschen Politik*, Köln, Kiepenheuer und Witsch

Fischer, J. (1999) 'Kluge Selbstbeschränkung, Multilaterale Interessenvertretung', *Frankfurter Allgemeine Zeitung*, 26 November 1999, p. 8

Flockhart, T. (1996) 'The Dynamics of Expansion: NATO, WEU and EU', *European Security*, 5: 2 (summer), 196–218

Flockton, C. (1996) 'Economic Management and the Challenge of Reunification', in Smith, Paterson and Padgett, 211–32

Francke, K. (1997) 'Rebalancing Transatlantic Relations', *NATO Review*, 45: 5 (September–October), 17–20

Frankel, B., ed. (1996a) *Roots of Realism*, London, Frank Cass

Frankel, B., ed. (1996b) *Realism: Restatements and Renewal*, London, Frank Cass

Freudenstein, R. (1998) 'Poland, Germany and the EU', *International Affairs*, 74: 1, 41–54

Friis, L. and Murphey, A. (1999) 'The European Union and Central and Eastern Europe: Governance and Boundaries', *Journal of Common Market Studies*, 37: 2 (June), 211–32

Gaddis, J.L. (1992) 'International Relations Theory and the End of the Cold War', *International Security*, 17: 3, 5–58

Gaddis, J.L. (1996) 'History, Science, and the Study of International Relations', in Woods, 32–48

Garton Ash, T. (1988) 'Reform or Revolution?', *New York Review of Books*, 27 October, 47–56

Garton Ash, T. (1990) *We the People: The Revolution of 1989*, Harmondsworth, Penguin

Garton Ash, T. (1994) *In Europe's Name: Germany and the Divided Continent*, London, Vintage

Garton Ash, T. (1996) 'Germany's Choice', in Mertes, Muller and Winkler, 79–94

Geipel, G. (1994) 'Germany: Urgent Pressures, Quiet Change', *Current History*, November, 358–63

Geiss, I. (1997) *The Question of German Unification: 1806–1996*, London, Routledge

Genscher, H.-D. (1991) 'Preface' to *Deutsche Aussenpolitik 1990/91. Auf dem Weg zu einer europäischen Friedensordnung. Eine Dokumentation*, Bonn, Auswärtiges Amt

George, A. (1969) 'The "Operational Code": A Neglected Approach to the Study of Political Leaders and Decision-Making', *International Studies Quarterly*, 13, 190–222

George, A. (1988) 'Strategies for Facilitating Cooperation', in *US–Soviet Security Cooperation: Achievements, Failures, Lessons*, edited by Alexander George, Philip Farley and Alexander Dallin, Oxford, Oxford University Press

Geremek, B. (1999) 'Europäische Politik zwischen Ost und West: Polens geostrategische Chancen', *Internationale Politik*, 54: 11 (November), 35–40

Gillessen, G. (1994) 'Germany's Position in the Centre of Europe: the Significance of Germany's Position and Misunderstandings about German Interests', in Baring, 21–34

Gilpin, R. (1996) 'No One Loves a Political Realist', in Frankel (1996b), 3–27

Goetschel, L. (1999) 'Aussenpolitikanalyse in der Schweiz: Paradigma oder Sonderfall? Zum Einfluss von Entscheidungsprozessen auf nationale Rollenkonzepte', *Zeitschrift für Internationale Beziehungen*, 6: 2 (December), 349–70

Goetz, K. (1996) 'Integration Policy in a Europeanized State: Germany and the Intergovernmental Conference', *Journal of European Public Policy*, 3: 1, 24–40

Goldberger, B. (1993) 'Why Europe Should Not Fear the Germans', *German Politics*, 2: 2 (August), 288–310

Goldgeier, J. (1998) 'NATO Expansion: The Anatomy of a Decision', *The Washington Quarterly*, 21: 1 (winter), 85–102

Goldhagen, D. (1996) *Hitler's Willing Executioners: Ordinary Germans and the Holocaust*, New York, Alfred Knopf

Goldmann, K. (1997) 'Nationalism and Internationalism in Post-Cold War Europe', *European Journal of International Relations*, 3: 3, 259–90

Goldstein, J. and Keohane, R. (1993) *Ideas and Foreign Policy: Beliefs, Institutions and Political Change*, New York, Cornell University Press

Gordon, P. (1994) 'Berlin's Difficulties: The Normalisation of German Foreign Policy', *Orbis*, 38: 2 (spring), 225–44

Grass, G. (1990) *Two States – One Nation? The Case against German Reunification*, London, Secker & Warburg

Gray, J. (1993) 'From Post-Communism to Civil Society: The Reemergence of

History and the Decline of the Western Model', *Social Philosophy and Policy*, 10: 2 (summer), 26–50

Grewe, W. (1986) *Die Deutsche Frage in der Ost-West-Spannung: Zeitgeschichtliche Kontroversen der achziger Jahre*, Herford, BusseWald

Grieco, J. (1996) 'State Interests and Institutional Rule Trajectories: A Neorealist Interpretation of the Maastricht Treaty and European Economic and Monetary Union', in Frankel (1996b), 261–306

Gustavsson, S. and Lewin, L., eds (1996) *The Future of the Nation-State: Essays on Culturalism, Pluralism and Political Integration*, Stockholm, Nerenius & Santerus

Guzzini, S. (1998) *Realism in International Relations and International Political Economy: the Continuing Story of a Death Foretold*, London, Routledge

Habermas, J. (1999) 'Destialität und Humanität', *Die Zeit*, no. 18, 29 April 1999, p. 1

Hacke, C. (1993) *Die Aussenpolitik der Bundesrepublik Deutschland: Weltmacht wider Willen*, Berlin, Ullstein Verlag

Hacke, C. (1997a) 'Die neue Bedeutung des nationalen Interesses für die Aussen-politik der Bundesrepublik Deutschland', *Aus Politik und Zeitgeschichte*, B1-2/97 (3. January), 3–14

Hacke, C. (1997b) *Die Aussenpolitik der Bundesrepublik Deutschland: Weltmacht wider Willen?*, Aktualisierte Aufgabe, 4th edition, Berlin, Ullstein Verlag

Haftendorn, H. (1997) *German Foreign Policy in a Strategic Triangle: Bonn–Washington–Paris*, Thyssen Lecture, Washington, Georgetown University, Center for German and European Studies

Halliday, F. (1994) *Rethinking International Relations*, London, Macmillan

Hall, J. (1996) *International Orders*, Cambridge, Polity Press

Hampton, M. (1998) 'Poland, Germany and NATO Enlargement Policy', *German Comments*, no. 49, 85–94

Handl, V. (1997) 'Czech–German Declaration on Reconciliation', *German Politics*, 6: 2 (August), 150–67

Handl, V. and Zaborowski, M. (1999) *Comparative Czech and Polish Perspectives and Policies on the Eastern Enlargement of the EU and the Prominence of the 'German Factor'*, Birmingham, Paper sponsored by the Research Support Scheme of Open Society Foundation

Hanrieder, W. (1989) *Germany, America, Europe: Forty Years of German Foreign Policy*, New Haven, Yale University Press

Hanrieder, W. (1995) *Deutschland, Europa, Amerika: Die Außenpolitik der Bundesrepublik Deutschland 1949–1994*, 2nd edition, Paderborn, Ferdinand Schöningh

Hanson, M. (1993) 'Democratisation and Norm Creation in Europe', *European Security Beyond the Cold War: Part One*, Adelphi Paper 284, London, Brassey's for the IISS, 28–41

Hartmann, J. (1998) 'Organisierte Interessen und Aussenpolitik', in Eberwein and Kaiser, 239–52

Haslam, J. (1998) 'Russia's Seat at the Table: A Place Denied or a Place Delayed?', *International Affairs*, 74: 1, 119–30

Hasenclever, A., Mayer, P. and Rittberger, V. (1997) *Theories of International Regimes*, Cambridge, Cambridge University Press

Hassner, P. (1968) *Change and Security in Europe*, Adelphi Paper no. 45, London, International Institute for Strategic Studies

Hassner, P. (1993) 'Beyond Nationalism and Internationalism: Ethnicity and World Order', *Survival*, 35: 2 (March–April), 49–63

Hauner, M. (1993) 'The Czechs and the Germans: A One Thousand Year Relationship', in Verheyen, D. and Soe, C., 251–78.

Hay, C. (1995) 'Structure and Agency', in Marsh and Stoker, 189–208

Hayes-Renshaw, F. and Wallace, H. (1996) *The Council of Ministers*, London, Macmillan

Heinelt, H. (1996) 'Multilevel Governance in the European Union and the Structural Funds', in *Policy Networks and European Structural Funds*, edited by Hubert Heinelt and Randall Smith, Aldershot, Avebury, 9–25

Held, D. and McGrew, A. (1993) 'Globalization and the Liberal Democratic State', *Government and Opposition*, 28, 261–85

Hellmann, G. (1996) 'Goodbye Bismarck?: The Foreign Policy of Contemporary Germany', *Mershon International Studies Review*, 40, 1–39

Hellmann, G. (1997a) 'Jenseits von "Normalisierung" und "Militarisierung": Zur Standortdebatte über die neue deutsche Aussenpolitik', *Aus Politik und Zeitgeschichte*, B1-2/97 (3. January), 24–33

Hellmann, G. (1997b) 'The Sirens of Power and German Foreign Policy: Who is Listening?', *German Politics*, 6: 2 (August), 29–57

Hellmann, G. (1998) 'Die Prekäre Macht: Deutschland an der Schwelle zum 21. Jahrhundert', in Eberwein and Kaiser, 265–82

Hellmann, G. (1999) 'Nationale Normalität als Zukunft? Zur Aussenpolitik der Berliner Republik', *Blätter für Deutsche und Internationale Politik*, 44: 7 (July), 837–47

Herbert, U. (1998) 'Der Judenmord war das Kernereignis des Jahrhunderts', *Die Welt*, 16 March 1998, p. 9

Herdegen, M. (1994) 'Maastricht and the German Constitutional Court: Constitutional Restraints on an "Ever Closer Union"', *Common Market Law Review*, 31, 235–62

Herzog, R. (1995) *Die Globalisierung der deutschen Aussenpolitik ist unvermeidlich*, Bonn, Bulletin: Presse- und Informationsamt der Bundesregierung, vol. 20, 161–5

Heurlin, B. (1996) *Germany in Europe in the Nineties*, London, Macmillan

Heurlin, B. (1997) *Military Command Structures in the Baltic Sea Area*, Copenhagen, Danish Institute of International Affairs

Heuser, B. (1998) *Nuclear Mentalities? Strategies and Beliefs in Britain, France and the Federal Republic of Germany*, London, Macmillan

Heydrich, W., Krause, J., Nerlich, U, Nötzold, J. and Rummel, R., eds (1992)

Sicherheitspolitik Deutschlands: Neue Konstellationen, Risiken, Instrumente, Baden-Baden, Nomos Verlagsgesellschaft

Hildebrand, K. (1994) *Deutsche Aussenpolitik 1871–1918*, Munich, Oldenbourg Verlag

Hill, C., ed. (1996) *The Actors in Europe's Foreign Policy*, London, Routledge

Hill, C. and Wallace, W. (1996) 'Introduction. Actors and Actions', Hill, C., 1–18

Hilsman, R. (1990) *The Politics of Policy Making in Defence and Foreign Policy*, Englewood Cliffs, Prentice-Hall

Hirschman, A. (1970) *Exit, Voice, and Loyalty: Responses to Decline in Firms, Organizations, and States*, Cambridge, Mass., Harvard University Press

Hobsbawm, E. (1994) *Age of Extremes: The Short Twentieth Century, 1914–1991*, London, Michael Joseph

Höffe, O., ed. (1995) *Zum Ewigen Frieden*, Berlin, Akademie Verlag

Hoffmann, S. (1990) 'Reflections on the "German Question"', *Foreign Affairs*, 32: 4 (July–August), 291–8

Hoffmann, S. (1995) *The European Sisyphus: Essays on Europe, 1964–1994*, Oxford, Westview Press

Holland, M. (1994) *European Integration: From Community to Union*, London, Pinter

Hollis, M. and Smith, S. (1990) *Explaining and Understanding International Relations*, Oxford, Oxford University Press

Holst, C. (1998) 'Einstellungen der Bevölkerung und der Eliten: Vom Alten zum Neuen Aussenpolitischen Konsens?', in Eberwein and Kaiser, 227–38

Holsti, K. (1987) 'Toward a Theory of Foreign Policy: Making the Case for Role Analysis', in *Role Theory and Foreign Policy Analysis*, 1st edition, edited by Stephen Walker, Durham, Duke University Press

Holsti, K. (1991) *Peace and War: Armed Conflicts and International Order 1648–1989*, Cambridge, Cambridge University Press

Holsti, K. (1993) 'International Relations at the End of the Millennium', *Review of International Studies*, 19: 4 (October), 401–8

Holtbrügge, D. (1996) 'Ökonomische Voraussetzungen und Folgen einer Osterweiterung der Europäischen Union', *Osteuropa*, 46: 6 (June), 537–47

Hombach, B. (1999) 'The Stability Pact: Breaking New Ground', *NATO Review*, 47: 4 (winter), 20–3

Honig, J.W. (1996) 'Totalitarianism and Realism: Hans Morgenthau's German Years', in Frankel (1996a), 283–313

Hopmann, P. (1994) 'French Perspectives on International Relations After the Cold War', *Mershon International Studies Review*, 38, 69–93

Hoyer, W. (1998) 'Nationale Entscheidungsstrukturen Deutscher Europapolitik', in Eberwein and Kaiser, 75–86

Hubert, H.-P., ed. (1993) *Grüne Aussenpolitik: Aspekte einer Debatte*, Göttingen, Die Werkstatt

Hudson, V. and Vore, C. (1995) 'Foreign Policy Analysis Yesterday, Today and Tomorrow', *Mershon International Studies Review*, 39: 2, 209–38

Hupchick, D. (1994) *Culture and History in Eastern Europe*, London, Macmillan

Hurrell, A. (1993) 'International Society and the Study of Regimes: A Reflectivist Approach', in Rittberger, 49–72.

Hurrell, A. and Menon, A. (1996) 'Politics Like Any Other? Comparative Politics, International Relations and the Study of the EU', *West European Politics*, 19: 2, 386–402

Huysmans, J. (1998) 'Revisiting Copenhagen: Or, On the Creative Development of a Security Studies Agenda in Europe', *European Journal of International Relations*, 4: 4 (December), 479–505.

Hyde-Price, A. (1991) *European Security beyond the Cold War: Four Scenarios for the Year 2010*, London, Sage

Hyde-Price, A. (1996) *The International Politics of East Central Europe*, Manchester, Manchester University Press

Hyde-Price, A. (1997) 'The New Pattern of International Relations in Europe', in Landau and Whitman, 15–35

Hyde-Price, A. (1998) 'The International Politics of Central and Eastern Europe', in *Developments in Central and Eastern Europe 2*, edited by S. White, J. Batt, and P. Lewis, London, Macmillan, 255–75

Hyde-Price, A. (1999) 'Berlin Republic Takes to Arms', *The World Today*, 55: 6 (June), 13–15

Huysmans, J. (1998) 'Revisiting Copenhagen: Or, On the Creative Development of a Security Studies Agenda in Europe', *European Journal of International Relations*, 4: 4 (December), 479–505

Jachtenfuchs, M. and Kohler-Koch, B. (1996) 'Regieren im dynamischen Mehrebenensystem', in Jachtenfuchs and Kohler-Koch, eds, *Europäische Integration*, Opladen, Westdeutscher Verlag, 15–44

Jachtenfuchs, M., Dietz, T. and Jung, S. (1998) 'Which Europe? Conflicting Models of a Legitimate European Political Order', *European Journal of International Relations*, 4: 4, 409–45

Jacobsen, C., ed. (1990) *Strategic Power: USA/USSR*, London, Macmillan

Janning, J. (19994) 'Europa braucht verschiedene Geschwindigkeiten', *Europa-Archiv*, no. 18, 527–36

Janning, J. and Algieri, F. (1996) 'The German Debate', in *The 1996 IGC – National Debates (2): Germany, Spain, Sweden and the UK*, Chatham House Discussion Paper 67, London, Royal Institute of International Affairs, 1–21

Jeffery, C. (1996) 'Towards a "Third Level" in Europe? The German Länder in the European Union', *Political Studies*, 44, 253–66

Jepperson, R., Wendt, A. and Katzenstein, P. (1996) 'Norms, Identity and Culture in National Security', in Katzenstein (1996), 33–75

Jervis, R. (1976) *Perception and Misperception in International Politics*, Princeton, Princeton University Press

Jervis, R. (1983) 'Deterrence and Perception', *International Security*, 7: 3, 3–30

Joffe, J. (1994) 'German Grand Strategy After the Cold War', in Baring, 79–106

Joffe, J. (1996) 'Goldhagen in Germany', *New York Review of Books*, 28 November 1996

Johnstone, D. (1984) *The Politics of Euromissiles: Europe's Role in America's World*, London, Verso

Jönsson, C. (1984) 'Perceptions in International Politics and National Security', in *Security in the North*, edited by Bo Huldt and Atis Lejins, Stockholm, Swedish Institute of International Affairs, Conference Papers 5, 1–18

Jopp, M. and Arnswald, S., eds (1998) *The European Union and the Baltic States. Visions, Interests and Strategies for the Baltic Sea Region*, Bonn and Helsinki, Institut für Europäische Politik and Ulkopoliittinen instituutti

Jopp, M. and Lippert, B. (1998) 'Towards a Solution of the Baltic Issue: The EU's Role', in Jopp and Arnswald, 9–18

Jopp, M. and Warjovaara, R. (1998) *Approaching the Northern Dimension of the CFSP. Challenges and Opportunities for the EU in the Emerging European Security Order*, Helsinki, Finnish Institute of International Affairs (Ulkopoliittinen instituutti) and the Institut für Europäische Politik (Bonn)

Jönsson, C. and Westerlund, U. (1982) 'Role Theory in Foreign Policy Analysis', in *Cognitive Dynamics and International Politics*, edited by C. Jönsson, London, Frances Pinter

Judt, T. (1996) *A Grand Illusion. An Essay on Europe*, London, Penguin

Juricic, M. (1995) 'Perception, Causation and German Foreign Policy', *Review of International Studies*, 21: 1, 105–15

Kaelberer, M. (1997) 'Hegemony, Dominance or Leadership? Explaining Germany's Role in European Monetary Cooperation', *European Journal of International Relations*, 3: 1, 35–60

Kaiser, K. and Roper, J., eds (1988) *British-German Defence Cooperation*, London, Jane's for the Royal Institute of International Affairs (RIIA) and German Society for Foreign Policy (DGAP)

Kaiser, K, and Schwarz, H.-P., eds (1995) *Die Neue Weltpolitik*, Baden-Baden, Nomos Verlagsgesellschaft

Kaiser, K. and Krause, J., eds (1996) *Deutschlands Neue Außenpolitik. Band 3: Interessen und Strategien*, Munich, Oldenbourg Verlag

Kaiser, K. and Maull, H., eds (1997) *Deutschlands Neue Außenpolitik. Band 1: Grundlagen*, 3. Auflage, Munich, Oldenbourg Verlag

Kaletsky, A. (1997) 'Eastern Front', *Prospect*, 22 (August/September), 34–8

Kamp, K.-H. (1997) 'NATO-Russland-Gundakte: Trojanisches Pferd oder Meilenstein des Ausgleichs?', *Aussenpolitik*, 48: 4, 315–24

Kamp, K.-H. (1998) 'NATO Entrapped: Debating the Next Enlargement Round', *Survival*, 40: 3 (autumn), 170–86

Kamp, K.-H. (1999) 'A Global Role for NATO?', *The Washington Quarterly*, 22: 1 (winter), 7–11

Kant, I. (1795) [1992] *Perpetual Peace: A Philosophical Essay*, Bristol, Thoemmes Press

Kapteyn, P. (1996) *The Stateless Market*, London, Routledge

Kato, J. (1996) 'Institutions and Rationality in Politics: Three Varieties of Neo-Institutionalists', *British Journal of Political Science*, 26: 4, 553–82

Katzenstein, P., ed. (1996) *The Culture of National Security: Norms and Identity in World Politics*, New York, Columbia University Press

Katzenstein, P., ed. (1997) *Tamed Power: Germany in Europe*, Ithaca and London, Cornell University Press

Kennard, A. (1996) 'Issues of Identity in the Polish–German Border Region', *Journal of Area Studies*, issue 8: Citizenship in Contemporary Europe (spring), 106–19

Kennedy, P. (1988) *The Rise and Fall of the Great Power: Economic Change and Military Conflict From 1500 to 2000*, London, Fontana

Kennedy, P. (1991) 'Grand Strategy in War and Peace: Toward a Broader Definition', in *Grand Strategies in War and Peace*, edited by Paul Kennedy, New Haven, Yale University Press, 1–11

Keohane, R. (1984) *After Hegemony: Discord and Cooperation in the World Political Economy*, Princeton, Princeton University Press

Keohane, R. (1988) 'International Institutions: Two Research Programmes', *International Studies Quarterly*, 32, 379–96

Keohane, R. (1989) *International Institutions and State Power: Essays in International Relations Theory*, Boulder, Westview Press

Keohane, R. (1993a) 'The Analysis of International Regimes: Towards a European-American Research Programme', in Rittberger, 23–48

Keohane, R. (1993b) 'Internationalist Theory and the Realist Challenge after the Cold War', in Baldwin, 269–300

Keohane, R., ed. (1986) *Neorealism and Its Critics*, New York, Columbia University Press

Keohane, R. and Nye, J. (1977) *Power and Independence: World Politics in Transition*, New York, Scott-Foresman

Keohane, R., Nye, J. and Hoffman, S., eds (1993) *International Institutions and State Strategies in Europe, 1989–1991*, Cambridge, Mass., Harvard University Press

Keohane. R. and Martin, L. (1995) 'The Promise of Institutionalist Theory', *International Security*, 20: 1, 39–51

Keynes, J.M. (1919) *The Economic Consequences of the Peace*, London, Macmillan

Kiep, W. (1985) 'The New Deutschlandpolitik', *Foreign Affairs*, 63: 2 (winter), 316–29

Kiesinger, K. (1967) 'Rede anlässlich des Staatsakt zum Tag der deutschen Einheit', *Bulletin*, 17 June

Kindelberger, C. (1973) *The World in Depression*, Berkeley, University of California Press

Kindelberger, C. (1981) 'Dominance and Leadership in International Economy: Exploitation, Public Goods, and Free Rides', *International Studies Quarterly*, 25 (June), 242–54

Kindelberger, C. (1986) 'Hierarchy versus Inertial Cooperation', *International Organization*, 40, 841–7

Kintis, A. (1997) 'The EU's Foreign Policy and the War in Former Yugoslavia', in *Common Foreign and Security Policy: The Record and Reforms*, edited by M. Holland, London, Pinter

Kirste, K. and Maull, H. (1996) 'Zivilmacht und Rollentheorie', *Zeitschrift für Internationale Beziehungen*, 3: 2, 283–312

Kissinger, H. (1994) *Diplomacy*, New York, Simon and Schuster

Knodt, M. (1998) 'Auswärtiges Handeln der Deutschen Länder', in Eberwein and Kaiser, 153–66

Knudsen, B. (1987) 'The Paramount Importance of Cultural Sources: American Foreign Policy and Comparative Foreign Policy Research', *Cooperation and Conflict*, 22: 2, 81–113

Knutsen, T. (1999) *The Rise and Fall of World Orders*, Manchester, Manchester University Press

Kohl, H. (1998) 'Sicherheit für die Zukunft', *Europäische Sicherheit*, 47: 3 (March), 9–12

Köhler, H. and Fankhauser, S. (1999) 'Die Transformation Mittel- und Osteuropas: Die Mitwirkung Deutschlands', *Internationale Politik*, 54: 11 (November), 28–34

Kohler-Koch, B. (1996a) 'The Strength of Weakness: The Transformation of Governance in the EU', in Gustavsson and Lewin, 169–210

Kohler-Koch, B. (1996b) 'Catching up with Change: The Transformation of Governance in the European Union', *Journal of European Public Policy*, 3: 3, 359–80

Kohn, H. (1944) *The Idea of Nationalism: A Study in Its Origins and Background*, New York, Macmillan

Kolboom, I. (1996) 'Frankreich und Deutschland: Die Neue Akzente', in Kaiser and Krause, 123–28

Konrad, G. (1984) *Antipolitics*, London, Quartet Books

Korte, K. (1998) 'Unbefangen und Gelassen: Über die Aussenpolitische Normalität der Berliner Republik', *Internationale Politik*, 53: 12 (December), 23–43

Kowert, P. and Legro, J. (1996) 'Norms, Identity, and Their Limits: A Theoretical Reprise', in Katzenstein, 451–97

Kramer, M. (1996) 'The Soviet Union and Eastern Europe: Spheres of Influence', in Woods (1996b), 98–125

Krasner, S., ed. (1983) *International Regimes*, Ithaca, Cornell University Press

Krause, J. (1998) 'Die Rolle des Bundestages in der Aussenpolitik', in Eberwein and Kaiser, 137–50

Kreile, M. (1996) 'Verantwortung und Interessen in der deutschen Aussenpolitik', in *Aus Politik und Zeitgeschichte*, B5/96, 21 January

Krippendorff, E. (1999) 'Unzufrieden: Vierzig Jahre Politische Wissenschaft', *Blätter für deutsche und internationale Politik*, 8 (August), 991–1,001.

Kumar, K. (1992) 'The 1989 Revolutions and the Idea of Europe', *Political Studies*, 40, 439–61

Kupchan, C. and Kupchan, C. (1991) 'Concerts, Collective Security and the Future of Europe', *International Security*, 16: 1 (summer), 114–61

Landau, A. and Whitman, R., eds (1997) *Rethinking the European Union: Institutions, Interests, Identities*, London, Macmillan

Langguth, G. (1998) 'Rüchschau auf die Zukunft: Deutschland im Zeichen der "Globalisierung"', *Europäische Rundschau*, 26: 1 (winter), 49–68

Lankowski, C., ed. (1993) *Germany and the European Community: Beyond Hegemony and Containment*, New York, St Martin's Press

Lantis, J. (1996) 'Rising to the Challenge: German Security Policy in the Post-Cold War Era', *German Politics and Society*, 14: 2 (summer), 19–35

Larsen, H. (1997) *Foreign Policy and Discourse Analysis: France, Britain and Europe*, London, Routledge

Le Prestre, P., ed. (1997) *Role Quests in the Post-Cold War Era: Foreign Policies in Transition*, Montreal, McGill Queen's

Lefebvre, S. and Lombardi, B. (1996) 'Germany and Peace Enforcement: Participating in IFOR', *European Security*, 5: 4 (winter), 564–87

Leonhard, E. (1999) 'Schärfung des Profils: Die Deutsche Auswärtige Kulturpolitik', *Internationale Politik*, 54: 11 (November), 47–52

Lepgold, J. (1998) 'NATO's Post-Cold War Collective Action Problem', *International Security*, 23: 1 (summer), 78–106

Lepsius, R. (1990) *Interessen, Ideen und Institutionen*, Opladen, Westdeutscher Verlag

Libal, M. (1997) *Limits of Persuasion: Germany and the Yugoslav Crisis, 1991–1992*, Westport, Praeger

Lichback, M. and Zuckerman, A., eds (1997) *Comparative Politics: Rationality, Culture and Structure*, Cambridge, Cambridge University Press

Lindfors, B. (1999) *The Blind Men and the Elephant and Other Essays in Biographical Criticism*, Eritrea, African World Press

Linklater, A. (1998) *The Transformation of Political Community: Ethical Foundations of the Post-Westphalian Era*, Cambridge, Polity

Lipschutz, R., ed. (1995) *On Security*, New York, Columbia University Press

Lipski, J. (1996) *Wir Müssen Uns Alles Sagen … Essays zur Deutsch-Polnischen Nachbarschaft*, Warsaw, Deutsch-Polnischer Verlag

Little, R. and Smith, M., eds (1991) *Perspectives on World Politics*, 2nd edition, London, Routledge

Lübkemeier, E. (1998) *Interdependenz- und Konfliktmanagement: Deutsche Außenpolitik am Beginn des 21. Jahrhunderts*, Studie zur Außenpolitik no. 74, Bonn, Friedrich Ebert Stiftung

MacKinder, H. (1942) *Democratic Ideals and Reality*, 2nd edition, New York, Henry Holt

Maeder-Metcalf, B. (1997) 'The Organisation for Security and Cooperation in Europe', in *Baltic Security: The Long View from the Region*, Conflict Studies Research Centre, Conference Papers G58, Royal Military Academy Sandhurst

Magris, C. (1990) *Danube*, London, Collins Harvill

Maland, D. (1968) *Europe in the Seventeenth Century*, London, Macmillan

March, J. and Olsen, J. (1983) *Institutional Perspectives on Governance*, Bergen, LOS-senter

March, J. and Olsen, J. (1984) 'The New Institutionalism: Organizational Factors in Political Life', *American Political Science Review*, 78, 734–49

March, J. and Olsen, J. (1989) *Rediscovering Institutions: The Organizational Basis of Politics*, New York, Free Press

March, J. and Olsen, J. (1998) *The Institutional Dynamics of International Political Orders*, ARENA Working Paper no. 5 (April), Oslo, University of Oslo

Marks, G. (1993) 'Structural Policy and Multilevel Governance in the EC', in *The State of the European Community, Vol. 2: The Maastricht Debates and Beyond*, edited by A. Cafruny and G. Rosenthal, Harlow, Longman, 391–410

Marks, G., Hooghe, L. and Blank, K. (1996) 'European Integration from the 1980s: State-Centric v. Multilevel Governance', *Journal of Common Market Studies*, 34: 3 (September), 341–78

Markovits, A. and Reich, S. (1991) 'Should Europe Fear the Germans?', *German Politics and Society*, no. 23, 1–20

Markovits, A. and Reich, S. (1998) *Das Deutsche Dilemma: Die Berliner Republik zwischen Macht und Machtverzicht*, Berlin, Alexander Fest Verlag

Markovits, A., Reich, S. and Westermann, (1996) 'Germany: Hegemonic Power and Economic Giant?', *Review of International Political Economy*, 3: 4 (winter), 698–727

Marsh, D. and Stoker, G., eds (1995) *Theory and Methods in Political Science*, London, Macmillan

Marx, K. and Engels, F. (1968) [1848] *Selected Works in One Volume*, London, Lawrence and Wishart

Masty, W. (1988) 'Europe in US–USSR Relations: A Topical Legacy', *Problems of Communism*, 37: 1 (January–February), 16–29

Mathiopoulos, M. (1988) 'The US Presidency and the German Question During the Adenauer to Kohl Chancellorships', *Aussenpolitik*, 39: 4, 348–64

Mathiopoulos, M. and Gyarmati, I. (1999) 'Saint Malo and Beyond: Towards European Defense', *The Washington Quarterly*, 22: 4 (autumn), 65–76

Maull, H. (1990) 'Germany and Japan: The New Civilian Powers', *Foreign Affairs*, 69: 5, 91–106

Maull, H. (1993) 'Civilian Power: The Concept and its Relevance for Security Issues', in *Mapping the Unknown: Towards a New World Order*, Yearbook of the Swedish Institute of International Affairs, edited by Lidija Babic and Bo Huldt, Stockholm, Swedish Institute of International Affairs, 115–31

Maull, H. (1995) 'Germany in the Yugoslav Crisis', *Survival*, 37: 4 (winter), 99–130

Maull, H. (1997) 'Zivilmacht Deutschlands. Vierzehn Thesen für eine neue deutsche Aussenpolitik', in *Frieden Machen*, edited by D. Senghaas, Frankfurt am Main, Suhrkamp, 63–76

Maull, H. and Kirste, K. (1997) 'Zivilmacht und Rollentheorie', *Zeitschrift für Internationale Beziehungen*, 3: 2 (December), 283–312

Mayall, J. (1998) 'Globalisation and International Relations', *Review of International Studies*, 24: 2 (April), 239–50

Mayer, H. (1997) 'Early at the Beach and Claiming Territory? The Evolution of German Ideas on a New European Order', *International Affairs*, 73: 4, 721–37

Mayer, P. (1999) 'War der Krieg der NATO gegen Jugoslawien moralisch gerechtfertigt?: Die Operation "Allied Force" im Lichte der Lehre vom gerechten Krieg', *Zeitschrift für Internationale Beziehungen*, 6: 2 (December), 287–322

Mayhew, A. (1998) *Recreating Europe: The European Union's Policy Towards Central and Eastern Europe*, Cambridge, Cambridge University Press

McGrew, A. (1992) 'Conceptualizing Global Politics', in *Global Politics*, edited by A. McGrew and P. Lewis, Cambridge, Polity, 312–30

McKenzie, M. (1996) 'Competing Conceptions of Normality in the Post-Cold War Era: Germany, Europe and Foreign Policy Change', *German Politics and Society*, 14: 2 (summer), 1–18

McKenzie, M. and Loedel, P., eds (1998) *The Promise and Reality of European Security Cooperation: States, Interests, and Institutions*, Westport, Praeger

McManus, C. (1998) 'Poland and the Europe Agreements: the EU as a Regional Actor', in *A Common Foreign Policy for Europe?*, edited by J. Peterson and H. Sjursen, London, Routledge, 115–32

McSweeney, B. (1999) *Security, Identity and Interests: A Sociology of International Relations*, Cambridge, Cambridge University Press

Mearsheimer, J. (1990) 'Back to the Future: Instability in Europe after the Cold War', *International Security*, 15: 1 (September), 5–56

Mearsheimer, J. (1994–95) 'The False Promise of International Institutions', *International Security*, 19: 3 (winter), 5–49.

Mearsheimer, J. (1995) 'A Realist Reply', *International Security*, 20: 1, 82–93

Medick-Krakau, M., ed. (1999) *Aussenpolitischer Wandel in Theoretischer und Vergleichender Perspektive: Die USA und die Bundesrepublik Deutschland*, Baden-Baden, Nomos Verlagsgesellschaft

Meiers, F. (1995) 'Germany: The Reluctant Power', *Survival*, 37: 3 (August), 82–103

Mertes, M., Muller, S. and Winkler, H. (1996) *In Search of Germany*, New Brunswick, New Jersey, Transaction Publishers

Miller, L. (1994) *Global Order: Values and Power in International Politics*, 3rd edition, Boulder, Westview

Milner, H. (1998) 'Rationalizing Politics: The Emerging Synthesis of International, American and Comparative Politics', *International Organization*, 52: 4, 759–86

Milward, A. (1992) *The European Rescue of the Nation-State*, London, Routledge

Milward, A. (1993) 'Conclusions: the Value of History', in Milward and Sørensen, 182–201

Milward, A. and Sørensen, V., eds (1993) *The Frontier of National Sovereignty: History and Theory 1945–1992*, London, Routledge

Moravcsik, A. (1998) *The Choice for Europe: Social Purpose and State Power from Messina to Maastricht*, London, UCL Press

Moreton, E., ed. (1987) *Germany Between East and West*, Cambridge, Cambridge University Press

Morgan, R. (1987) 'West German Foreign and Security Interests', in Moreton, 97–108

Morgenthau, H. (1993) [1948] *Politics among Nations: The Struggle for Power and Peace. Brief Edition*, New York, McGraw-Hill

Mörth, U. (1998) *EU Policy-Making in Pillar One and a Half: the European Commission and Economic Security*, Stockholm, ÖCB Forskningsrapport

Mouritzen, H. (1997) 'Kenneth Waltz: A Critical Rationalist Between International Politics and Foreign Policy', in Neumannn and Waever (1997), 66–89

Mueller, J. (1989) *Retreat from Doomsday: The Obsolescence of Major War*, New York, Basic Books

Mueller, J. (1994) 'The Catastrophe Quota', *Journal of Conflict Resolution*, 38, 335–75

Müller, H. (1994) 'Military Intervention for European Security: The German Debate', in *Military Intervention in European Conflicts*, edited by Laurence Freedman, Oxford, Blackwell, 125–41

Müller, H. (1999) 'Sicherheit für das Vereinte Deutschland', in Medick-Krakau, 1,455–70

Münkler, H. (1998) 'Opfer der Geschichte? Das Jahr 1945 im Gedenken und Erinnen der Deutschen', *Die Zeit*, no. 46, 5 (November), p. 13

Murray, W. and Grimsley, M. (1994) 'Introduction: On Strategy', in *The Making of Strategy: Rulers, States, and War*, edited by W. Murray, M. Knox and A. Bernstein, Cambridge, Cambridge University Press, 1–23

NATO (1994) 'Declaration of the Heads of State and Government Participating in the Meeting of the North Atlantic Council Held at NATO Headquarters', Brussels, 10–11 January, *Europe Documents*, no. 83, Brussels, 12 January 1994

NATO (1997) 'Madrid Declaration on Euro-Atlantic Security and Cooperation', NATO Press Release M-1(97)81, Madrid, 8 July 1997

NATO (1999) 'The Alliance's Strategic Concept', Approved by Heads of State and Government at the Washington NAC, 23–4 April 1999, *Atlantic News*, no. 3105 (Annex), 5 May 1999–11–25

Naumann, F. (1916) *Mitteleuropa*, Berlin, Verlag von Georg Reimer

Naumann, K. (1998) *Der Krieg als Text. Das Jahr 1945 im kulturellen Gedächtnis der Presse,* Hamburg, Hamburger Edition

Neack, L, Hey, J. and Haney, P., eds (11995) *Foreign Policy Analysis: Continuity and Change in Its Second Generation*, Englewood Cliffs, Prentice-Hall

Nelson, D. (1997) 'Germany and the Balance Between Threats and Capacities in Europe', *International Politics*, 34 (March), 63–78

Neumann, I. and Welsh, J. (1991) 'The Other in European Self-Definition: An Addendum to the Literature on International Society', *Review of International Studies*, 17: 4, 327–48

Neumann, I. and Waever, O., eds (1997) *The Future of International Relations: Masters in the Making*, London, Routledge

Niedhart, G. (1997) 'Deutsche Aussenpolitik: Vom Teilstaat mit begrenzter Souveränität zum postmodernen Nationalstaat', *Aus Politik und Zeitgeschichte*, B1-2/97 (3. January), 15–24

Nye, J. (1990) *Bound to Lead*, New York, Basic Books

O'Neill, S. (1999) 'Rationality', in Ashe et al., 1–24

Olsen, J. (1996) 'Europeanization and Nation-State Dynamics', in Gustavsson and Lewin, 245–85

Onuf, N. (1998) *The Republican Legacy in International Thought*, Cambridge, Cambridge University Press

Papcke, S. (1998) 'Zur Neuorientierung deutscher Aussenpolitik' *Aus Politik und Zeitgeschichte*, B12/98, 13 March, 3–13

Paret, P., ed. (1986) *Makers of Modern Strategy from Machiavelli to the Nuclear Age*, Oxford, Clarendon Press

Paterson, W. (1996) 'Beyond Bipolarity: German Foreign Policy in the Post-Cold War World', in Smith, Paterson and Padgett, 134–55

Patton, D. (1999) *Cold War Politics in Postwar Germany*, London, Macmillan

Paul, T. and Hall, A., eds (1999) *International Order and the Future of World Politics*, Cambridge, Cambridge University Press

Pedersen, T. (1998) *Germany, France and the Integration of Europe: A Realist Interpretation*, London, Pinter

Peters, I. (1997) 'Vom "Scheinzwerg" zum "Scheinriesen: deutsche Außenpolitik in der Analyse', *Zeitschrift für Internationale Beziehungen*, 4: 2 (December), 361–88

Pflüger, F. (1995) 'Poland and the European Union', *Aussenpolitik*, 3, 225–31

Phillips, A. (1998) 'The Politics of Reconciliation: Germany in East Central Europe', *German Politics*, 7: 2 (August), 64–85

Pichugin, B. (1996) 'Russia and the European Union's Eastward Expansion', *International Affairs* (Moscow), 42: 1 (January–February), 90–7

Piper (1987) *'Historikerstreit': Die Dokumentation der Kontroverse um die Einzigartigkeit der Nationalsozialistischen Judenvernichtung*, Munich, R. Piper Verlag

Pommerin, R., ed. (1995) *The American Impact on Postwar Germany*, Oxford, Berg

Pond, E. (1996) 'Germany Finds its Niche as a Regional Power', *The Washington Quarterly*, 19: 1 (winter), 25–43

Pond, E. (1997) 'Letter from Bonn: Visions of the European Dream', *The Washington Quarterly*, 20: 3 (summer), 65

Powell, W. and DiMaggio, P., eds (1991) *The New Institutionalism in Organizational Analysis*, Chicago, University of Chicago Press

Pradetto, A. (1999) 'Zurück zu den Interessen: Das Strategische Konzept der NATO und die Lehren des Krieges', *Blätter für Deutsche und Internationale Politik*, 44: 7 (July), 806–15

Pradetto, A., ed. (1997) *Ostmitteleuropa, Rußland und die Osterweiterung der*

NATO: Perzeptionen und Strategien im Spannungsfeld nationaler und europäis-cher Sicherheit, Opladen, Westdeutscher Verlag

Preston, P. (1997) *Political/Cultural Identity: Citizens and Nations in a Global Era*, London, Sage

Preuß, U. (1999) 'Zwischen Legalität und Gerechtigkeit: Der Kosovo-Krieg, das Volkerrecht und die Moral', *Blätter für Deutsche und Internationale Politik*, 44: 7 (July), 816–28

Pflüger, F. and Lischer, W., eds (1993) *Feinde Werden Freude*, Bonn, Bouvier

Pridham, G., Herring, E. and Sandford, G., eds (1994) *Building Democracy? The International Dimensions of Democratization in Eastern Europe*, London, Leicester University Press

Pritchard, G. (1996) 'National Identity in a United and Divided Germany', in *European Integration and Disintegration: East and West*, edited by R. Bideleux and R. Taylor, London, Routledge, 154–73

Pritzel, I. (1998) *National Identity and Foreign Policy: Nationalism and Leadership in Poland, Russia, and Ukraine*, Cambridge, Cambridge University Press

Puchala, D. (1972) 'Of Blind Men, Elephants and International Integration', *Journal of Common Market Studies*, 10, 267–84

Pulzer, P. (1995) 'Nation-State and National Sovereignty', review article, *German History Institute*, London, 17: 3 (November), 5–14

Pulzer, P. (1996) 'Model or Exception: Germany as a Normal State?', in Smith *et al.*, 303–16

Putnam, R. (1988) 'Diplomacy and Domestic Politics: The Logic of Two-Level Games', *International Organization*, 42: 3, 427–60

Rachwald, A. (1993) 'Poland and Germany: From Foes to Friends?', in Verheyen and Soe, 231–50

Rattinger, H. (1994) 'Public Attitudes to European Integration in Germany after Maastricht: Inventory and Typology', *Journal of Common Market Studies*, 32: 4 (December), 525–40

Rees-Mogg, W. (1989) 'Year of Change that Heralds a German Age', *The Independent*, 4 December 1989

Reinicke, W. (1993) *Building a New Europe: The Challenge of System Transformation and Systemic Reform*, Washington, The Brookings Institution

Rengger, N. (2000) *International Relations, Political Theory and the Problem of Order: Beyond International Relations Theory*, London, Routledge

Rietbergen, P. (1998) *Europe: A Cultural History*, London, Routledge

Risse, T. (1997) *Between the Euro and the Deutsche Mark: German Identity and the European Union*, Thyssen Lecture, Washington, Center for German and European Studies, Georgetown University

Risse, T. and Sikkink, K. (1999) 'The Socialization of International Human Rights Norms into Domestic Practices: Introduction', in Risse *et al.*, 1–38

Risse, T., Ropp, S. and Sikkink, K., eds (1999) *The Power of Human Rights: International Norms and Domestic Change*, Cambridge, Cambridge University Press

Risse-Kappen, T. (1996) 'Exploring the Nature of the Beast: International Relations Theory and Comparative Policy Analysis Meet the European Union', *Journal of Common Market Studies*, 34: 1, 53–79

Risse-Kappen, T., ed. (1997) *Bringing Transnational Relations Back In*, Cambridge, Cambridge University Press

Rittberger, V., ed. (1993) *Regime Theory and International Relations*, Oxford, Clarendon Press

Roberts, J. (1996) *The Penguin History of Europe*, London, Penguin

Robertson, B., ed., (1998) *International Society and the Development of International Relations Theory*, London, Cassell

Rometsch, D. (1996) 'The Federal Republic of Germany', in *The European Union and Member States: Towards Institutional Fusion?*, edited by D. Rometsch and W. Wessels, Manchester, Manchester University Press

Rosamond, B. (1999) 'Discourses of Globalization and the Social Construction of European Identities', *Journal of European Public Policy*, 6: 4, 652–68

Rose, G. (1998) 'Neoclassical Realism and Theories of Foreign Policy', *World Politics*, 51: 1 (October), 144–72

Rose, R. and Haerpfer, C. (1995) 'Democracy and Enlarging the European Union Eastwards', *Journal of Common Market Studies*, 33: 3, 427–50

Rosecrance, R. (1985) *The Rise of the Trading State: Conquest and Commerce in the Modern World*, New York

Rosenau, J. (1990) *Turbulence in World Politics: A Theory of Change and Continuity*, New Jersey, Princeton University Press

Rosenau, J. (1997) *Along the Domestic–Foreign Frontier: Exploring Governance in a Turbulent World*, Cambridge, Cambridge University Press

Rosenau, J. and Czempiel, E.-O., eds (1992) *Governance Without Government: Order and Change in World Politics*, Cambridge, Cambridge University Press

Ross, M. (1997) 'Culture and Identity in Comparative Political Analysis', in Lichbach and Zuckerman, 42–80

Rotfeld, A. (1991) 'New Security Structures in Europe: Concepts, Proposals and Decisions', in *SIPRI Yearbook 1991: World Armaments and Disarmament*, Stockholm, Stockholm International Peace Research Institute (SIPRI), 585–600

Rueb, M. (1999) 'Reconstructing Kosovo: On the Right Track: But Where Does It Lead?', *NATO Review*, 47: 3 (autumn), 20–3

Ruggie, J. (1993) 'Multilateralism: The Anatomy of an Institution', in *Multilateralism Matters*, edited by J. Ruggie, New York, Columbia University Press

Ruggie, J. (1998) *Constructing the World Polity: Essays on International Institutionalization*, London, Routledge

Rühe, V. (1993) 'Shaping Euro-Atlantic Policies: A Grand Strategy for a New Era', *Survival*, 35: 2 (summer), 129–37

Rühl, L. (1992) 'Einige Kriterien Nationaler Interessenbestimmung', in Heydrich *et al.*, 741–59

Rühl, L. (1994) 'European Security and NATO's Eastward Expansion', *Aussenpolitik*, 45: 2, 115–22

Rühl, L. (1996) *Deuschland als europäische Macht: Nationale Interessen und Internationale Verantwortung*, Bonn, Bouvier Verlag

Rühle, L. and Williams, N. (1995) 'NATO Enlargement and the European Union, *The World Today*, May, 84–8

Rummel, R. (1995) 'The German Debate on International Security Instititions, in *European Security after the Cold War*, edited by M. Carnoval, New York, St Martin's Press, 177–97

Rummel, R. (1996) 'Germany's Role in the CFSP: "Normalität" or "Sonderweg"?', in *The Actors in Europe's Foreign Policy*, edited by C. Hill, London, Routledge, 40–67

Safranski, R. (1998) *Martin Heidegger: Between Good and Evil*, Cambridge, Harvard University Press

Sager, K. (1996) 'Grüne Friedens- und Sicherheitspolitik', *Internationale Politik*, 51: 8 (August), 43–8

Schaber, T. and Ulbert, C. (1994) 'Reflexivität in den Internationalen Beziehungen: Literaturbericht zum Beitrag kognitiver, reflexiver und interpretativer Ansätze zur dritten Theoriedebatte', *Zeitschrift für Internationale Beziehungen*, 1: 1, 139–69

Schariot, K. (1997) 'The PFP and the OSCE: Key Elements of European Security', in *First Annual Stockholm Conference on Baltic Sea Security and Cooperation*, edited by Bo Huldt and Ulrika Johannessen, Stockholm, Utrikespolitiska Institutet, 33–6

Scharping, R. (1998) 'Die Zukunft der Bundeswehr Mitgestalten und Mitverantwortung', Festansprache Bundesminister der Verteidigung Rudolf Scharping, anläßlich der Universität der Bundeswehr Hambury am 11 November 1998 in Hamburg

Scharping, R. (1999) *Wir Dürfen Nicht Wegsehen: Der Kosovo-Krieg und Europa*, Berlin, Ullstein Buchverlage

Schäuble, W. (1998) *Und der Zukunft Zugewandt*, 2nd edition, Berlin, Siedler Verlag

Schäuble, W. and Lamers, K. (1994) 'Überlegungen zur europäischen Politik', Position paper of the CDU/CSU Bundestag Faction, 1 September 1994, reprinted in *Blätter für Deutsche und Internationale Politik*, 10/1994, 1,271–80

Schenfield, S. (1987) *The Nuclear Predicament: Explorations in Soviet Ideology*, London, Routledge and Keegan Paul for the RIIA

Schimmelfennig, F. (1998) 'NATO Enlargement: A Constructivist Explanation', *Security Studies*, 8: 2–3,

Schissler, H. (1997) 'Postnationality: Luxury of the Privileged? A West German Generational Perspective', *German Politics and Society*, 15: 2 (summer), 8–27

Schlör, W. (1993) *German Security Policy*, Adelphi Paper 277, London, Brassey's for the IISS

Schmidt, P. (1996) 'German Security Policy in the Framework of EU, WEU and NATO', *Aussenpolitik*, 47: 3, 211–22

Schneider, G. (1997) 'Die bürokratische Politik der Außenpolitikanalyse. Das

Erbe Allisons im Licht der gegenwärtigen Forschungspraxis', *Zeitschrift für Internationale Beziehungen*, 4: 1 (June), 107–23

Schöllgen, G. (1993) *Angst vor der Macht: Die Deutschen und ihre Außenpolitik*, Berlin, Ullstein Verlag

Schöllgen, G. (1994) 'National Interest and International Responsibility: Germany's Role in World Affairs', in Baring, 35–50

Schöllgen, G. (1999) *Die Aussenpolitik der Bundesrepublik Deutschland: Von den Anfängen bis zur Gegenwart*, Munich, Verlag C.H. Beck

Schrade, C. (1997) 'Machtstaat, Handelsstaat oder Zivilstaat?', *Zeitschrift für Internationale Beziehungen*, 4: 2 (December), 255–94

Schröder, G. (1999) 'Die Grundkoordinaten deutscher Aussenpolitik sind unverändert: Frieden und Sicherheit und Stabiles Umfeld für Wohlstand festigen', *Bulletin*, Bonn, Presse- und Informationsamt der Bundesregierung, no. 83/S, 6 December 1999

Schulte, G. (1997) 'Bringing Peace to Bosnia: A Basis for the Future?', *NATO Review*, 45: 2, 22–5

Schwarz, H.-P. (1985) *Die gezähmten Deutschen: Von der Machtbessenheit zur Machtvergessenheit*, Stuttgart, DVA

Schwarz, H.-P. (1991) 'Deutschlands Aussenpolitik im Strukturwandel Europas', in *Europäische Friedenssicherung im Umbruch*, edited by Andreas Rauch, Munich, Verlag für Wehrwissenschaften, 97–115

Schwarz, H.-P. (1994) *Die Zentralmacht Europas: Deutschlands Rückkehr auf die Weltbühne*, Berlin, Siedler Verlag

Schwarz, H.-P. (1995a) 'Die neue Weltpolitik am Ende des 20. Jahrhunderts – Rückkehr zu den Anfängen vor 1914?', in Kaiser and Schwarz, 15–33

Schwarz, H.-P. (1995b) *Konrad Adenauer: A German Politician and Statesman in a Period of War, Revolution and Reconstruction. Volume 1: From the German Empire to the Federal Republic, 1876–1952* (two volumes), Oxford, Berghahn

Schwarz, H.-P. (1999) 'Die Zentralmacht Europas auf Kontinuitätskurs: Deutschland stabilisiert den Kontinent', *Internationale Politik*, 54: 11 (November), 1–10

Schweller, R. (1996) 'Neorealism's Status-Quo Bias: What Security Dilemma?', in Frankel (1996b), 90–121

Schweller, R. and Priess, D. (1997) 'A Tale of Two Realisms: Expanding the Institutions Debate', *Mershon International Studies Review*, 41, (May), 1–32

Schwilk, H. and Schacht, U., eds (1994) *Die Selbstbewußte Nation: 'Anschwellender Bockgesang' und weitere Beiträge zur einer deutschen Debatte*, Berlin, Ullstein Verlag

Seidelmann, R., ed. (1996) *Crisis Policies in Eastern Europe: Imperatives, Problems and Perspectives*, Baden-Baden, Nomos Verlag

Sen, A. (1999) 'Die Freiheit gleicher Lebenschancen', *Frankfurter Allgemeine Zeitung*, 31 December, p. 15

Senghaas, D., ed. (1995) *Den Frieden Denken*, Frankfurt am Main, Suhrkamp

Senghaas, D., ed. (1997) *Frieden Machen*, Frankfurt am Main, Suhrkamp

Singer, M. and Wildavsky, A. (1996) *The Real World Order: Zones of Peace, Zones of Turmoil*, revised edition, New Jersey, Chatham House Publishers

Siwert-Probst, J. (1998) 'Die Klassischen Aussenpolitischen Institutionen', in Eberwein and Kaiser, 13–28

Skocpol, T. (1985) 'Bringing the State Back In: Strategies of Analysis in Current Research', in Evans, Rueschemeyer and Skocpol, London, Macmillan, 13–32

Sloan, S. and Forrest, M. (1997) 'NATO: What Is It?', *CRS Report for Congress*, 17 July

Smith, G., Paterson, W. and Padgett, S., eds (1996) *Developments in German Politics II*, London, Macmillan

Smith, M. (1996) 'The European Union and a Changing Europe: Establishing the Boundaries of Order', *Journal of Common Market Studies*, 43: 1, 5–28

Smith, S. (1989) 'Foreign Policy Analysis and International Relations', in Dyer and Mangasarian, 375–9

Smith, S. (1995) 'The Self-Images of a Discipline', in Booth and Smith, 1–37

Smith, S. (1999) 'Is the Truth Out There? Eight Questions about International Order', in Hall and Paul, 99–120

Snyder, J. (1996) 'Process Variables in Realist Theory', in Frankel (1996b), 167–92

Snyder, T. (1999) 'Special Report: Czechs, Poles Ten Years On', *Prospect*, 38 (February), 54–7

Solana, J. (1999) 'Growing the Alliance', *The Economist*, 13 March 1999, 23–9

Sørensen, G. (1997) 'An Analysis of Contemporary Statehood: Consequences for Conflict and Cooperation', *Review of International Studies*, 23, 253–69

Sperling, J. (1994) 'German Foreign Policy after Unification: An End of Cheque Book Diplomacy', *West European Politics*, 17: 1 (January), 73–97

Sperling, J., ed. (1999) *Europe in Change: Two Tiers or Two Speeds? The European Security Order and the Enlargement of the European Union and NATO*, Manchester, Manchester University Press

Spirtas, M. (1996) 'A House Divided: Tragedy and Evil in Realist Theory', in Frankel (1996b), 385–424

Stark, H. (1999) 'France and Germany: a New Start?', *The International Spectator*, 34: 2 (April–June), 21–8

Steinfeld, J. (1996) 'Schweden, Deutschland und die Ostsee-Region', in *Deutschland, Schweden und die Ostsee-Region*, edited by B. Henningsen and B. Stråth, Baden-Baden, Nomos Vergesellschaft, 23–34

Stent, A. (1999) *Russia and Germany Reborn: Unification, the Soviet Collapse, and the New Europe*, New Jersey, Princeton University Press

Stoessinger, J. (1991) 'The Anatomy of the Nation-State and the Nature of Power', in Little and Smith, 23–35

Strange, S. (1988) *States and Markets: An Introduction to International Political Economy*, London, Blackwell

Stratman, P. (1988) 'Arms Control and the Military Balance: the West German Debate', in *British-German Defence Co-operation: Partners Within the Alliance*, edited by Karl Kaiser and John Roper, London, Jane's

Szücs, J. (1988) 'Three Historical Regions of Europe', in *Civil Society and the State*, edited by J. Keane, London, Verso, 291–332

Taylor, A.J.P. (1955) *Bismarck: The Man and the Statesman*, London, Penguin

Taylor, A.J.P. (1967) 'German Unity', in his collection of essays *Europe, Grandeur and Decline*, London, Pelican

Taylor, R. (1997) 'Global Claptrap', *Prospect*, 25 (December), 62–3

Tedstrom, J. (1997) 'NATO's Economic Challenges: Development and Reform in East-Central Europe', *The Washington Quarterly*, 20: 2, 3–19

Tewes, H. (1997a) 'Das Zivilmachtkonzept in der Theorie der Internationalen Beziehungen. Anmerkungen zu Knut Kirste und Hanns W. Maull', *Zeitschrift für Internationale Beziehungen*, 4: 2 (December), 347–59

Tewes, H. (1997b) 'The Emergence of a Civilian Power: Germany and Central Europe', *German Politics*, 6: 2 (August), 95–116

Tewes, H. (1998) 'Between Deepening and Widening: Role Conflict in Germany's Enlargement Policy', *West European Politics*, 21: 2 (April), 117–33

Thatcher, M. (1993) *The Downing Street Years*, London, Harper Collins

Timmermann, H. (1997) *Die Reformstaaten Mittel- und Osteuropas und die Euro-Atlantischen Integrationsprozesse*, Berichte des Bundesinstituts für ostwissenschaftliche und internationale Studien, no. 18/1997

Treverton, G. (1992) 'The New Europe', *Foreign Policy*, 71: 1, 94–112

Treverton, G. (1993) 'Finding an Analogy for Tomorrow', *Orbis*, winter, 1–20

Van Evera, S. (1991) 'Primed for Peace: Europe after the Cold War', *International Security*, 15: 3, 7–57

Van Ham, P. (2000) 'Europe's Common Defence Policy: Implications for the Transatlantic Relationship', *Security Dialogue*, 31: 2 (June)

Van Ham, P. and Grudzinski, P. (1999–2000) 'Affluence and Influence: The Conceptual Basis of Europe's New Politics', *The National Interest*, no. 58 (winter), 81–7

Vasquez, J. (1998) *The Power of Power Politics: From Classical Realism to Neotraditionalism*, Cambridge, Cambridge University Press

Verheyen, D. and Soe, C., eds (1993) *The Germans and Their Neighbours*, Boulder, Westview

Vernet, D. (1999) 'Kluge Ausschöpfung begrenzter Soveränität: Die Europa-Politik der rot-grünen Koalition', *Internationale Politik*, 54: 11 (November), 11–18

Vincent, J. and Miller, J., eds (1990) *Order and Violence*, Oxford, Clarendon Press

Vogel, H. (1997) 'Opening NATO: A Cooperative Solution for an Ill-defined Problem', *Aussenpolitik*, 48: 1, 22–30

Voigt, K. (1997) 'Die Künftigen Wege der NATO', *Europäische Rundschau*, 25: 2 (spring), 33–9

Volmer, L. (1998) *Die Grünen und die Aussenpolitik – ein Schwieriges Verhältnis: Eine Ideen-, Programm- und Ereignisgeschichte grüner Aussenpolitik*, Münster, Westfälisches Dampfboot

Waever, O. (1997) 'Figures of International Thought: Introducing Persons Instead of Paradigms', in Neumann and Waever, 1–38

Wagenlehner, G., ed. (1988) *Die Deutsche Frage und Die Internationale Sicherheit*, Koblenz, Bernard & Graefe Verlag

Walker, S. (1979) 'National Role Conceptions and Systemic Outcomes', in *Psychological Models in International Politics*, edited by L.S. Falkowski, Boulder, Westview

Wallace, H. (1985) 'Negotiation and Coalition Formation in the European Community', *Government and Opposition*, 68: 1 (autumn), 452–73

Wallace, H. (1999) 'Whose Europe is it Anyway? The 1998 Stein Rokkan Lecture', *European Journal of Political Research*, 31:1, 1–20

Wallace, W. (1990) *The Transformation of Western Europe*, London, Pinter for the RIIA

Wallace, W. (1999) 'The Sharing of Sovereignty: The European Paradox', *Political Studies*, 47, 503–21

Walt, S. (1987) *The Origins of Alliances*, London, Cornell Univesity Press

Walter, F. (1996) 'Rußland und die NATO-Osterweiterung', *Osteuropa*, 46: 8 (August), 741–57

Waltz, K. (1959) *Man, the State and War*, New York, Columbia University Press

Waltz, K. (1979) *Theory of International Politics*, Reading, Addison-Wesley

Waltz, K. (1993) 'The Emerging Structure of International Politics', *International Security*, 18: 2, 44–79

Webber, D. (1999) 'Franco-German Bilateralism and Agricultural Politics in the European Union: The Neglected Level', *West European Politics*, 22: 1 (January), 45–67

Wehler, H.-U. (1988) *Entsorgung der Deutschen Vergangenheit? Ein Polemischer Essay zum 'Historikerstreit'*, Munich, Beck'sche Reihe

Weidenfeld, W. and Janning, J. (1997) 'Das Europa der differenzierten Integration', in Senghaas, 77–101

Weiss, L. (1998) *The Myth of the Powerless State: Governing the Economy in a Global Era*, Cambridge, Polity Press

Weizsäcker, R. von (1991) 'Gulf War Not a Sign of Things to Come', *German Comments*, 9: 22 (April), 6–14

Wellershoff, D. (1999) *Mit Sicherheit: Neue Sicherheitspolitik zwischen Gestern und Morgen*, Bonn, Bundeszentrale für politische Bildung

Wendt, A. (1992) 'Anarchy is What States Make of It: the Social Construction of Power Politics', *International Organisation*, 46: 2, 391–425

Wendt, A. (1994) 'Collective Identity Formation and the International State', *American Political Science Review*, 88: 2, 384–96

Wendt, A. (1995) 'Constructing International Politics', *International Security*, 20: 1, 71–81

Wendt, A. (1999) *Social Theory of International Politics*, Cambridge, Cambridge University Press

Wight, M. (1966) 'Western Values in International Relations', in *Diplomatic Investigations*, M. Wight and H. Butterfield, London, Allen and Unwin

Williams, H. (1992) *International Relations in Political Theory*, Milton Keynes, Open University Press

Williams, M. (1997) 'The Institutions of Security: Elements of a Theory of Security Organizations', *Cooperation and Conflict*, 32: 3 (September), 287–308

Wish, N. (1980) 'Foreign Policy Makers and Their National Role Conceptions', *International Studies Quarterly*, 24: 4, 532–54

Wittgenstein, L. (1953) *Philosophical Investigations*, Oxford, Blackwell

Wolfers, A. (1962) *Discord and Collaboration: Essays in International Politics*, Baltimore, John Hopkins University Press

Wolff, L. (1994) *Inventing Eastern Europe: The Map of Civilisation in the Mind of the Enlightenment*, Stanford, Stanford University Press

Woods, N. (1996a) 'The Uses of Theory in the Study of International Relations', in Woods, eds (1996b), 9–31

Woods, N., ed. (1996b) *Explaining International Relations Since 1945*, Oxford, Oxford University Press

Wyatt-Walter, A. (1996) 'The United States and Western Europe: The Theory of Hegemonic Stability', in Woods (1996b), 126–54

Young, O. (1989) *International Cooperation: Building Regimes for Natural Resources and the Environment*, Ithaca, Cornell University Press

Young, O. (1994) *International Governance: Protecting the Environment in a Stateless Society*, Ithaca, Cornell University Press

Zaborowski, M. (1998) 'Does Germany Support the Eastern Enlargement of the European Union?', *The Polish Quarterly of International Affairs*, 7: 4, 77–92

Zacher, M. (1992) 'The Decaying Pillars of the Westphalian Temple: Implications for International Order and Governance', in Rosenau and Czempiel, 58–75

Zaslavsky, V. (1992) 'Nationalism and Democratic Transition in Postcommunist Societies', *Daedalus*, 121: 2 (spring), 97–121

Zelikow, P. (1992) 'The New Concert of Europe', *Survival*, 34: 2 (summer), 12–30

Zelikow, P. and Rice, C. (1995) *Germany Unified and Europe Transformed: A Study in Statecraft*, Cambridge, Mass., Harvard University Press

Zimmer, M. (1997) 'Return of the Mittellage? The Discourse of the Centre in German Foreign Policy', *German Politics*, 6: 1 (April), 23–38

Zitelmann, R., Weissmann, K. and Grossheim, M., eds (1993) *Westbindung. Risiken und Chancen für Deutschland*, Berlin, Propyläen Verlag

Index

Index